Talking About Feelings and Values With Children

Michael Schleifer

with

Cynthia Martiny

Detselig Enterprises Ltd.
Calgary, Alberta

Talking About Feelings and Values with Children

Library and Archives Canada Cataloguing in Publication

Schleifer, Michael
  Talking about feelings and values with children / Michael Schleifer with
Cynthia Martiny
Includes bibliographical references and index.
ISBN 1-155059-303-X

  1. Children – Conduct of life. 2. Moral education. I. Martiny, Cynthia
II. Title

BF721.S287 2006   649'.7   C2005-906685-7

210, 1220 Kensington Road NW
Calgary, Alberta
T2N 3P5

Phone: (403) 283-0900
Fax: (403) 283-6947
Email: temeron@telusplanet.net
Website: www.temerondetselig.com

We acknowledge the financial support of the Government of Canada through the Book Publishing Industry Development Program (BPIDP) for our publishing activities.

We also acknowledge the support of the Alberta Foundation for the Arts for our publishing program.

1-55059-303-X   SAN 113-0234   Printed in Canada

Preface

Why I wrote this book: How my grandchildren helped

My first motivation for working on this book came from personal experience. When I was growing up, topics such as divorce and illness (both physical and mental) were never discussed. I remember hushed tones and evasive answers at certain times. Only later did I come to figure out that an aunt and uncle were divorcing, a relative was being treated in hospital for depression or some close friend of the family was dying of a serious disease. While I think that this silence was unhealthy and extreme, speaking with friends and family from my generation (born in the 40's, growing up in the 50's and 60's), I discovered that my experiences were not at all uncommon.

All these delicate issues are, of course, still with us at the beginning of the twenty-first century. Illness and death will always (alas!) be part of life. Divorce occurs more frequently than in the past. Times have changed, indeed these topics are prevalent in a different way. Both adults and young children are constantly exposed through television to all of the afore-mentioned topics (plus sex and drugs!). The popular TV show "Seinfeld" discussed such topics as nose-picking and masturbation in episodes still available in re-runs, and OPRAH devoted an entire show to bowel movements. My children and their friends, the new generation of parents, have the desire to talk to their children openly and honestly about these sensitive topics. Despite this desire, many young parents hesitate as they are still not sure how to talk about these issues with their children. Talking about divorce, clinical depression or cancer is not an easy task. It is even a more formidable undertaking when talking about these subjects with young children. The present book offers some suggestions on how to have a parent-child dialogue, not only about divorce and illness but, generally speaking, about values, and feelings. Judgment and empathy are the two key ingredients that facilitate dialogue. The most popular parental advice books do not cover this perspective. The present book will offer practical suggestions on how to develop (in children and in ourselves) these two key components, namely good judgment and genuine empathy.

I have been encouraged to write this book by my children, wife, sister and friends, as well as by colleagues and students. The main inspiration for this book comes, however, from conversations and discussions about moral issues with my three grandchildren, Hannah, Joseph and Rachel. I hope and believe that they benefited, and will continue to benefit, from these kinds of discussions with me. I know that I have learned from them. Here are some recent examples:

Pride

Scene 1

Six-year old grand-daughter Rachel was able to solve a complicated puzzle which older friends and cousins had failed to do. The following conversation occurred:

Proud Grandfather Michael: "Well done Rachel, did you work hard at it?"

Rachel: "No, not much"

Michael: "How did you find the solution when nobody else could?"

Rachel: "I am good at this, I am smart."

Bystander: (admonishingly) "Don't boast, that's not nice" (addressed to Rachel) "You shouldn't encourage bragging" (addressed to Michael).

Scene 2 (a soccer field)

Proud Grandfather Michael: "What a fantastic goal you scored Joseph! That was great! You have really improved since last summer, did you have a very good coach?"

Joseph: "We got special training because I was put on the elite team."

Michael: "What does 'elite' mean?"

Joseph: "We were the best in the school, and will compete against other counties."

Bystander: (admonishingly) "There you go encouraging boasting again."

The ensuing discussion revolves around the appropriateness of being proud of one's accomplishments and achievements. Is pride, as some say, a sin, or a vice? Is pride to be associated with bragging, boasting and arrogance? When is pride a good thing? Is it linked to confidence and self-esteem? When is pride a predictor of success – whether in sports, games or academics? When is it appropriate to speak to others of our pride? How is self pride different than pride in others? For some of our answers see Chapter 8, section 6 (Moral Emotions).

Politeness

All 3 grandchildren have been asked by their parents and grandparents to show forms of politeness. For example, saying "thank you" or giving an elderly aunt a desired kiss on the cheek when a gift has been given. All three have argued (particularly the two girls) that they do not always want to show any kind of physical affection, and have made me aware of their point of view. This ongoing dialogue continues between grandparents and grandchildren on different aspects of politeness, rudeness, gratitude, and limits of physical demonstration. In one of the most important discussions in my university class on moral education, we offer our views on the case of Lisa, who is asked by her date, a boy who paid for the movie, to be "polite" and give him a kiss. She refuses but is very sad, angry, and confused. Many of the participants in my university course (particularly the women), relate the episode to experiences where they were asked as children to be "polite" by kissing a relative. This issue is discussed more fully in Chapter 4 (Politeness), Chapter 12, section 2 (Friends, Relatives and Strangers) and Chapter 9, section 3 (Abuse, incest, harassment and violence).

Honesty

My 12 year old granddaughter Hannah and 9-year old grandson Joseph live with their mother in the United States. In 2002, I was asked to drive them across the border from Canada, and given the appropriate documentation. We knew, however, that because of terrorism and kidnapping concerns, there might be questioning by the American authorities. We prepared how to answer their questions, treating it as a little bit serious but also as a fun thing. The role-playing inevitably involved how much of the truth to disclose. How "honest" were we to be in our answers? If we failed to volunteer certain details about our lives (or didn't answer fully) were we lying? What would constitute "deception" in these circumstances, and would it be right? How were we going to feel (fearful? guilty? angry?), and what could we do to control our emotions? These questions which we enjoyed discussing and debating inspired some of the ideas in Chapter 2 (Judgment), Chapter 3, (Honesty), Chapter 8, section 3 (Controlling emotions).

Emotions

My grand-daughter, Rachel, at age 4 drew a picture for my wife Carole and me which she called "cloud-people." She explained that the cloud-people were having different feelings. There is only one girl who is happy because of the rainbow. The other four are boys. One boy is sad and angry because the rainbow was gone; one other guy is also angry and sad, but also happy because he threw a tantrum (which feels good and makes you a bit happy even if you are sad and angry); a third boy stole a star from another, so the victim was angry and sad, but the perpetrator was angry, sad and afraid all at once. Her drawing, not surprisingly, followed an incident at pre-school involving a conflict with a friend.

Rachel and I discussed her drawing and some of its implications. We noticed that one can be sad, glad and mad all at once. We can be confused about what we feel; we can feel different things at the same time; we can shift quickly from one emotion to another; sometimes we don't know what we are feeling; sometimes others tell us what we are feeling although they may get it wrong.

My discussion with Rachel happened at about the same time as my colleague Cynthia Martiny and I were writing up our research papers on the development and education of emotions. Cynthia mentioned that confusion about basic emotions (anger, fear and sadness) is a key ingredient in her clinical work (she leads groups with men who have committed conjugal or familial violence). My granddaughter's insights are in direct parallel to the lack of clarity many adults display. We have been discussing this (and related) issues for a few years now. Chapter 7 of the present book (Understanding emotions) presents some of these ideas.

1   For everything there is a season,
     And a time for every matter under heaven:
2   A time to be born, and a time to die;
     A time to plant, and a time to pluck up what is planted;
3   A time to kill, and a time to heal;
     A time to tear down, and a time to build up;
4   A time to weep, and a time to laugh;
     A time to mourn, and a time to dance;
5   A time to throw stones, and a time to gather stones together ;
     A time to embrace, and a time to refrain from embracing;
6   A time to seek, and a time to give up as lost;
     A time to keep, and a time to throw away;7
7   A time to tear apart, and a time to sew together;
     A time to keep silent, and a time to speak;
8   A time to love, and a time to hate;
     A time for war, and a time for peace.

(Ecclesiastes 3: 1-8)

Acknowledgments

As stated in the Preface, my conversations with three grandchildren inspired several chapters of this book. Over the years, my children have also been part of an ongoing dialogue about values and feelings. I thank them as well as those friends who have discussed "Scruples" questions with me (both the game and real life moral dilemmas). I am grateful, as well, to other family members, friends, colleagues and students who have encouraged me to write this book.

Cynthia Martiny and I have discussed most of the issues in this book over the past few years. She particularly collaborated in the writing of Chapters 6 through 12. I want to express gratitude to my secretary Diane Amatuzio and research assistant, Lee Londei who were active participants in discussing many of the ideas in the book, and helped with suggestions about organization and presentation. My wife Carole, proofread the manuscript and suggested ideas for improvement. For all her support, often in difficult circumstances, I thank her!

Michael Schleifer, Montreal, 2005

Copyrights

We thank Torstar Syndicate Sales for permission to use three Hagar cartoons, Universal Press Syndicate for permission to use *Real Life Adventures,* United Media for permission to use four *Peanuts* comic strips, and Creators Syndicate for *Wizard of JD* cartoon. Our thanks also goes to the Institute for the Advancement of Philosophy for Children for permission to use sections from novels and manuals.

About the Author

Michael Schleifer is a Professor in the Faculty of Education at the Université du Québec à Montréal (Sections Foundations, Epistemology, and Educational Psychology). He obtained his BPhil in Oxford (Philosophy) and his PhD at McGill (Psychology). He has taught Ethics at McGill University (Philosophy Department) and worked as a Clinical Psychologist at the Montreal Children's Hospital (Department of Psychiatry). He has published numerous articles in Educational, Philosophical and Psychological journals. He has also edited books on Identity, Cooperation, and the Development of Judgment. He is a grandfather of three children with whom he enjoys conversing about feelings and values.

About the Co-Author

Cynthia Martiny is a Professor in the Faculty of Education at the Université du Québec à Montréal (Section Counselling). Her published articles concern the verbal and non-verbal manifestations of empathy. She leads counselling groups for men who have committed conjugal violence. Her professional experience includes therapeutic foster care with children, mediation between parents and children, group home care for delinquent adolescent girls, and counselling for perpetrators and victims of sexual assault. She is a mother of four children with whom she discusses emotions and morality.

Contents

      * P4C refers to philosophy for children. These questions are used in guides for teachers which accompany the novelettes for older children. We have often modified or adapted them for use with younger children

Introduction

Who is this book for?

This book is for anyone who wants to help children to become good people, to help them in choosing to do the right thing. In short, this book is meant for educators, those working as nursery school teachers, day care workers, and parents. It is intended to provide material focusing on the age group 0 to 5, which will fill a gap in the literature. As well, it will provide specific advice, exercises, and questions, which can be used to help develop good judgment and empathy. Although the book is primarily intended for use with the very youngest children, all the topics discussed will be relevant for teachers in elementary schools, continuing the moral education of children aged 5 to 12. The book is about how to dialogue and converse about moral values and emotions. In regard to early childhood education, there is an attempt, wherever possible, to distinguish between what is appropriate during the ages 0 to 2, where the child is listening and understanding, and the later stage of ages 2 to 5, where the verbal skills of the child allow the beginnings of a give-and-take communication. In my Early Childhood Education and Child Development courses, we discuss practical suggestions concerning moral education,[1] and education of the emotions,[2] in conjunction with psychological research and philosophical analysis. Material for these courses comes from many different sources. This book is intended to provide a text integrating these ideas, which can be helpful for this kind of university course.

Early childhood educators are particularly in need of direction concerning talk about values and feelings. In recent years, we have become aware of the importance of the first five years of development. Consequently, we want our preschool educators and other caregivers to be equipped for the task. *Educators include, of course, parents, who will continue to play a primary role in discussing and dialoguing with their children.*[3] This book is, therefore, also intended to help mothers and fathers and any other relatives or friends who find themselves substituting in this role. Speaking as a grandfather of 3 (see Preface), I particularly offer this book to my fellow grandparents.

As parents, we want our children to be happy, and ultimately be successful, at school, with friends, and in life generally – however we define "success." Moreover, we may want to see them develop what Robert Coles and Michele Burba have called their "moral intelligence,"[4] that elusive goodness which is different than other forms of intelligence, and from happiness. Regardless of how we define this "goodness," the question remains how can we help our children be good people, as well as happy ones? I will assume that we want a caring child, that is to say, a child who is kind, considerate, and certainly not cruel. In addition, as I hope to show, we want our child to be a thinking person. In other words, the caring and kindness will be genuine, and therefore also long-lasting.[5]

At how young an age should children be talking about feelings and values?

This book is offered to educators who want to talk about moral values and feelings to children from ages 0 to 12. As mentioned above, we are targeting the neglected period of early childhood ages 0 to 5. The emphasis in the present book is on discussion and dialogue. A child is (generally) ready to talk from the age of 2 onwards, although, of course, he will comprehend a great deal long before that! This book is not about child-rearing as such, nor does it deal (except indirectly) with extreme or problem behaviors. Some of the suggestions for improving judgment (see Chapter 2) refer to the period from birth to two years of age, and parental reactions to the expressed feelings[6] and values[7] of infants are important. Questions of toilet training, discipline, safety and protection are not covered in the present book. Doctor Spock's classical book,[8] now in its seventh edition (and available on the internet), covers these topics as well as any parent would need. Spock and his successors offer rudimentary advice about how to handle values including such issues as honesty and responsibility. These, however, are offered as brief "recipes." Parents know that talking about moral values and feelings is often much more complicated. Topics such as honesty, politeness and responsibility each deserve at least a chapter in order to fully explore the complex issues.

At the upper end of the age spectrum, I am not going to make any recommendations (again except obliquely) about adolescents or young adults. Here the age restriction is more a matter of my personal experience and expertise. I have worked for almost 40 years on learning about the development of moral reasoning, judgment, and emotions from ages 2 to 12. My research and teaching has concentrated on two developmental periods; namely preschoolers[9] (2 to 5) and children in elementary schools[10] (5 to 12).

Although this book will not refer specifically to adolescence, many of the issues discussed, will, nevertheless, apply to teenagers – particularly the most sensitive topics of Part IV (for example Chapter 12 on "touching"). *Rather than wait for the turbulent teen years, the idea is to begin the dialogue about values and feelings (including topics such as drugs, safety and sexuality!) as early as possible.* As one author stated "Adolescence looms ahead, which nowadays can begin at around the age of 8. Drug dealers lurk in the alley; nihilist rock 'n' roll wafts up from the storm sewer; the culture of covetousness is everywhere."[11] There is no way to stop our children from being exposed to the very explicit and sometimes the very worst of sexual and violent content, as well as the multi-faceted drug culture. My grandchildren listen to Eminem's music (and alas the lyrics!) before parents or grandparents catch up. All that we can do is point out the risks and consequences of drug use, respond to questions about sexual activity, and talk about the violence, both physical and verbal; all of which are explicit in Eminem's music as well as in the available video "Eight Mile." The bottom line is we must be available to talk about these issues!

In this book, we do ask parents to examine and clarify their own values and feelings. In fact this is part of the process in learning how to better talk to young children about these matters (Chapter 2 deals with this issue in detail). The key is developing good judgment, both for ourselves as adults and for our children. In fact, many of the same issues involving judgment concern both parents and children. For example, when to speak up and when to keep silent is a problem for the young child but no less for the adult. In the classroom, the question of when the teacher should state his or her own opinion is a very difficult one. What is not good is a teacher introducing his or her own opinion before the children have had a chance to respond, thus foreclosing genuine consideration of alternatives. On the other hand, if the teacher feels that the children have been able to develop their own ideas, and can hold them in a strong and confident fashion, then the teacher should not feel hesitant about introducing his or her own ideas, where the children themselves have failed to bring forth such a point of view. In classroom discussions, children should understand that the teacher has temporarily abandoned the role of moderator in order to assume that of co-participant. Parents have the analogous choice to make when talking with their children: *Be forthcoming and honest with your views, but also do not play the role of supreme authority, which will surely inhibit the children from expressing their views.*

Similar questions of judgment arise for adults and children in regard to most of the themes of this book. We all struggle with the complicated task of doing the right thing, not always so obvious as it may have been for our grandparents in another age. Both we and our children learn that it is sometimes good to keep quiet (for reasons of tact or perhaps not hurting the feelings of another), and that it is sometimes right to speak up (to point out unjust or unfair behavior, or to protect someone's rights). We encourage children to play with others, but also to play by themselves, we teach the importance of keeping a secret, yet also want the child to report bad behavior by peers, or dangerous strangers. For each of these antinomies, which is the right choice? The answer, of course, is that either choice could be right or wrong. (Of course, they may both be right or wrong,) depending upon many factors. We all have rules and principles to apply to difficult decisions, but these are only helpful up to a point; as are our traditions, beliefs, intuitions, and experience. What we invariably need, in addition to all this, is good judgment! As educators, our role is to help our children by improving their judgment, and their ability to reflect on these matters. *In fact that is the main message of this book: All we can do is help provide our children with good judgment. The choice will be theirs!* The suggestions offered for developing judgment (Chapter 2 and subsequent chapters) are aimed at very young children. They are meant, however, to be applicable also to situations discussed by adolescents and young adults. An added bonus: As parents try to help their children hone their judgment skills, they will also, at the same time, be developing their own competence and judgment.

Children wonder at the world, are curious about it, and try to make sense of it. There is the world as it is, the facts of the case, nature, causal relations, etc. But even more complex, complicated and difficult to comprehend are feelings and values. This world of good and bad, right and wrong, and the feelings which go along, is much more difficult to get straight. This parallels the state of affairs of the world. In the 21st century it is generally acknowledged that our coping with questions of value lags way behind our grasp of nature, science and technology. We sent a man to the moon, probed Mars and figured out the genetic code of the human body. We are, however, still witnessing wars, violence, intolerance, and cruelty. In our new scary world, children have to be protected from "cyber-bullying," where they are harassed by e-mail or may incur racial slurs or sexist language.[12] Here is the point we must stress: *whether our child is listening to music, watching television, reading books, or surfing the Internet, we must try to accompany him as he begins the activity, in order to talk about the values and feelings connected with the stimuli.*

How many of us have children at ages 2 or 3 who master programming the VCR (it is a standing joke that children are often better at modern gadgets than many adults), yet the world of morality remains very foreign for them? We have to use their competence with visual stimuli for moral education. Elliot Turiel and his associates at Harvard University have created a number of films, which elicit conversations about values and feelings.[13] In 1971 I made use of films, created in collaboration with the National Film Board, for my research on the moral development of children as young as two years of age.[14] Parents, in addition to these materials can (and should) use movies and books as rich sources for instigating discussion about values and feelings. (A list of some of my favorite films is provided at the end of the book after the section on "Recommended Readings").

Can *any* parent talk about feelings and values with their children?

I accept that there are mothers and fathers who love their children, and are concerned with protecting them, but are content to leave their (moral) education to others. Among this group, there may be those who believe that the question of values should be left to the church, synagogue or mosque; they may think that moral values are based upon (or synonymous with) a set of religious values. I present why my own orientation is different (see Chapter 1), and perhaps may convince some readers (if they have an open mind about the subject) that the moral values we want to discuss with our children transcend the religious and cultural ones. It may also be, I know, that some parents are not ideologically opposed to doing some kind of moral education with their children, but rather do not have the temperament for it. This is quite legitimate and relevant. For those, however, who like talking to children, and feel that they want to engage in dialogue even about these serious matters (like honesty, politeness, responsibility, cooperation and the emotions – even the most difficult topics like illness, death, separation and divorce), then I know you can find some helpful ideas in the pages that follow. The temperament of children can be a factor from birth onwards,[15] relevant to the development of emotion (see Chapter 8) as well as the ability to discuss values. With rare exceptions, however, all children need these discussions, and are ready for them very soon.

Didn't Jean Piaget show that up to a certain age, children are not capable of moral judgment and moral reasoning?

Before proceeding, there is one dogma or myth which must be dispelled. You may believe, or have heard that "young children cannot or should not talk about moral values." I have had this slogan repeated to me by parents seeking counselling, by teachers in preschools, students in my university classes, and even occasionally by some psychologist at an academic conference.[16] All of these may invoke the authority of Jean Piaget who has supposedly said (or supposedly shown) that young children are not capable of the kind of thought needed for moral discussion. This may have led to irrational worry that discussing moral values and feelings with young children could be dangerous. Let me state categorically: there is no danger! Those who invoke the dogmatic authority of Piaget (or Freud, Montessori, Erikson and anyone else who offers us the "stages" of the child) are simply adhering to an unthinking orthodoxy.

Piaget was a great thinker, and has influenced the course of child psychology in this century. My doctoral dissertation, and many of my publications,[17] are inspired by his important book on the development of moral judgment.[18] *On Piaget's pronouncements, however, about what a child cannot do at a precise age, he is simply wrong.*[19] In almost every domain where Piaget tells us, for example, that a 5 year-old child is incapable of a certain kind of thought, research has shown that it was Piaget's methodology, rather than the 5 year-old, which was lacking.[20]

When discussing how to help develop good judgment and empathy in the following chapters, we will use three major age divisions: 0-2, 2-5 and 5-12. These are meant to be taken as broad, common-sense age periods. We do not want to make Piaget's mistake mentioned above, which rigidly overstates a specific age, leading to underestimation of the child's capacities.

The consensus in 2004 concerning the moral development of a child: although very young children (2 to 5) generally cannot articulate or verbalize certain values or emotions as well as older children or adults, they are capable of a very sophisticated thinking about these notions.[21] From 2 to 5 they are aware of, and competent in, recognition of values, including rules and important behaviors like cooperation and sharing.[22] They are also, even from these earliest ages, learning about feelings and emotions.[23] They need guidance, however, from adults on these matters. So by all means, do not talk to your children if you are disinclined. If, however, you enjoy talking about values or feelings with your girls and boys, go for it! There are no legitimate age restrictions: whether we are 3 years old, 30 years old, or 60 years old, it is the right time for dialogue about these matters.

What did Piaget *really* show us?

Although we must reject the dogmatic "orthodox" interpretation of Piaget, there are nevertheless important lessons that he has left for educators. Despite differences between those early childhood educators who were followers of Piaget, and those more inspired by Maria Montessori,[24] their ideas form a consensus. Here is a summary of the most relevant principles:

1. Listen and observe carefully when talking to a child.

2. The child is a philosopher with a point of view – take it seriously![25]

3. Enjoy what children say, how they reason and how they argue. Have fun with the discussion and dialogue.

4. Focus on arguments, justifications, and explanations rather than a simple response.

5. Any "errors" made by a child at any level of development are very important, and should not be dismissed or neglected.

6. The notion of development is important to consider.[26]

Didn't Aristotle (or somebody) show that young children have to practice good habits before we offer explanations or discuss values and feelings?

No matter what Aristotle said (or what some may think he said) instilling habits in young children without offering explanation is not a good idea. Furthermore, as we will see when discussing gratitude, greetings (Chapter 4) and apologies (Chapter 5), moral values left unexplained and undiscussed are worse than no moral values at all. Another way to make the same point is to contrast education and socialization. Whenever we are interested in education, we want to offer the reasons for choosing a particular value. There is, of course, a place for socialization, which emphasizes behavior; particularly with very young children. The opportunity to educate should not, nonetheless, ever be missed. *Children who are told "Say thank you" or "Say you are sorry" or "Say Hello," without an attempt to explain why this is desirable, will often not mean or feel the required politeness and respect. A sullen politeness is worse than no politeness at all.*

Is there anything new to be learned about feelings and values not covered in other books for parents?

1. There are many good books, including some recent ones, which offer suggestions on how to talk to children.[27] However, none of these specifically show parents how to develop the crucial ingredient in ourselves and our children; namely *judgment*. This is the key to talking about values and feelings and trying to do the right thing. I discuss the questions about judgment in Chapter 2, and then again in regard to every specific value in Chapters 3, 4, 5 and 6, and finally in connection with feelings and emotions (Chapter 8) and the most difficult and delicate questions (Part IV, Chapters 9 to 12).

2. Some of the best books are written from within a particular religious perspective,[28] even those which attempt to transcend the particular, and discuss *universal values. We will discuss moral values and feelings in a way which is compatible with religious belief, but can be useful for those without any religious affiliation or persuasion.* This is discussed more fully in Chapter 1. Let us simply emphasize that we want children to think for themselves. This implies trying to avoid indoctrination, whether as teachers or parents. [29] Similarly, in our work with therapists and guidance counsellors in high school, we stress the need to point out the consequences for their clients, but leave the ultimate choices to the individual.

3. Many books aimed at parents focus on discipline, and reacting to bad behavior.[30] Perhaps the best books of this sort are by Chaim Ginott, and his disciples. Most of us who have worked as clinicians have made use of his great examples on how to communicate with a child. One favorite example concerns the child who is kicked off the school bus. Instead of saying, as we are all tempted to say: "What did you do?," Ginott suggests that we start with:"You must feel awful, don't you?"[31]

   In the present book, we are interested in how to talk to children about values and feelings independently of any specific incident. Discussion is important about these matters at any time, with the bonus that it will also have an effect on behaviors when they occur, as well as decisions and choices which have to be made in the future. There is no guarantee, of course, that talking to children will help them later on as adolescents and young adults. There are, however, indications that sometimes early interventions often do have a good effect. Daniel Goleman has shown this in the field of emotional intelligence, where children able to delay gratification in his "marshmallow test" cope better with moral dilemmas later in life.[32] Similarly, early childhood intervention programs have been shown to be beneficial in certain circumstances in regard to later cognitive development.[33] In our own research on prevention of violence, we have shown that philosophical discussions with 5 year-olds had a dramatic impact on their judgment, moral autonomy, empathy and emotion-recognition.[34]

4. *What we say as parents must be connected to what we do and vice-versa.* Although the focus of this book is on talking, we are aware of the importance of modelling in the moral judgments and moral behavior of children.[35] Generally when children want to know what is right to do, they do not bother to ask you: They just observe what you do and do likewise. For example, suppose you frequently stress to them the importance of honesty, and they also observe that you snatch other people's property (such as a pillow from a hotel). What will they learn from you? Not just two things, but three. They will learn to advocate honesty,

just like you, they will learn to respect (or disrespect) other's property – just like you, and they will learn how to keep their actions consistent (or inconsistent) with their pronouncements – just like you. An understanding of consistency is important if children are to learn moral integrity. But the consistency has to be practiced by those whom the children take as their models of correct conduct, it will not be effective if it is merely advocated to them.[36] *Behavior alone, however, without reflection is worthless.* Such behavior may last a while, but will inevitably be susceptible to influences by peers, propaganda and various authorities. Thinking about moral issues is no guarantee that one will make the right choices, and behave well. Thinking well (thinking for oneself) is, however, a necessary condition for moral action.[37]

5. Other books, some very excellent ones,[38] focus on moral education, discipline, character training, and communication skills. What the present book offers, in addition to these important dimensions, is a focus on *dialogue,*[39] whereby we adults often learn from our children about how to cope with difficult situations at the same time that they are learning from us (see Preface). Dialogues are conversations, but of a particular sort. When we engage in dialogue, we must listen carefully to others (for listening is thinking) and we must weigh our words (for speaking is thinking), we must rehearse in our minds what we and others have said, and reconsider what we might have said. Thus, to engage in dialogue is to explore possibilities, to discover alternatives and to recognize other perspectives.[40]

6. Feelings and values are intertwined in our perspective. Unlike others who discuss either values alone, or feelings alone, we believe that one must treat both together. A growing consensus among philosophers[41] and psychologists[42] is that moral virtues inevitably involve emotions, and emotions are themselves a form of moral choice. In talking about values, one must talk about feelings. Talking about the right thing to do invariably involves talking about how one feels about doing the right thing, or some other thing. Also one has to invariably consider other's feelings in addition to one's own. Judgment and emotion are inextricably combined (see Chapter 2). Furthermore, judgment is tied to empathy (see Chapter 6). There is an indissoluble bond between thinking and feeling. There is little value instructing a child in what would be right to do in a given situation, when a child does not care about anyone. It is hard to see how a child who is not interested in other people's feelings would have any sympathy with their needs. Moreover, the feelings necessary to moral conduct are not restricted to particular sympathies to this person or that person, since it is equally indispensable that one be sensitive to the entire situation to which one is a part. Strategies for developing this relevant sensitivity will be presented in Chapter 2 on judgment, Chapter 6 on empathy and Part III on feelings. Books and movies are abundantly available and offer a rich source for the development of the kind of sensitivity we are discussing.[43] What must be emphasized is that we be present with our children and engage them in dialogue about the material arising from these media.

7. In this book, we will provide an up-to-date *synthesis of research on values and emotions.* There has been a lot of exciting new discovery and analysis in the last twenty years concerning the development and education of moral reasoning, judgment and the emotions,[44] including the latest work on the emotional brain.[45] I have not only been studying these findings and theories, but I have been an active participant in the process. I have contributed to the discussion among philosophers,[46] as well as to the research in psychology[47] and educa-

tion.[48] In addition, Cynthia Martiny (my colleague and collaborator) and I have worked as clinical psychologist and group counselor respectively, with a focus on problems of impulsivity, aggression and violence.

Do I have to be a philosopher or have taken a philosophy class?

As we have already noted, young children are philosophers; they wonder at the world, play around with language, and reflect about every subject under the sun. In the 1920's Piaget's young children asked questions like "Why is the moon following me?" or "What are dreams?" Montessori's children, rescued by her from the slums to be cared for in the first preschools, discuss the relative importance of play versus work. In the twenty first century, there is no reason to doubt that this kind of philosophizing is still there for most children. We as parents or teachers only have to join in this half fun, half serious enterprise. Children don't have to take a philosophy class or read any of the great philosophers to do philosophy. So as parents, let us not worry that we won't be able to do philosophy without any reading of philosophy texts. Of course if any reader would like to do some reading, by all means go ahead! To this end, wherever possible, the philosophical debates and references are relegated to the footnotes and bibliography at the end of the book. There is, nevertheless, a remaining kind of necessary philosophy, particularly in the first six chapters. This is because it is essential to look at the meaning of the terms. Words are important, not only to philosophers, but to anyone wanting to deal with values, and talk about them with children. Do we want our children to be honest, polite, responsible, and cooperative? It will depend on what we (and they) mean by "honesty," "politeness," "responsibility" and "cooperation." This is not linguistic nitpicking; it is a crucial point. When we say, for example, "don't lie," "don't cheat," "cooperate," "be polite," "be responsible," we must think about what we mean, and sometimes more importantly, what we do *not* mean. Finally, it is essential to understand that the young child will inevitably understand the key notion (lying, cheating, responsibility, cooperation, politeness, respect, etc.) in a somewhat different way (maybe a very different way!) than we as parents or teachers.

How is this book organized?

Part I of the book is divided into two chapters entitled: Which Values? (Chapter 1) and How to Discuss Values: The Role of Judgment (Chapter 2). Chapter 1 deals with the central issue in ethics, namely the status of values: Are they always subjective and "relative," as one side contends? Or can there be objective and universal values, as others maintain? (I side with this latter group). The text focuses on the practical implications of this philosophical issue for educators (parents and teachers). Chapter 2 is concerned with the key concept of this book, namely judgment. It looks at the concept of judgment, as well as specific ways to develop good judgment for ourselves and our children.

Part II looks at three specific values namely, honesty (Chapter 3), politeness (Chapter 4), responsibility (Chapter 5). In all these chapters, the crucial ingredient is the role of "judgment." An Interlude Chapter is entitled "To Speak or to Keep Silent." Part III concerns feelings and is divided into three chapters on Caring (Chapter 6), Understanding Emotions (Chapter 7), and Emotions and Morality (Chapter 8). Part IV treats The most difficult subjects, and is divided into four chapters, Chapter 9 "Separation," Chapter 10 "Illness," Chapter 11 "Touching" and Chapter 12 "Beliefs." For the last four chapters, once again the key is "good judgment!"

There is much overlap between chapters, and, wherever possible, we have tried to supply cross-references. For example, Chapter 3 (Honesty) is linked to Chapter 8 (Moral virtues) and all of the chapters in Part IV (The most difficult subjects). Another example is Chapter 4 (Politeness) whose themes reoccur in the discussions of "Friends, relatives and strangers" (Chapter 11, section 2) and "Abuse, incest, harassment and violence" (Chapter 11, section 3). Notes to all the chapters appear at the end of the book along with a selected bibliography (recommended reading) an index, and appendices.

Note: Throughout the book "he" will be used to refer to boys and girls, mothers and fathers, etc.

Part I

Values

Chapter 1 will ask what values are, what *moral* values are, and discuss the questions of relativism and objectivity. These questions are central in moral philosophy; it is crucial for educators to be aware of them. For those of us working with teachers, the ultimate challenge is to show that there is objectivity and truth not only to facts, but also to values. Furthermore, there exists a set of fundamental universal values. Teachers and animators of philosophical discussions in the classroom learn to avoid the extremes of relativism (anything goes, any opinion is as good as any other) and the other twin danger of dogmatism. For parents to talk about values with children, they need to find a path between admitting uncertainty and doubt on the one hand, but expressing an appropriate certainty at other times.

Chapter 2 deals with the question: how to talk about values? The key concept is "judgment." Judgment will be defined and contrasted with reasoning and the use of rules. Specific suggestions for helping develop good judgment will be offered.

1

Which Values

"Value judgments" raise questions not about facts but about how men feel about facts, not about what man can do but about what he ought to do. (B.F. Skinner)

What are values?

Values are desires, preferences and tastes: they are the things we consider "good." In the widest sense, little babies and many animals have values. Some foods taste sweet, some objects feel smooth and some things look nice. As Skinner reminds us, we say that things taste "good," feel "good" and look "good."[1] Obviously, the very young baby has values in a sense but cannot yet talk about them. We might even, in an extreme way, talk of animals having values; this is akin to saying we have an "educated" dog. Those of us who find this notion absurd will also see the humor in the Peanuts cartoons. This is because we want to talk about training or conditioning of our dogs, cats and hamsters, but not use the term "education" or "values" for anyone but human beings. We will see in the next section why moral values are necessarily human.

Although Skinner is correct to remind us that feelings and values are inextricably intertwined, he is wrong to insist that what we consider as "good" (what we value) is equivalent to what we feel. Nor is what we consider "good" to be reduced, as Skinner would like, to what has been positively reinforced.[2] Those following Skinner do not see anything funny about Snoopy, Charles Schultz's famous dog, calling himself educated because he was conditioned in obedience school. This is because behaviorists consider that conditioning is only one form of education. Most psychologists have, however, rejected behaviorism.[3] Values for humans are different than animals conditioned behavior; values are linked to beliefs and choices.

Where Skinner's analysis fails can be seen by considering some of his basic examples. Let us say that a child finds some candies sweet, likes them, and, when he begins to talk, even may use the word "good" when eating them. As parents, we may have said to our very young child, as he eats the candy, "that's good!". However, we quickly will want to make a distinction between "good" in the sense of pleasant taste, and "good" referring to what is more valuable (perhaps we will consider the candy, or at least too much candy, as unhealthy and therefore, "bad"). It is precisely the distinction between what we find pleasant and often want to do as opposed to what we should do which brings us to the relevant sense of value we are discussing in this book.

Unlike Skinner, most philosophers and psychologists consider values to be more than taste, preferences and desire.[4] We can agree with Skinner that there is not too much rational discussion possible concerning whether red or green candies are "better." We do not agree with him, however, that all discussions of values make no sense. Contrary to Skinner, most philosophers and educators accept that we can try to persuade each other that a car, painting, food item or piece of music is better than another.[5] In short, taste and some preferences may be entirely subjective, as Skinner insists; values, however, have a certain objectivity. Values can be discussed, whether they are of the educational ("this is a good text book"), aesthetic ("this is a good painting or piece of music") or other varieties. The values that will concern us most specifically in the chapters of this book are moral values.

What are moral values?

The simple answer to this question is that, just as educational values deal with education, and aesthetic values with aesthetic, moral values concern "morality." What, then, is "morality"? "Morality" is concerned with what an individual ought personally to do in situations that typically involve inner conflict. Both as adults and as children, we are aware of situations where we must, for example, decide to keep a promise to a friend or tell the truth to someone else, thereby perhaps betraying our friend. This is precisely the kind of moral dilemma which we will treat in the following chapters. The roots to our moral conflicts may occur at very young ages, and in regard to relatively easier choices. Take for example Daniel Goleman's famous "marshmallow challenge."[6] The "marshmallow test" concerns impulse control. The essence of this test is, following Goleman, as follows:

> Just imagine you're four years old, and someone makes the following proposal: If you'll wait until after he runs an errand, you can have two marshmallows for a treat. If you can't wait until then, you can have only one – but you can have it right now. . . . Which of these choices a child makes is a telling test; it offers a quick reading not just of character, but of the trajectory that child will probably take through life.

Goleman's child is four years old when he makes this choice whether or not to delay gratification. Rudimentary values of this sort occur even earlier, with children as young as two and a half to three years of age. What is important is that we can discuss these moral values with very young children. They can understand the difference between doing what tempts us at the moment and choosing what may be better in the long run. It is of interest to note that no animal - even the smartest of our pet dogs or cats – can reflect about the future in this way. This is, of course, connected to the fact that human language is not available to other animals, even those with fascinating communication skills.[7]

Are moral values just a matter of opinion? Aren't they always "subjective"? Isn't it "all relative"?

Skinner would argue that this is the case, and some "postmodernist" philosophers also hold that there is no truth (in morals or even in science).[8] In the view adopted in this book, however, and supported by a majority of philosophers and educators, values are more then opinions and beliefs. Values are connected with our choices and can often be formulated and justified; they are not simply matters of opinion or belief, or attitudes, any more then they are simply tastes or preferences. Taste and preferences, as seen in section 1, can be entirely "relative" and "subjective." Opinions and beliefs can often be entirely "relative" to the person as well. Values, however, are not "relative" or "subjective" in the same way. There is an objectivity to values which is crucial for education. We want our children, for example, to consider what is important and relevant. Notions of importance and relevance are tied to a consensus, and therefore "objective."[9]

The Oxford Dictionary defines objectivity as "exhibiting facts uncolored by feelings or opinions." Webster tells us that it is the state or quality of being objective. The word "objective" is defined in turn as "not influenced by personal feelings or prejudice." It adds that objective opinions are unbiased ones.

These definitions already highlight some of the important points on both sides of the debate. On the positive side (for "objectivity") we have the notion of being unbiased, without prejudices. We ask journalists, judges, teachers reading exams, and research grant committee members to strive for objectivity in this sense. This is reflected in the American presidential election of 2000, where a majority wanted recounts done by machines. The above definitions go further, however. They mention not only bias and prejudice, but also feelings and opinions. If objectivity is to mean looking at facts without feelings, then the negative side of objectivity is highlighted. How can we diminish the passions people have for their points of view? Do we want to? Does objectivity equate with coldness and distance? This would make many of us non-objectivists in most spheres, but particularly in regard to moral values, where strong feelings and opinions are typical. These are two extremes of course. The most relevant meaning of objectivity in discussions and debates emphasises a third view, namely that which surpasses personal taste or opinion. For the objectivist side, one looks for a truth or a reality, which goes beyond opinion or preference. For the subjectivist, "it is impossible to separate reality and our opinions."[10]

For those of us who have worked in the area of Philosophy for Children, we believe that all discussions must have an element of objectivity to them. Discussions may often begin with personal opinions, but not to go beyond this level would be considered as unsuccessful. This is the case for a discussion of a concept or controversy in science as well as one in morals. At the very least, participants are encouraged to see what their opinion and other opinions have in common, or how they differ. These similarities and differences can already be considered as objective features going beyond their own tastes, feelings, or opinions. Children may say that they like being in the playground more than the classroom; the philosophical discussion should bring out features about the classroom and the playground.[11] These objective features lead one to values, which are things of importance, and differ from desires feelings and preference. At the level of this new reflection about these concepts, there is again a kind of objectivity, which is linked to the truth about these concepts. Subscribing to this view commits one to a certain notion of education. Specifically, one accepts that there is more to a discussion of values than simply "the clarification" of one's personal views.

This debate between the relativists, on the one hand, and those of us who, on the other side, see values as much more like facts, has been called the most important philosophical topic of this century.[12] I have argued about this issue elsewhere, and I am content to leave the reader to pursue the philosophical battle, if interested, via the footnotes[13] and suggested readings. As noted here, this philosophical question has practical implications which are relevant for parents and other educators.

As professors, we have often had to confront the view of the university student who says, "it's all a matter of opinion" or "it's all relative."[14] Similarly, the teachers we train to do moral education or introduce philosophical dialogue in the classroom must cope with the child in class who only wants to know the teacher's answer, because he thinks it must always have more weight than his own (he may be looking, mistakenly, for the one "right" or "correct" answer, where this is inappropriate in the context of a discussion about moral values, choices, or dilemmas.)

The university student who says: "it is all relative," often is really saying: "What good is any kind of discussion about morals (or anything?)." This point of view must be confronted, discussed, and shown to be faulty. For the child, one must also be prepared to explain that the teacher is not an extreme authority on the kind of matters often discussed about values.

Discussions are only possible if we accept that, although all opinions should be respected (none should be laughed at or ridiculed, for example), there will be some points of view which are better justified, more profound, and provide more insight than others. Furthermore, a point of view may even achieve a consensus among a group, and people (children or adults) can change their mind. The argument does not have to be that of the teacher in the classroom. It is a fundamental tenet of our approach to discussion that the teacher is not the supreme authority, particularly on moral values and dilemmas. Parents, like teachers, must also approach discussing values with this outlook; their own opinion is important, but so is that of the child. It is often, although by no means always, possible to have an open mind about the matter at hand, change one's mind, and even reach a compromise, agreement, or consensus. This openmindedness, it must be stressed, is for all participants, whether adults (teacher or parent) or child.

In discussing a moral issue, one will often begin by expressing one's opinion or belief. As stated here, any opinion is to be respected, in the sense of not being ridiculed – no person (child or adult) should be subjected to a personal attack. Sometimes an extreme view may be expressed, perhaps some racist or sexist belief. This is the most delicate of issues to be confronted in moral or philosophical discussions. There are many ideas about the best way to handle this situation. *My own suggestion is that no view (even a racist one, however damaging to others who hear it) should be silenced, or the person made to feel humiliated.* One must, however, be prepared to show that such utterances are at the very limits of tolerance, and are fundamentally wrong, harmful to others, and obstacles to the goal of rational dialogue.

Is spanking a child right or wrong? Why "relativism" doesn't work

A recent debate in Canada has reached the level of the Supreme Court. The ruling of this highest body (Spring 2004) is that Canadian parents must spare the belt, the ruler and other objects when disciplining children, and any physical punishment of babies, children and teens is off limits. By a six to three margin, the court upheld the *Criminal Code* defence-known widely as the "spanking law" that allows parents and teachers to use "reasonable" force "by way of correction." Not surprisingly, no one is happy with the compromise. Passions are very strong on both sides of the issue, for those who believe parents should be able to use corporal punishment, as they always have, and those who oppose any use of force by parent or teacher at any time.[15] We can use this issue to illustrate what goes wrong with relativism.

Suppose I believe that spanking children at any age is wrong, and should be prohibited. And then I come across someone who holds that it is not wrong, and should be allowed. Suppose now a relativist[16] comes in, and mocks our conversation. "You absolutists," she says "always going on as if there is just one truth. What you don't realize is that there is a plurality of truths. It's true for one of you that spanking should be prohibited, but it's also true for the other guy that it should be allowed."

How does the relativist's contribution help? Indeed, what does it mean? When he tells me that it is "true for me that spanking is wrong" doesn't that just mean that I think spanking should be prohibited. Furthermore, my opponent just means that he believes the opposite. But we already knew that: That's why we are in disagreement.

Perhaps the relativist is trying to get us to see that there is no real disagreement. But how can this be so? I want people to aim at one outcome, that spanking should be prohibited, and my opponent wants another outcome. At most one of us can succeed, and I want it to be me. Therefore the relativist cannot stop us from seeing each other as opponents.

Perhaps the relativist is trying to get us to tolerate the other person's point of view. However, why should I tolerate a point of view which I consider to be very wrong. As many philosophers have argued,[17] toleration is a virtue, but it must have its limits.

Perhaps the relativist wants to stop the conversation: She is like someone asking "Will you two just stop bickering?" This can sometimes be a good thing to say. Some conversations are pointless. If we are music lovers, and I say Mozart is better than Schubert, and you say Schubert is better than Mozart, and we start fighting about it, the best advice may well be that we stop. Perhaps we can agree to disagree. In *moral* issues, however, we often cannot agree to differ. Agreeing to differ with my opponent about spanking is in effect agreeing to tolerate spanking, and my whole stance was against that. Moral issues are frequently ones where we want to coordinate, and where we are finding what to forbid and what to allow. Naturally, the burden falls on those who want to forbid. In liberal democratic societies, freedom is the default. The Supreme Court of Canada had to spell out under what conditions spanking is against the law. It is just not true that anything goes. So conversation has to go on among citizens concerning what to allow and what to forbid. Once again, the relativist is not helping. Relativism seems to simply be a distraction. As Blackburn states:

> If relativism is just a distraction is it a valuable one or a dangerous one? It all depends. Sometimes we need reminding of alternative ways of thinking, alternative practices and ways of life ... We need to appreciate our differences. Hence in academic circles, relativism has often been associated with the expansion of literature and history to include alternatives that went unnoticed in previous times. This is a good thing. Sometimes however, we need reminding that it is time to draw a line and take a stand; ... the alternative way of looking at things might be corrupt, ignorant, out of touch, or plain evil. It is a moral issue, whether we tolerate and learn, or regret and oppose.[18]

Another way to show how the relativist's stand is irrelevant is via a story told by Blackburn which is worth repeating here:

> At a high-powered ethics institute, representatives of the great religions held a panel. First the Buddhist talked of the ways to calm, the mastery of desire, the path of enlightenment. The panellists all said: "Wow, terrific, if that works for you that's great." Then the Hindu talked of the cycles of suffering and birth and rebirth, the teachings of Krishna and the way to release, and they all said: "Wow, terrific, if that works for you that's great." And so on, until the Catholic priest talked of the message of Jesus Christ, the promise of salvation and the way to life eternal, and they all said: "Wow, terrific, if that works for you that's great." And he

thumped the table and shouted: "No! It is not a question of if it works for me: It is the true word of the living God, and if you don't believe it you are all damned to Hell!" And they all said: "Wow, terrific, if that works for you that's great."

The joke here lies in the mismatch between what the priest intends – a claim to unique authority and truth-and what he is heard as offering, which is one more saying like all the others. The relativist wants to emphasize that this is just *his* certainty and truth, which he has made absolute. It is of course true that people put the word "true" to their doctrines, because to have a belief and to hold it to be true are the same thing. What the relativist misses, however, is that the priest is not the only one who seizes on the word "true." A Buddhist will hold the Buddhist doctrine to be true, and the Hindu, the Hindu doctrine, etc. As we have argued here, there is justification for talking about truth and objectivity, despite the objections from the "post-modernists."[19]

Facts and values

Another dichotomy that is an underlying assumption of many moral education programs is the dichotomy between fact and value. This assumption has often led teachers to believe that somehow value education can be treated entirely separately from other subjects. This is connected, of course, with the dichotomy discussed above where values were taken to be "subjective" and facts "objective." We have already made clear that values are as objective in the relevant sense as facts.

Of course facts and values are not identical. That you are now reading this page is a fact. That you find it worthwhile to do so makes reading the page not just a fact but a matter of value. The existence of the eggs you consider purchasing is a fact, but the store identifies them as "Grade A" and thereby cites their grade of value. So fact and value are nothing but the same thing viewed in different perspectives.

For purposes of analysis, we can isolate an order of "facts," and likewise, for purposes of analysis, we can isolate an order of value, but matters that concern us are always at the intersection of those orders.[20]

In my class, Ethics for Counsellors, we discuss the use of tests to predict violent behavior, on the basis of the unstable personality of the client. Important decisions are made about whether or not to testify in court about the results of these personality tests. In cases like these, clearly facts and values are inextricably combined. A similar controversy in education concerns the use of I.Q. tests to determine the relevance of early childhood compensatory preschool programs.[21]

Facts and values are similar in another way as well. They are both needed for stability in the world. With facts, we are looking for the truth about the world, or at least an approximation of the truth in order to get on with living. Science is always redefining its consensus about what the facts are. We need, however, to agree about some things to allow us the necessary validity, reliability and communication between laboratories. We act as if we can know about the world even if the ultimate reality escapes us. In exactly the same way, values and virtues need a consensus in order to get on with life. Minimum agreement about universally accepted core values allows people to live in relative stability.

We may not achieve certainty about the facts of the world, but that is okay. The sun, we say, will rise the next day because we are quite confident that the earth is going on spinning in its axis – the universe is unfolding as it should. Similarly we place confidence in the actions and emotions of others although absolute certainty will escape us here as well.

Religious and cultural values

There is another kind of relativism which is not as extreme as that discussed above. This concerns culture and religion. For some people, eating pork is wrong, for others not; for some, hiding one's hair (of a woman) is mandatory, for others this practice is offensive. We are talking about values here, often religious or cultural. These values are relative, not to the individual but to the group. They are often, as we know, held very strongly, and have led to clashes, and even wars. Religion and culture exist, and these kinds of values are very important. Furthermore, parents will often want to talk to their children about them. The present book is going to discuss values which transcend religion or culture. Although there is a diversity of morals between cultures and religions, which relativists stress, the similarity of values across cultures is far greater. Anthropologists[22] have shown that the moral codes of most societies do not differ appreciably from one another. Our studies on causal and moral responsibility in children[23] (to be discussed in more detail in Chapter 5) have similarly been tested across cultures, and shown to be universal. There will be components of honesty, politeness, responsibility, cooperation, and the emotions, which are culturally specific to countries or groups. These will be mentioned when relevant. Most of the time, they will be impediments to discussing the universal aspects of these values, as well as of virtues and emotions. The emphasis in the following chapters will be on the universal core fundamental values, those which any parent (grandparent or teacher) from any culture or religion can want to talk about with children. Universal values do not have to necessarily oppose specific religious or cultural ones, although often they do. Universal values do transcend cultures and groups, and should be for any adult or any child. Parents who have no particular religious persuasion should find the discussion of values and emotions relevant to their concerns, as much as those who also have a specific religious set of values or cultural ones to offer their children. *In talking about core values, we must make it very clear that we are not talking about absolute values, or any kind of absolutism.* As will be seen in Chapter 2, moral values often have to be discussed in contexts of ambiguity and uncertainty. There is no place, in our perspective, for the dogmatic certainty associated with absolute values.

Fundamental universal values

There are of course philosophers who will deny that universal values exist.[24] Even those who will acknowledge that values can be objective, and are more than opinions (thus not "simply relative"), sometimes balk at the notion of universality. Here again, I will refer to the reader via a footnote and the suggested readings to the philosophical debate.[25] I will simply summarize here the impact on education. In any case, whatever the philosophers say, young children get it: Three year olds can readily understand the difference between rules regarding nudity on the one hand, and rules concerning hurting others on the other. In Turiel's experiments,[26] children understood that the latter rules (about hurting others) were universal and more important than the former (about nudity) which could be cultural or conventional. When asked whether hitting was permissible if those were the rules, most children insisted it was still wrong, as opposed to codes permitting nudity which might make it right.

I will argue in the chapters that follow that it is the universality of the values, virtues and emotions which justify imparting them to the next generations. We do not, as argued above, simply want to indoctrinate our children to have certain beliefs (without seeing why), nor to behave in certain ways without seeing the reasons for it. No humanely concerned adult wants children to be slaves to any prior programming any more than they want them to be slaves to their youthful impulses. *What adults truly wish is that in a given situation boys and girls would have done the right thing, not because they were programmed to do so, but because they believe it to be right and because they choose to do it.* Even if adults as parents have certain clear, firm, and well-defined beliefs and values, they should not take the entire package, and make it part of their children. First, if they do that, these will never be the beliefs and values of the individual child; they will remain forever the parent's beliefs and values. Second, adult conviction in the rightness of certain beliefs and values is the product of a long process (experiences, maturation, thought and reflection, trial and error). No one can simply graft the result onto children. Finally, a great danger is inherent in trying to impose an entire set of beliefs and values en bloc without allowing for assessment and then critical acceptance by children. *Almost inevitably at some point a child will reject some particular teachings of his or her parents.* If these teachings are part of a total set of teachings which were merely passed *en bloc* to the child, it is quite likely that the child will tend to reject the entire set of teachings *en bloc*.[27] Of course, as parents (and other educators) we often must (particularly with very young children) tell them what to do for their protection and safety. We want, however, as soon as we can (and one can begin as early as 2 years of age) to talk to the child about every one of the values we consider important.

We will want children to understand about honesty, politeness, responsibility (including following rules), cooperation and sharing. We will also want them to see the importance of a number of personal virtues, including consideration, generosity and kindness, as well as appropriately understanding and handling their feelings. As the leading French and English philosophers of education have both stressed[28] the only values that we should reasonably impart are the universal ones. How, then do we go about doing this?

2
How to Discuss values: The Role of Judgment

What is Judgment?

Before giving a definition, try your hand at a test of judgment which we used in a recent research project1 concerning the prevention of violence [see page 163]. For each of the four items, pick the one that is "not like the others" (like on Sesame Street). After you have made your choices, think about why you picked that item. The "correct" responses can be found in the footnotes.[2] (Try the examples on pages 164, 165.) The test compares items which are intentionally somewhat ambiguous. Judgment, in its very essence, deals with uncertainty, contradiction and ambiguity.

To explore the notion of ambiguity, let us begin with the famous Gestalt example in human perception [see Figure 2-1]

Figure 2-1. The contour which divides figure from ground "belongs" to the figure only and changes its shape radically if a figure-ground reversal occurs. Thus the figure has specific determinate characteristics, while the background can be characterized only as that-which-is-not-the figure. This indeterminacy plays a crucial role in human perception; most of what we experience must remain in the background so that something can be perceived in the foreground (Neisser, 19904, cited by Dreyfus, 1979).

When looking at this figure, we are confronted with having to take a stand between two different choices or perspectives. The picture can be seen as either a vase or as two women. It is not that one or the other perspective is better, or more correct. They are both equally possible, and equally "right" and only by sliding in and out of background and foreground do we choose one interpretation rather than another. We never resolve which perspective is "better," if that question has any meaning. We certainly do not justify our choice by any form of reasoning. It should be noted that the insights of Gestalt theory have stood the test of time: Philosophers like

33

Merleau-Ponty[3] and psychologists like Neisser[4] stress their continued and central relevance. More recently, the Nobel prize winner Bernard Crick[5] makes the Gestalt Laws of Perception the centre-piece for understanding human vision.

Turning from psychology to a very different field, it has been argued that the essence of mathematics also involves ambiguity.[6] Human mathematicians thrive on ambiguity (and contradiction!) which allows them to have ideas and intuitions about a mathematical proof or mathematical concept long before they can demonstrate the proof of the theorem or the appropriateness and legitimacy of the concept. It has been convincingly argued that true breakthroughs in math come about because the human mathematician is challenged by some contradiction or ambiguity. As these theorists argue, machine mathematics is essentially different in this way from human mathematics. Computers detest ambiguity, uncertainty, and especially contradiction; whereas humans live with these throughout life.

When Gestalt theory informs us that a figure on background is the simplest sense-datum available to us, we reply that this is not a contingent characterization of factual perception, which leaves us free, in an ideal analysis, to bring in the notion of impression. It is the very definition of the phenomenon of perception . . . The perceptual "something" is always in the middle of something else; it always forms part of a "field" (Merleau-Ponty, 1962[3], cited by Dreyfus, 1979).

The notion of ambiguity used by both the Gestalt theorists and the mathematicians is captured by the Oxford Dictionary definition. "Ambiguity" is defined as: "admitting more than one interpretation or explanation: having a double meaning or reference." It must be stressed, then, that ambiguous situations always contain two aspects. On the one hand, they contain an apparently unified situation or idea. On the other hand, they carry with them a duality, two frames of reference that are usually seen as incompatible or even contradictory. The duality can be reconciled via the single situation or single idea, yet can still be interpreted in two different ways.[7]

A very different area of human experience from these two fields (Psychology and Mathematics) concerns political debate. Complicated issues like the Middle East conflict invariably involve (at least) two clashing contradictory points of view, in this case that of the Israelis and that of the Palestinians. Both cannot be (entirely) right, and yet we must somehow judge between them. In these types of situations, we need a special creativity to inspire solutions towards resolving the conflict. One must see that both sides do have a legitimate point, and somehow forge a higher or more integrated point of view than each side on its own. Reaching a political "synthesis" is, of course very difficult, yet is probably the only way out of these ongoing intractable conflicts, with their unfortunate consequences of violence, war and human misery.

A final example comes from the Philosophy for Children Program, an approach to education developed by the philosopher/educators Matthew Lipman and Ann-Margaret Sharp. The development of judgment is helped by exercises, questions, and guided discussions.[8] Here, too, the concept of ambiguity is highlighted. I quote from the introduction to the novelette *Pixie*:

Learning a new word is not more important, in and of itself, than learning that a familiar word has not just one but a variety of meanings and can have several such meanings in a given context. When children learn about language, people, and the world in general, there is a danger that they will acquire a severely over-simplified view of these matters. They may assume, for example, that people always mean what they say and that things are always what they appear to be. The naïve trust of the child in a just and benevolent order must sooner or later come to grief, as the child attempts to impose a grid of orderly understanding upon a world that is many-levelled, turbulent in its alterations, and frequently absurd. Therefore, equipping children with an understanding of ambiguity is a valuable preparatory discipline which readies the child not only for the puns, equivocations, and double-entendres of everyday discourse, but also for the rich allusiveness of literature, the double-binds of human relations, and the covertness of nature itself. Moreover, while learning about ambiguity prepares children to deal with the duplicity that frequently characterizes the world around us, it also helps children discover the relationships of words with words, things with things, and words with things.

What all four examples have in common (from psychology, mathematics, politics and education) is that reasoning alone does not suffice.[9] We have to compare like and unlike situations and relationships to make our choice. We cannot avoid the ambiguities and contradictions. Rather we must thrive on these, take inspiration from them, be challenged by them, and make use of them to come up with a solution. This is, in short, what judgment is all about. *A consensus definition of judgment*[10] *is "the consideration of like and unlike situations and relationships." Judging essentially involves looking at differences and similarities where these are not obvious.*

Judgment is the essential characteristic of what educators call critical and creative thinking."[11] Training children to be better in their judgments is different than training them in logic, or in general forms of reasoning."[12] Ten specific exercises for developing good judgment will be provided in the section following; additional ones can be found in the appendices at the end of the book.

It has already been noted that judgment is different than reasoning. Nevertheless, judgment makes use of reasoning, as well as intuition, "heuristics" (making good guesses and estimates), experience and good old common sense. A good judge, however, must develop other abilities in addition to all these. These other abilities will include a competence in being able to decide what is appropriate in the context, where the situation may appear as relatively or completely new. The training of these abilities in children closely mirrors the training in fields needing expert judgment to make important practical decisions. Nurses, fire-fighters, psychotherapists, laboratory diagnosticians, and teachers all must use their judgments in their specific field, often in the heat of action, and often to make important decisions. Experts in all these fields testify[13] that their judgments often go beyond the lists of rules they have set up for themselves or for teaching novices and less experienced practitioners. One set of judgments which particularly concern us in this book, are moral judgments: here, too judgments are more than reasoning.

Moral judgments are more than reasoning

One of the objectives of a moral education program is to help children perceive situations accurately and to make sound moral judgments. For example, if a teacher were to ask the children of his class if cruelty is wrong, possibly they would all agree, although such agreement may not be very important. If they were presented with a situation in which a student was punished and the children claimed that the student was being treated cruelly, the question would be whether what happened to the student was in fact an instance of cruelty. We can modernize Aristotle[14] at this point:

1. All cruelty is wrong.

2. This is a case of cruelty.

3. Therefore this case is wrong.

We may all accept the first premise (all cruelty is wrong) just as we accept that all love is good, all justice is good, and so on. But the real heart of ethics is in trying to determine the factual second premise. Was this *in fact* an instance of cruelty? If so, it was wrong. But, in fact, was it? Here only sensitivity in our *judgment* – only the ability to perceive and read the situation in all its complexity – can help us. Parents interested in helping their child to both understand cruelty, and oppose it, must do similar work to that of the teacher.

Another example of the primacy of judgment over reasoning regarding moral values comes from Chinese philosophy.[15] One model (Zhuangzi's) is based on rules, and tries to derive particular judgments from these rules or general principles. The second model (Mencius's), in contrast, places trust in particular judgments and feelings that arise in response to particular situations. People who see a child about to fall into a well react with alarm and distress. A king who looks into the eyes of an ox being led to slaughter, and is reminded of an innocent man being led to execution, spares the ox. The story of the ox is part of the famous legend associated with Mencius. Mencius reminds the king to take the feeling of compassion he had for the ox and apply it to his people by sparing them from over-taxation, and drafting them for war. We can summarize this approach in an Aristotelian syllogism again:

1. The King should have spared the ox from its suffering.

2. The case in which the king could do something about his people's suffering is relevantly similar to the case in which the king should have spared the ox.

3. Therefore the king should spare his people.

This Mencien approach to morality is based primarily on one's judgment of the relevance of two cases, and two cases only. It is opposed to the other model mentioned above sometimes described as "top-down reasoning." An interesting feature stressed by Mensius' model is the confidence one has about one's particular judgment. So in the case of the above syllogism, I am very confident that the two cases (that of the ox and that of the people) are relevantly similar. In the same way, I could have a great deal of confidence in the relevant similarity between my judgment that I have reason to help a child falling into a well, and another judgment that I have reason to spare an innocent person from being executed (remember the ox's eyes reminded the king of an innocent man about to be executed). That confidence I feel about my judgment is often greater than any confidence I might feel about rules or general principles.

Judgments are different than moral dilemmas

Just as judgment is more than reasoning, as we have discussed in the last section, it is also more than the use of hypothetical moral dilemmas, associated with the work of Lawrence Kohlberg. In Kohlberg's theory, moral reasoning is advanced by being thrown into "disequilibrium."[16.] Children find that their customary modes of reasoning are not adequate for handling certain moral problems. Successful resolution of such problems requires advancing to the next stage of moral reasoning. A situation poses a moral dilemma when there are competing moral values, which in more ordinary circumstances are decisive. For example, Kohlberg's famous

Heinz dilemma (Should Heinz steal a cancer-curing drug to save his wife? Is this is the only way he can obtain it for her?) presupposes that property is an important value, that stealing is generally wrong, and that saving a life, especially a loved one, is very important. It is precisely because these are all morally important considerations that Heinz is faced with a moral dilemma.

However it isn't just moral dilemmas that give rise to moral puzzlement and call for careful thinking. For example, there is a passage in *Lisa* (one of the novelettes from philosophy for Children) in which the children wonder when it is right to "return in kind" and when it is not – and, equally important why it is or is not. The passage involves a child retaliating after being tripped, children discussing trading stamps and lending money and Lisa's discussion about paying back her boyfriend on her date (see Preface). How does discussing a passage like this differ from discussing a moral dilemma? As we have noted, when we face a moral dilemma we are pulled in conflicting directions. We think we have reasons for going either way, or for avoiding both ways. None of the choices seem to be without moral cost and we are very likely perplexed about what the right choice is, or even whether there is a right choice. However, children often do not think about these situations as any kind of dilemma at all. Many children have no doubt that, for example, retaliation is called for. Their thinking is about what it means to retaliate or "get even." Other children have no doubt that acts of retaliation are inappropriate, that trading stamps is appropriate, and that one ought to repay borrowed money and that Lisa does not have to offer her date his demanded affection. What puzzles them is how to explain the differences among these instances of returning in kind.[17]

A number of educators and philosophers have pointed out that children are very much aware of the limitation of traditional ethical theories, including the most popular, namely the utilitarian or non utilitarian approaches. Children concerned with difficult moral issues, like the ones discussed here, seem to realize that the full description of the case they are discussing does not allow, without significant over-simplification, for the direct application of any of the general principles associated with these two main ethical traditions (utilitarian or non utilitarian).[18]

Why do we need judgment? The limits of rules

Everyone is acquainted with the expression "rules are made to be broken." Some rules, however, must not be broken; they are needed for protection and safety. A good example is a convention of the road, whereby red lights mean "stop" and green ones mean "go." This conventional but important rule is taught to pre-schoolers as it should be. To many people, rules are not a problem; they see rules as permanent, universal, and not to be broken. Children, however, understand that this is not always so. When discussing rules in the classroom, children often wonder whether the given rules are the best rules for dealing with the issue at hand. Rules of a game, like baseball, or rules for a game like making up sentences, that the children themselves have devised, can have a different status; they can be temporary, modified, or more long lasting. *When children raise questions about the status of rules, they are not being disrespectful of authority;* it is simply that they feel more inclined to go along with rules that they understand, rather than with rules they do not understand, and they see no harm in asking for explanations.[19] In discussing rules, it is important that parents and children see that there are many different kinds. Some rules are simply conventions, which are agreed upon for the common good (like the red light example mentioned here). Some rules are generalizations based upon experience (don't touch the hot stove is a good practical rule). Other rules can be traditional recipes for conduct that may or may not prove successful in a given situation (for example the rules of etiquette).[20] A fourth kind of rule has been called "a personal strategy" type of rule.[21] For example, I may have a rule of getting up at 6 am everyday in order to have time to eat breakfast and get to work. For the person who dislikes rising early, this self-imposed rule was intentionally set up after considering the alternatives.

Rules (or "laws") can be regularities describing the way things work, they can be conventional regulations, for example "go on green, stop on red" or descriptions such as "the sun rises as a rule" or objects "obey the laws of gravity," they may be the rules of the game, either descriptive as "the bishop moves diagonally in chess" or prescriptive as "move your king pawn before your knight." There are finally moral rules, for example: "Keep your promises!" All forms of rules make life simpler. We need however, to apply and interpret them case by case. We live in an increasingly uncertain and complex world. Ethical systems and codes of ethics may give us rules and principles for morality, but we need to interpret and apply these rules in various situations and contexts.[22]

The use of rules is also complicated by the fact that other considerations, including other rules, are always relevant to a decision. A rule that seems to apply to a situation provides a starting point or general direction for making a decision. But if we want to be sure that we are making the right decision, we should bring other facts, ideas, feelings, and rules to bear on the problem. Application of a rule to a decision is only one way of thinking about it; the more corroboration we can get from other ways of thinking, the better.

Of course, there are practical limits to the amount of thought we can put into a decision. The decision might not be very important, so that it is not worth our while to carry out an extensive check on the course of action suggested by the rule. Or we may be too limited in our knowledge of the situation to devise other approaches to the problem, however, if we do cut short our deliberations in order to save time, or because of lack of knowledge, we should be aware of the risk that is involved. We should not think that because we have "applied a rule," we must be right.

In discussing rules with our young children, it is important to look at the origin of the rules, the penalties and rewards (if any) normally associated with the rules, and the consequences for individuals and groups of the observance, or non observance of the rule. Against this background we want to encourage our children to decide what place any rules are going to have in their own life, and to what extent they might be supplemented with rules that they themselves develop.

An important distinction, which we must make, is that between rules and standards. Rules tell one how to act ... a standard is a measure you use when you judge.[23] In other words, one obeys a rule, but one does not obey a standard. A standard is a criterion by means of which one can distinguish one kind of thing from another, or tell the better from the worse. *As children become practised in distinguishing rules from standards, they begin to realize that rules too must be judged, and that we judge them by certain standards.* These standards in turn must be apd by still other criteria. This entire process involves *judgment.*

Judgment for moral virtues and moral emotions

Children are very much aware that, when considering a moral dilemma, the facts of the specific case are very relevant to deciding what is the right thing to do [24] In regard to each of the moral virtues, it is not enough to simply avoid the corresponding vices, as Aristotle argued 2500 years ago.[25] Aristotle's famous quote to illustrate all this refers to anger:

> Anyone can become angry – that is easy. But to be angry with the right person, to the right degree, at the right time, for the right purpose, and in the right way – this is not easy. (*The Nicomachean Ethics*)

We can, in the twenty-first century, paraphrase Aristotle by substituting the moral values and emotions, which we find important. For the word "anger" in the above quote, we can substitute our own moral values. So for example, we could say:

> But to be *honest* with the right person, to the right degree, at the right time, for the right purpose, and in the right way – this is not easy.

Our 21st century version can use other moral values; all we have to do is plug in, for example, the words "polite," "responsible" and "cooperative" in place of "honest" in this above quote. We can continue our paraphrasing by using various emotions. Now, for instance, the quotation will become:

> But to be *proud* (or *humble*) with the right person, to the right degree, at the right time, for the right purpose, and in the right way – this is not easy.

Finally, we can create similar versions in regard to some of the most difficult topics that we want to discuss with our children. These can include for example "touching," that delicate set of issues which will be discussed in Chapter 10. The formulation will now look something like this:

> To touch the right person, to the right degree, at the right time, for the right purpose, and in the right way – this is not easy.

Aristotle, in one of his most celebrated rejections of his teacher Plato, reminds us that there are no hard and fast rules for the moral and social life. Disagreeing with Plato, Aristotle insists that calculation may work in mathematics, but to get things right in regard to moral values and emotions, we need judgment.[26]

Children, rules and judgment

If morality were simply a matter of knowing rules and obeying them, then moral education would consist of developing in children a conscientiousness that would permit them to carry out these rules in a happy, unquestioning fashion. But morality is not so simple. It is not clear that there are rules for every situation, nor is it clear that it contributes to children's development that they should accept uncritically those rules that apply. Consequently, the child must be equipped to cope with situations lacking clear guidelines, situations that nevertheless require that one makes choices, and that one accepts responsibility for the choices one makes. As we have pointed out before, children can develop rules on their own initiative, without having them laid down by anyone; and children can begin to have a somewhat independent attitude towards rules, provided, however, that they are aware of the consequences for themselves and others for deviance of the rules.

Children find themselves in various situations during the course of a day. Some of these situations call for action; some do not. But children can hardly know what actions or decisions are called for or appropriate unless they have developed an awareness of the dimensions of each situation, its complexity, and its various nuances and subtleties.[27] In the novelette *Lisa*, children discuss the complexity of certain rules and situations (see Appendix G). For example, they condone Mark's behavior when he tells the truth about his sister's whereabouts, although shortly before he answered the same question in a very misleading way. The children perceive that in one situation an honest answer was called for, whereas, in the other, an honest answer would have been inappropriate since it would have resulted in possible harm to his sister. The question arises whether in fact Mark has been guilty of inconsistency. The complex answer of course, is that sometimes it is right to be inconsistent. (We will return to a fuller discussion of the complexities of honesty in Chapter 3).

Counselling and therapy: Judgment at work

In a class Cynthia and I teach on the Ethics for Counsellors and Therapists, the key notion is judgment. Time and again, in interpreting the codes, edicts, laws and rules pertaining to ethical questions involving clients or patients, the ambiguities and contradictions are flagrant. For example, one article of the code for clinical psychologists says "keep absolute confidentiality," but one also has a major responsibility to reveal and report what happens in therapy or counselling in cases of harm, possible harm, or when subpoenaed by the law court. Results of tests are secret, yet one is morally (and often legally) obliged to report the details in custody cases, or civil proceedings, or criminal process. How to decide what to do? Another set of problems concerns on the one hand the obligation to stick with one's client, and never abandon him, especially where there is danger (for example suicide). On the other hand, the codes demand that the therapist have the competence to treat the client, with relevant knowledge of specific circumstance and cultural background, including sexual orientation. If not competent, one is obliged to refer the client to another therapist. Once again two sets of opposing demands. These problems facing the 21st century clinician can only be resolved by hard reflection, and improving the only competence which can deal with them, namely good judgment. One has to look at the various experiences and contexts of one's own, and other therapists and see to what degree they are relevantly similar or relevantly different. If therapists and counsellors, with all their experience, need to work with ambiguities, interpret and apply the rules, how much more difficult is this for children whose experiences are obviously limited.

Why computers cannot play bridge; judgment at work

The game of bridge, like chess, provides an immediate challenge to computer programmers solely because of the very large number of possibilities. It is estimated that the number of possible positions in chess is 10^{120}. Bridge, similarly, offers a huge number of possible hands. The official *Encyclopedia of Bridge* calculates the number of possible hands which one player can hold as 5×10^{28} (this is the possible number of 13 cards out of the 52; clearly the number is greater if one calculates for all four players). The number of possible bridge positions is approximately 10^{80}. These very large numbers are not infinite or indefinite. They are so very big, however, that neither a person nor a machine could ever have the time to consider all the possible positions in either chess or bridge (No game could ever be completed in less than hundreds of years).[28] This feature of chess alone marks how much progress has been made, from the early algorithms to the "heuristics"[29] of Simon and others, and finally in 1999, after about 40 years of effort, culminating with the success of the machine beating the best human beings. Why should one not expect that sooner or later similar ingenuity will lead to success in bridge? In fact, bridge programs are not successful, and as I have argued in detail elsewhere,[30] computers will never play high level bridge as humans can. It is worth summarizing that argument here, since the bridge example illustrates the limits of rules, and the importance of human judgment in an area other than values and feelings.

The more competent the player, the more often the decision to bid or not to bid, and what to bid, is based on factors such as "table feel," which encompasses noticing those almost imperceptible pauses and hesitations which human beings display when bidding, or not bidding. These factors are not extraneous to the game, but are part of bridge competence. The top players are almost certainly those who can bring into play these abilities, which go beyond reasoning, inferences, deductions, memory of system, and the set of prescriptive rules. In bidding, as in the more difficult aspects of the game (defence and play of the hand), that extra something which goes beyond reasoning is best captured by the notion of "judgment."

If judgment is crucial for bridge, and the computer is not capable of judgment, then it follows that it cannot and will not play bridge; the machine can play some form of the game, but it will never play the bridge game played by human beings. Judgment is different than reasoning, as already noted. Therefore, computers, although they are excellent at following rules, are not capable of judgment. With all this in mind, educators are beginning to introduce the game of bridge to children at school, and at home. Just as the game of chess helps develop logical reasoning, bridge stimulates the development of judgment. It should be said that workers in artificial intelligence, and those working on bridge robots are ready to bet that I am wrong. They predict that within the next few years computers/robots will beat any human being at bridge.[31]

Judgment and emotion

Let us assume that the argument of the above section is correct. Machines, including the most sophisticated computers (and eventually robots), will not be able to exhibit human judgment, and will never, for that reason, be able to play high-level bridge. Most bridge players agree with me, but most artificial intelligence programmers are equally convinced that I am wrong. The bets are on the table, and only time will tell whether success in bridge (or in the game "Go")[32] will be achieved as it has in chess. The same controversy applies to emotion. In our view, machines (and even robots) will not have human emotion (notwithstanding the Robin Williams character in the movie "Bicentennial Man").

Robots are portrayed by Isaac Aasimov, both in the book and the movie, *I Robot*, as having judgment and emotion. These make them like humans. In the Foundation series, the ability to detect emotions for the Mule and the Second Foundation (super psychologists) is tied to their ability to alter them. In general, it is true in real life (forget science fiction) that the ability to feel is linked to the ability to better able to influence others. Feeling more, unfortunately also leads to greater suffering since the pain of some emotions is magnified.

We have to take science fiction with a grain of salt of course. In the Star Trek T.V. series and movies, we have Mr. Spock who makes moral decisions, has judgment without emotion. He is portrayed as having good moral reasoning (a la Kohlberg) without the emotions of a human being. It must be emphasized that this fictional portrayal does not even begin to show what humans can be like.[33]

Maybe robots will have emotions, and maybe machines and bodiless gods might have feelings. Philosophers and psychologists continue to debate this issue.[34] In the meantime, we will continue to deal with real human beings where feelings are inextricably tied to our bodies and brains.

We return to emotions, and their link to values and virtues in Part III. Here I only wish to stress that judgments are inextricably linked to emotions. In the first place, as mentioned above, judgments involve certain emotions, particularly doubt, uncertainty, and confidence. These feelings that we have will appear at different levels, depending on the situation, the values, and many other factors. One cannot talk of judgment, or help impart it to our children, without this emotional component. In the other direction, emotions themselves are, on the best analysis, a form of judgment.[35] They are not simply "feelings" or physiological responses; they have a cognitive component involving appraisal, as well as considerations of relevance and importance (see Chapter 7). Finally, emotions play a role in our moral decisions, as sketched in the section above. Anger is not only a feeling, or even an emotion with a cognitive dimension; it is a moral emotion. As seen above, Aristotle's point is that we have to know when and how to express our anger, in the right degree, and with the right people. To this, and other moral emotions, we will return in part III, Chapter 8.

Ten ways to develop good judgment for ourselves and our children

Each of the following suggestions for improving judgment are based on the theoretical discussion above. To summarize: the key concepts are ambiguity, the limits of rules, uncertainty, and similarity / difference. These notions, along with the definition of judgment (see page 35) are assumed. A practical starting-place can be the test of judgment (page 163) which is discussed at the very beginning of the chapter (see page 33). All the elements for their development of judgment can be found in these drawings. For each of the 10 following suggestions, I will refer to this judgment test.

1. Classification, sorting, labelling, grouping

At the very earliest ages (from early infancy), even before there is any possibility of real dialogue, there are things parents can deliberately do to help in the later development of judgment. Obviously, many of these will be non-verbal, but are excellent activities to encourage and fun too! Whenever possible, group items by form and color, as you and your children play with blocks, crayons, and other items (including food items, why not?). Label the groupings as well, for children comprehend a great deal at very early ages, long before they can say much.[36] Say: "These are red things, those green. These are animals, and those animals are cats." Of course many parents already do this, and early childhood educators, whether influenced by Montessori or Piaget, know the importance of this kind of activity. What we often miss, however, is the importance of doing and talking at very young ages. By the time the child is 2 years old, he will be better able to classify and group for himself (see Appendix B for the practice judgment items used in the Prevention of violence test), if exposed earlier to this kind of operation. In pre-testing, many 5 year olds were better than others at these easier classifications (in terms of "animal" versus "human," or "alive," versus "not alive"). At ages 2 to 4, children may not have had the stimulation at even the easier items, like those involving form and color.[37] Of course, parents can help children classify using other modalities in addition to form and color. Let us not forget sounds, lullabies, speech rhythms and humming – all of which can occur very early on – even at a few days of age.

2. Similarity

From around age 2 onwards, the modality of communication becomes primarily verbal. Now, one not only wants to provide the labels ("these are red" or "animals are living things"); we can also begin to expect the child to begin his own verbal categories. Part of the crucial period in identity development occurs during these years,[38] and we often miss the opportunity to point out similarities to children, and encourage them to repeat the categories. It is important to stress that similarity precedes difference in the child's natural development; our verbal input should also put precedence on how things are alike, before we get to how they are different. So, for example, let us help the child refer to many different kinds of coins as money, before we tell him about dimes, nickels and quarters.

3. Differences

Hard on the heels of our talking a lot about the sameness of things, comes the differences and distinctions. Look once again at Figure 2-1. This Sesame Street type activity of finding the thing which "doesn't belong" is a very important indicator of cognitive development. Most children at age 5 have difficulty finding the "correct" answer to the four items, and even more difficulty giving an adequate explanation for why they chose one item rather than another. In regard to item 4, treating of violence, practically no child at age 5 (or younger) is capable of choosing the relevant picture, much less explaining why this is their choice. As mentioned before, after 1 year, many of them do develop their judgment so that they can pick drawing no. 3, and justify their choice. One of the ways this was achieved was via a discussion of the butterfly episode. See Appendix B for this discussion children have about tearing the wing of a butterfly, as opposed to tearing a doll or teddy bear. In the (philosophical) discussions children have about these matters, they learn to compare and contrast, and see the differences amongst the similarities. Thus, for example, they might begin to explore why it is okay to tear a piece of paper, and not a butterfly, why one feels badly when an animal is hurt, but perhaps also when a doll's arm is torn, and so on. Results with hundreds of young children clearly demonstrate that these kinds of considerations will make them better at their judgments, as measured by the violence drawings. As parents, we can offer the same kind of stimulation to our children at home, as is provided in schools, using this material.[39]

Situations can have much in common, and when they do, rules that have generally worked in like cases can be expected to work again. What parents must do, however, is equip the child to distinguish like from unlike situations, usual from unique situations, typical from atypical situations. The child should be prepared to confront the different, courageously and resourcefully, rather than trying to impose upon the unusual situation a rule that is doomed to fail.

So long as the child cannot distinguish similar situations (to which rules based on past experience may apply) from dissimilar situations (which require that something unique be devised), the whole question of the role of rules in moral behavior is mute.

Children are very ready to recognize that special cases require special solutions. In class, they may insist that teachers should treat all students alike and yet, if a child with a disability is part of the class, and therefore gets different treatment, they can understand and accept it, because the different treatment is justified by the differences in the children's situations. This obviously requires that children possess the capacity to perceive similarities and differences. Therefore one of the main objectives for parents is to help children read situations accurately so that they are aware of relevant similarities and differences.

An example from the novelette *Pixie* illustrates the importance of "difference" Miranda has criticized Pixie for putting the sugar over the cereal first rather than the milk first and then the sugar. Pixie argues that Miranda is blaming her for behavior that is neither right nor wrong. In fact, Pixie has pinpointed the criterion she uses to determine the difference between right and wrong when she asks "What difference does it make whether I put the sugar on first or the milk on first?" In other words, if something is to be called "right," it must be shown that its consequences are relevantly different than the consequences of something called "wrong." If the consequences of two actions are identical (or not relevantly different) then there is no justification for judging the two kinds of behavior differently.

4. Ambiguity

We need to provide as many ambiguous situations and examples as possible. Returning once again to an example of judgment test (see page 163) we see that there is a calculated uncertainty built in to the drawings. There are many ways to choose the item which is not like the others. One can use color (those guys are white, or yellow), or other criteria. Once one begins to get into the habit of exploring differences, one will see that one type of violence is different than the others. One may, as adults, use words like "unequal combat" or "dominant and submission." Children, of course, may not have the vocabulary of this sort. Nevertheless, those who see it are confident in their choice, and make their justifications very clear and in their own terms. "This kind of hitting is wrong," or they might say "it is not fair," or even "I know this is different but I can't say why." Whatever their linguistic ability, we have helped them by providing situations and contexts which are uncertain, and allow for different possible responses. Judgment is inevitably based on some kind of ambiguity, and we will help our children develop better judgments, as we provide more of this kind of example.

5. Language

We have already referred to the use of language in regard to classification, similarities, differences, and ambiguity. Another important task for parents is to introduce subtle nuances of language to underscore its conventional nature. Take the rule for example "red means stop, green means go." We know that this might have been "green means stop, red means go." Playing the game with children whereby they experiment with the inverted rules helps them to see that much of language is arbitrary. One advantage of this will be to downplay certain stereotypes and prejudices, for example that white is good and black is bad.[40] A second advantage to this playing around with language will be to increase the child's meta-cognitive consciousness and linguistic auto-regulation.[41] For example, it is very difficult for most children, and even many adults, to say "dogs meow" and "cats bark," even when trained to accept a make-believe world where this is the case.

We can, of course, also begin to help our children express similarities, differences, comparisons and contrasts if we focus on the parts of language which are often neglected during the very early years. In the Philosophy for Children Program used in many schools,[42] there is one particular story called *Pixie* which provides some of the ways children can become more adept at language. In particular, there are exercises which are used successfully by teachers to help children learn about these nuances. Some examples pertaining to contrasts, resemblances, ambiguity, comparisons, connectors, and relationships are provided in the appendices. Parents can use these, or modify, adopt, or invent their own. The importance is being aware of the kind of language sensitivity one is attempting to foster. As the creators of *Pixie* say in their introduction:

> If curiosity is the disposition which children and philosophers share, then concern with the nature of similarity and difference is their common intellectual interest. Either we compare things with one another, says Plato in *The States-man,* or we compare them with an ideal standard. The "we" here can stand indifferently for philosophers, for children, or, in fact, for anyone. We discover similarities and differences by making comparisons, and to make comparisons is therefore to uncover similar and different relationships. Hence, young children are intent upon examining the nature of exact and inexact (or literal and figurative) comparisons, and as they do so, they find themselves investigating similes, metaphors and analogie.

We must attempt to provide children with sequenced exercises which will give them practice in the making of comparisons both of "things" as well as "terms" and of relationships. Some children are prolific when it comes to producing fanciful or even extravagant associations; others are timid or inhibited. Nevertheless, the objective for all groups must be a competence in perceiving and expressing similarities and differences; those who use language with an exuberant flair for figurative expression will always feel free to go beyond such competence, while those who have been virtually inarticulate will find that practice in the making of comparisons suddenly opens new vistas in the description and explanation of the world around them.

Early childhood is a period in which language is being acquired at an incredibly rapid rate. We are inclined to take an indulgent view towards vocabulary expansion, even where it represents the acquisition of increasingly exotic terms by children whose proficiency in the use of such unglamorous terms as "all," "only," "because," "same" and "different" is uncertain and unsteady. This indulgence in novelty can be short-sighted, unwise and not enough: one has to work with children so that they can develop a firm command of the basic operations of a language, the addition of new terminology is more likely to aggravate the problem than to alleviate it.

It is when we contrast and compare that we discover relationships: faster than, busier than, equal to, later than. We also discover familial connections: mother of, cousin of, grandfather of. Likewise, we find that there are important linguistic relationships: the way some verbs "take objects" and others don't, the way nouns may be modified by adjectives and verbs by adverbs. Out of this potpourri emerges the astonishing and monumental fact of *resemblance:* of words with one another, of people with one another, of things and events with one another, of words with people and with things. These resemblances we express by means of literal comparisons, and by figurative means as well, *e.g.* similes, metaphors, and analogies.

Awareness of ambiguity, then, is the opening wedge of the struggle to establish a dynamic balance between the child's ability to function figuratively as well as literally. In a sense, simile is the inverse of ambiguity. An ambiguous word can have several distinct meanings in a particular context, whereas a simile suggests that two different things have a definite resemblance. So ambiguity sees difference in similarity, and simile sees similarity in difference.

In simile, comparison is explicit (whether one says "X is like Y," or "X is as _____ as Y.) In metaphor, however, comparison is suppressed. In metaphor, one wishes to call attention not to a resemblance between two things normally taken to be different but to the *identity* of those two different things. To say "George was angry" is clinical and remote, for it merely tells us that George was a member of the class of angry beings. "George's face was like a thundercloud" has more emotional effect, although it still involves us in the making of a conscious comparison. "George's face was a thundercloud" is still more dramatic because it eliminates the comparison and speaks of the two radically different things as if they were one. Writers accustomed to using figurative language find literal statements like "George was angry" pale and anemic. Writers accustomed to using literal language find metaphors to be examples of linguistic overkill. However, both forms of expression have their purposes, and it is only when used for the wrong purpose that either mode of expression may be found inappropriate.

A simile is a claim that two things normally taken to be different are in some respect similar; an analogy is a claim that two relationships are alike. Such, at least, is the minimal analogy, taking as it does the form A is to B as C is to D. Notice that analogies, like similes, involve likeness or similarity. Just as similes become radically dramatized when the similarity claim is replaced by an identity claim and they become metaphors, so analogies can take the form A:B :: C:D, where the relationships being compared are ratios and the alleged comparison is in fact a statement of equivalence. But the equivalence relationship is anything but dramatic: 3:6 :: 12:24 is simply a tautology, another way of saying $1/2 = 1/2$.

Not that small children – even those who are only three or four years of age – need to be counselled by us on the creation of similes and metaphors: Their fertility in these matters is far greater than that of adults. What they lack, however, is the critical sense which would enable them to judge the appropriateness or the inappropriateness of the figures of speech they can so elaborately construct. The strengthening of that critical sense can in turn help them become aware of whether their own analogical reasonings are being done well or badly.

6. Imagination

Moral problems are a subclass of human problems in general. It takes imagination to envisage the various ways in which an existing, unsatisfactory situation might be transformed. One has to be able to visualize what would happen if this were to be done or that were to be done, or if nothing were to be done at all. In other words, imagination is needed to anticipate the goals that individuals or groups might seek. At the same time, it takes imagination to review the alternative ways in which goals could be achieved. What steps would have to be taken? Who would have to be involved? What must be done first and then second, and so on? Exercises in moral imagination consist of two major varieties; first, there are those that involve consideration of different types of means-ends relations, and, secondly, there are those that involve different types of part-whole relations.[43]

One wants to encourage lots of make-believe, and story-telling. Here we part company with rigid adherents to some of Maria Montessori's dogmas. Some orthodox disciples have objected to this kind of activity by citing Montessori as an authority. Just like with Piaget (see introduction), one has to take the brilliant insights of Montessorri, but acknowledge where she was wrong. The importance of the relationship of make-believe to judgment is best brought out by considering the notion of hermeneutics, or if-then thinking. We want children to think about how things might have been, to use their imagination to consider reality and appearance, and many different possibilities. Research has shown that those children who have developed this ability will be the best at judgment, at critical and creative thinking. They will be able to evaluate arguments, consider the points of view of others, but maintain their own point of view. They will show what is called moral autonomy,[44] the conviction and strength of mind to hold a moral position, but not in a dogmatic way. Furthermore, they are those in the best position to resist slogans, peer pressure, and propaganda.[45] Similes and metaphors will have the added advantage, in addition to fostering critical and creative thinking, to get us to see the emotions of others, that is in developing empathy (see Chapter 6).

Before concluding this section, let us point out that there exists a danger in regard to the components of imagination. Although we have pointed out the benefit of imagination in regard to developing judgment, a too active imagination may lead to irrational fears.[46] Parents have to tread the fine line, as so often by distinguishing what is real from what is imaginary without disparaging either. Do not hesitate to use the phrase "you dreamt that" or "you imagined that" but be careful not to minimize the experience by saying for example "You only imagined that." Of course, when a child reports a nightmare, we want to calm them – and appropriately so – by saying "that was only a dream."

7. Relevance: Good and bad discrimination

Judgment, as we have seen, not only allows for, but encourages the making of distinctions. We want to learn to discriminate. However, we only want to do this when it is appropriate and justified. In short, there are good and bad discriminations. Boys and girls are different in some ways; the same in others. We want to teach our children that most activities should be available for girls and boys. Marla Thomas's tape-cassette Free To Be You And Me is an excellent educational device for discussing gender equality with very young children. The message is that there is nothing under the sun that a girl or a boy cannot be or achieve. The only exception is that girls, if they wish may become "mommies," and boys, "daddies." So much for the similarity part. Parents must also, however, acknowledge difference, where difference exists. At the very least anatomy is a fact, and should not be denied or ignored. In the twenty first century, we have more complex facts to introduce, including what is known about the brain and physiological aspects such as temperament.[47] For example boys are more active than girls from early infancy.[48] Leaving neurophysiology aside, there are the social conventions about gender. We have to explain to our children, for example that restaurants often have separate bathrooms for boys and girls although this is different than at home. We must be prepared for what to say when a boy wants to try on 'girls' clothes or makeup. A lot depends on the age of the child and the circumstances as well. Very young children (let's say 2-5) will experiment as part of make believe and in forming their identity, using adults as models. If one's 7 year-old boy, on the other hand, puts on a dress and lipstick before heading off to school, this is a bit more complicated. A conversation is needed. However liberal one may be about these matters, one has to ask questions about one's child's motivation, and be prepared to point out the consequences of this choice. For example, teasing, bullying and violence are all possible, and these risks should be considered. One had to mention that other people (children and adults) may be uncomfortable, and perhaps be ready to offer explanations for the embarrassment which some will feel. The ultimate choice of the parent, which cannot be avoided, even after the conversation, will be whether to allow the child to go to school, or insist on his staying home. These are very complicated matters about which well-meaning parents may have different views. We will return to this in Chapter 4. The bottom line is to at the very least make sure that you are ready to talk to your children about these questions.

Of course, this is precisely the situation for adult citizens considering issues such as same-sex marriage, or affirmative action. One has to ask whether treating some groups differently is justified or not. Is it right to allow more Blacks into some colleges, on the grounds of past injustice? Is it justified to treat gays who want to marry differently than others? These weighty matters have their counterpart among children. At a very early age, they have begun to adopt views about groups. Many of their attitudes and beliefs may be prejudices. A key component to helping develop good judgment is to examine these prejudices (notice the root "pre-judge"), and ask whether they are justified, or only based on hearsay or propaganda or inadequate evidence. One example we have used with fairly young children concerns handicaps. Children are different, and some may lack abilities of others. Does it justify treating them differently? These are questions very young children can understand. Another example came up in a research project with 7 to 8 year-olds.[49] They were told that many left handed people are bad drivers. Then they were asked whether they could say that Mary or John, who was left handed, was a bad driver. Were they sure? At first most children will say "Yes," and they are certain of their response. However, after a number of months of considering the issues of prejudices and relevance, a great number of the children insisted that one cannot say whether any individual left handed person is a bad driver, even if many are. Many educational programs looking at prejudice, school violence, racism, sexism, and stereotypes, have shown some success at helping children look at this issue of relevance, and the distinction between good and bad discriminations.[50] Parents can do similar things with children at home. Good reasons, criteria and burden of proof: these notions are the ones that we need in later life. Much better to begin introducing them at the very youngest age possible.

8. Analogies

Helen Keller, it is said, made her famous breakthrough along with her educator when she began to make use of analogical reasoning.[51] She did it, of course, being blind and deaf, without the help of language. Most people luckily do not suffer from these extreme handicaps, and can make use of analogies in verbal terms, situations and relationships. Some of these examples, again inspired, or borrowed from, the P4C Program are provided in the appendices at the end of the book. Analogical reasoning, is often considered as one of the best exercises for increasing judgment. Of course, it will only be used in a full blown verbal sense when children are a bit older, and can profit from the examples. Typically, I would suggest around 7 or 8 years of age.

9. Debate, Dialogue, Discuss

This suggestion is not a strategy but more an attitude which adults must be ready to adopt. Because of the very nature of judgment as a competence where rules no longer help, one must be ready to take some risks. Specifically, one has to be ready to talk about feelings, situations and values, much more than one might have in the past. One must not simply invoke the old "I said so" or other forms of authority. Nor can one simply invoke the rules without explanation (one exception, and it is important, concerns protection in case of immediate danger!).

In regard to each and every one of the values to be discussed in the chapters to follow, one must be prepared for a lot of debate, discussion and dialogue. The upside is that when our children are honest, polite, responsible and cooperative; when they are kind, caring people, it will be out of a reflection and awareness that comes from them and their own understanding. They will be better able to keep to rules and principles in the face of temptations, precisely because their values will be based, not on imposition and authority, but on a patient series of explanations and reasoning. It will often be difficult to have to discuss delicate matters like swearing, lying and cheating (see Chapter 3). One may be inclined simply to "lay down the law." However, the long-term benefits of doing more talking are well worth it. Particularly if whatever one says is reinforced by what one does (see modelling and behavior in the introduction).

There is nothing wrong with admitting that one is uncertain about some complicated moral issues. On the contrary it is very appropriate not to fake certainty when we don't feel it. In the first place, children are often not fooled, and we will lose their trust. Secondly, by feigning dogmatic certainty when inappropriate, we may lead our children into what Chopra calls "the Grip of Illusion."[52] The resulting perception of fakery by the child may reside in them for life.

To adopt this change in attitude may be difficult but essential. It is a true open-mindedness, which allows a parent to be ready to change one's view about matters concerning any value, or issues where one has had a longstanding point of view. One must genuinely consider the perspective, and arguments of the child, and consider the possibility that one might change one's decision or policy. Two of these examples which involved such a change in my life are discussed in the preface. In my case, the arguments of my grand-daughters led to reconsidering our view about politeness (see Chapter 4 and Chapter 10). Some of your own most cherished traditions, even about sexuality, religion, or cursing must similarly be open to possible revision!

10. Consult other judges

Whatever the issue where moral values may be colliding, ambiguous, or difficult to determine, we want to help our own judgment by consulting others whom we trust. As adults, when confronted by a moral choice, we will ask a friend (or perhaps 2 or 3 friends) their opinions, their experience, and their advice. Of course in the final analysis, we make our own choice and decision. But the input is very important. We may even have a panel of these judges, in a very informal way (perhaps 3 friends with different perspectives), whom we can consult when confronted with a difficult situation (perhaps they will reciprocate by asking us). So with children, let us be ready to see what other parents would say or do, and also encourage our children to see what a friend would do, we must encourage them to think for themselves. We will show them, however, that there is no shame (quite the contrary!) to see how others see it.

Consulting others can, and should be done long before the actual conversation occurs. Indeed, preparation is needed to know what one will say when questions arise about sexuality (what Mogel calls "The Big Hug"[53]) or all the other delicate subjects including the "G" question (see Part IV, Chapter 12, on God, Santa Claus etc.) This preparation can be supplemented, of course, by reading what others have written about these topics, in addition to the conversations with one's selected group of judges.

In discussing our ideas with others we must try to strike a balance with others, a balance from being too defensive and being too deferent. Our attitude should be that we are in a cooperative search for truth, and while every informed opinion is to be welcomed, no opinion is to be automatically adopted.

Some hints about whom to chose as our consulting judges: Try to find other parents who will be likely to argue for opposing points of view. Make a list of friends whom you trust to consult, trying for a gamut of perspectives. For example, it is an idea to have one friend/parent who is likely to be more cautious and conservative, and another friend/parent who might come down more on a liberal, risk-taking side. Another idea might be to include at least one woman and at least one man in your preferred list. Above all, it is important that the few other people you consult are people you trust, and are likely to be sensitive to your point of view and your particular family situation.

People whose judgment is prized will be those who have confidence, and inspire confidence. They will judge issues on their merit and not be frightened to voice an opinion even if it is a minority view, or politically incorrect. There is generally a consensus about these kinds of people; we see them as wise. King Solomon was known as a great judge and a wise man; as with all good judges, they were ready and willing to go beyond the rules. Wise people with the best judgment also have the capacity to listen well, and to formulate their point of view in a nuanced way. In other words, the best judges will also have the most highly developed empathy (more on this in Chapter 6).

As mentioned in the acknowledgments (see p. xiii), I discussed all these issues at great lengths with my collaborator Cynthia Martiny. In addition, we consulted friends and family about each of the issues discussed in this book. Concerning just one question namely: "Do we ask our children to show gratitude, or apologize even if they don't mean it?" I solicited the opinions of my daughter Miriam, my grand-son Joseph, my wife Carole and two friends, "one liberal," "one conservative." This group represented a diversity of ages and perspectives about child-rearing and other matters of value. There was some consensus about the matter, and some differences as well. The advice that we offer educators (see Chapters 4 and 5) reflect these various views. In the final analysis, of course, the judgment about the right thing to do is ours.

Part II
Specific Values

The following three chapters look at three core values; honesty, politeness, and responsibility. Each of these encompasses other related values of course. For example, honesty will include trust, truth, lying, cheating, stealing, promise-keeping, tact, diplomacy, hypocrisy, sarcasm and humor. Politeness involves the concepts of respect and consideration. Responsibility is a multifaceted notion, which includes questions of blame, praise, reward, punishment, autonomy, and obedience.

The perspective of values in the first chapter of this book is assumed. In other words, the focus will be on the universal aspects of these core values. Cultural aspects, where they exist, will serve as contrast to the universal features of each of the specific values and ideas explored.

The analysis of judgment in the second chapter of this book will be applied to each of the core concepts in Chapters 3 to 5. The general ways of developing judgment are put into practice as applied to honesty, politeness, responsibility, and the rest.

3
Honesty

Joke 1:

> Two merchants competing for the same business meet at the airport.
>
> "Where are you going?" asked the first.
>
> "Frankfurt" replied the other.
>
> "Liar" cried the first merchant. "You say that you're going to Frankfurt to make me believe that you are going to *Amsterdam*, but I know perfectly well that you are really going to Frankfort, so don't try to fool me."

The point of the joke, of course, is that we can try to deceive another person ("lie" to them) by telling the literal truth.[1] A more serious example of this is commonplace in theatre and the movies. The husband says to his wife "I was with a girlfriend today having an affair," as the best way to make her believe he was doing something else, whereas in fact, he had been with the girlfriend having an affair.

Is lying wrong? Why is lying wrong?

I recently was asked to speak on a television panel on the psychological effects of lying.[2] Two psychiatrists expounded their theories on the psychopathology of lying and liars. They were followed by a bright college student whose initial contribution was: "Everyone lies!," shocking the shrinks. On this point, I agreed with her. My own contribution, as the designated philosopher/psychologist was to insist that we first ask: "What is lying?" Before we can discuss the moral question about lying, whether and when it is wrong, we must try to answer the question about its meaning.

What is "lying"?

Before trying to answer, or giving a definition, try the following two examples taken from developmental research.[3]

Example A

Sally walks by a fence and peeks behind it, seeing an elephant.. Sally then meets Jimmy, who says: "What animal is there behind the fence?" She says "A dog." Is this a lie? Then Jimmy meets Annie, who asks: "What animal is behind the fence?" Jimmy says: "A dog." Did Jimmy lie? Try another scenario:

Example B

Sally begins the same way, seeing an elephant, meets Jimmy, and tells him it was a dog, Jimmy then meets Annie and tells her it is an elephant. Who lied? Did Jimmy lie when he said that it was an elephant? Have you made your choices?

Now the important thing is to know that most people cannot agree (at any age) about whether Jimmy lied or did not lie in Example B, or sometimes whether Sally or Jimmy lied in Example A. Children up to the age of 5 will inevitably think that Sally lied in the first case, and that Jimmy did not lie in the last case. For of course they are using "lying" in the literal sense of "not telling the truth" (it was, in fact, an elephant!). Children and adults at all ages will have different opinions on these matters, and I have had very lively debates on the matter in my moral education classes. Does one have to know the intentions of a person to determine if it was a lie? Is it deception which is crucial? How can we be sure that Sally or Jimmie wasn't mistaken, or telling a joke, etc. etc.

Why is lying wrong? Attempt no. 2

If we are trying intentionally to deceive someone, our act is wrong (we can tell our child "that was bad"), because it may lead to harmful consequences. The other person may need to need the truth, and we are not providing it. This may be harmful for the other person, because we told them it was a dog, they might be hurt by the elephant that was really there (see examples A and B). It may be harmful to ourselves as captured nicely in the "Cry Wolf" story, where one does not tell the truth a few times, yet when that person is in danger, and tells the truth, people will not believe the person. This leads to the question of trust. Keeping to the facts, saying it like it is, in general being respectful of the truth, allows others to trust one's word, and this is important. If we do not tell the truth frequently, we may get a reputation as a liar, as untrustworthy, and our friends and relatives will be less likely to like this part of our character. Children (and all of us) will also lie (attempt to deceive) because we may be trying to protect ourselves, in a self-serving way, so as to escape responsibility, blame and punishment. We do not "own up" to what we did. This issue will need an entire chapter (see Chapter 5, Responsibility). We ought to tell the truth to others, much as we expect them to give us the truth. So, in this Golden Rule version, it is a matter of fairness. Lying unto others (friends, parents) would presumably not be what we would wish others (friends, parents) to do unto us.

Each of these four general explanations of why lying is wrong can be used in talking to children, even very young children.

. 1. Lying may be harmful and dangerous.
2. Lying may lead to lack of trust.
3. Lying is not taking responsibility.
4. Lying may be unfair.

It should be noticed that we do not go along with those philosophers like Immanuel Kant and Saint Augustine who saw lying as absolutely and always wrong.[4] We take truth as a high value, but not an absolute one.[5] However, preparing to talk to children about why lying is wrong becomes even more complicated (alas!) because sometimes there are good reasons for lying, and justifications for doing so. The following two sections discuss some of these.

Humor, sarcasm, exaggeration, make-believe, imagination.

Children like to hear jokes, and to tell jokes. Furthermore, it is important to encourage this, both for their emotional and cognitive development. Joking, however, inevitably involves not telling the truth (or at least distorting it a bit) To take an obvious, (not very funny) example: one looks at the rain, and says: "What a beautiful sunny day!" This may be, in adult form, a kind of sarcasm or irony. For young children, it is telling an untruth. Of course in no case do we want to consider it a case of lying. This is because certain crucial features of the concept of lying, like intentionally deceiving, are missing.

Make-believe, similarly, and any kind of pretence makes use of the child's imagination, and is to be encouraged as well from earliest ages. Here too, there will be purposeful falsehoods, but they are in no ways blameworthy. The problem, of course, will be to distinguish the cases where we are talking about justified falsehoods, as in this section, and those cases which are unjustified as in the section above. Only judgment, which deals case by case, will solve this problem. There can be no absolutely clear rules to tell us when we are dealing with a serious situation (where lying is wrong) and a trivial or neutral situation where lying may be appropriate and good.

Children are quite able to tell the difference between a lie about a misdeed, and exaggeration or a mistaken guess. Of course, not only children but adults too will often confuse an exaggeration or a mistaken guess with a self-serving lie. We may misinterpret a person's remark which was meant as a joke, but taken it as serious, an attempt to deceive, or an outright lie. Notwithstanding these difficulties very young children are quite ready to begin to make the relevant distinctions. Jean

Piaget's work on lying in 1932 is very important but he made some definite errors.[6] The most important of Piaget's mistakes was to tell us that children (before about 9 years of age) could not understand the importance of intentions for wrong lying. Piaget found that children would decide something was a lie on the basis of whether the statement was believed or whether it was punished. *In 2006 we can assert unequivocally that children as young as five are very capable of making these distinctions.*[7] Piaget linked his conversations about lying with children, as he did with all his research about moral concepts, to his theory of stages. In regard to lying Piaget told us that at stage 1 (2 to about 5 or 6 years of age) the child will judge the wrongness of a lie in terms of it being imposed by an authority, along with the accompanying sanctions. At a second stage (at around 7 or 8 years of age) the child will be able to see a lie as wrong, even if there is no punishment or sanction. However, children from about 7 until about 11 or 12 years of age according to Piaget, continue to see the lie as absolutely wrong, coming from an adult or God. Only at Piaget's 3rd stage (11 or 12 years of age upwards) does a child begin to link the wrongness of lying to lack of trust, confidence and mutual affection. Let us emphasize again, that the consensus in 2006 is that the five-year old child is perfectly capable of making the distinctions which Piaget thought only possible from the age of about 11.

Joke 2:

Psychiatrist (to Patient): You are stupid!
Patient: I demand another opinion!
Psychiatrist: O.K., You are ugly too.

Tact and diplomacy: those "little white lies"

When a friend asks us whether we like their new dress or painting (which they like very much, and have purchased for a lot of money), we may not share their enthusiasm. Although we hate the painting or dress, we may have learned to be tactful, not to hurt their feelings. This may mean telling them that we do not like it, but trying to find soothing words to express the thought. Or it may depend on the relationship. Is this a friend who wants our clear opinion, or a friend (or perhaps just an acquaintance) who would prefer the little "white lie"? Furthermore, even as we tell the truth as we see it, to what degree are we bound to tell "the whole truth"? In a court of law, it is an obligation, but in most of our moral life, we have the choice about how much is right to say. Too much detail, like too little, may be equally mistaken. Every one of these complications arises early on, where as educators (parents or teachers) we must decide how to respond to the question about the child's dress, or painting. We want to teach children to be aware of other's feelings, and to occasionally lie when appropriate. Once again, only judgment of each case can begin to give us the path to the right response.

There are other reasons for justified lies in addition to those already mentioned. Two of these are lying to protect someone else's privacy and lying to appear humble, and avoid the sin of pride.[8] Each of these issues, that of privacy, and that of humility versus pride are quite complicated. Each will be treated in a later section of the book (for privacy see Chapter 11, for pride and humility see Chapter 8).

Hypocrisy

If tact and diplomacy are considered good things on occasion, we do not, however, want to encourage hypocrisy. What is "hypocrisy"? According to the Oxford dictionary it means saying what one does not believe. It also can mean "simulating or pretending virtue." Finally an actor in the original Greek meaning was known "as a hypocrite" (notice that the actor, in pretending, was not necessarily doing something bad). Our modern version of hypocrisy has extended the notion to include saying one thing and doing another. For example, if we tell our children don't steal, and they see us taking a pillow or ashtray from the hotel, they may accuse us of being guilty of hypocrisy. Other examples include preaching about health, including eating good food and not smoking, while engaging in these activities. This again is hypocrisy in the pejorative sense.

Although most of us strive not to be a hypocrite in any of the relevant senses just discussed, not all educators agree. In a recent book by Judith Shklar entitled *Ordinary Vices,*[9] she argues that hypocrisy should be encouraged. She says that in a liberal democracy, we need a certain amount of this trait. Shklar cites eighteenth century philosopher David Hume who asserted about hypocrisy that "the common duties of society usually require it" and that it was "impossible to pass through the world without it." She provides an episode of hypocrisy in a detailed example from the autobiography of Benjamin Franklin,[10] who insisted that in a liberal democracy one could not afford public sincerity. Franklin was against honesty which could humiliate and was arguing for compromise in a political society in which people have many serious differences of belief or interest.[11] We may all see the point, given the nature of politicians. The fact that most of them are hypocrites (saying what they do not believe) does not, for us, make hypocrisy a good thing, or a virtue to teach our children.

Deception as a cognitive skill

Research has shown conclusively that those children (as young as 3) who can lie about a transgression, even in a self-serving way, will be more advanced in their cognitive development, as well as in their emotional development.[12] It takes a certain amount of creativity, and one has to care enough on occasion to think of a good lie to fit a specific occasion. If the intention of the lie is to protect the feelings of another person we must have developed our empathy for others in the relevant way. The skills involved in lying (even self-serving lying to escape blame or punishment), are generalized to other facets of their intelligence, as well as to their level of empathy, i.e. their ability to put themselves in the other's shoes (more in Chapter 6). Those children who are best at deception tend to be able to pick up tones and facial expression better than others; this is part of "emotional intelligence" (more in Chapter 7).

What about cheating? Is it wrong?

A second major form of dishonesty involves cheating. We want our children to learn not to cheat. Why? But first, as usual, What is "cheating"?

What is cheating?

The Oxford dictionary tells us that it is breaking the rules of a game. So if we are playing Old Maid, and the child peeks at the other's hand, instead of just "guessing" which card to choose, this is "cheating." But who established the rules of Old Maid, and are they known to the young child playing? So we have to say that cheating involves going against the rules, provided these are known. But of course, there are games which encourage cheating. In fact one card-game called "Cheat" is mentioned specifically in the Oxford dictionary as an example of what cheating is. But of course, when playing a card, and saying it is a King (it was really a Queen) this is cheating (and lying) but permitted, even encouraged by the game. Furthermore, this is fun for us and the child, as well as good for cognitive development. Of course we can change the rules of any game, including Old Maid discussed above. Playing with a young child, one can play the game with peeking, and without. Of course, one should insist that both people (adult and child, or both children) play by the same rules. That, of course, will get us into issues of fairness (a version of the Golden Rule?). I have often played simple games like Old Maid with very young children, and more complicated games, like Master-Mind with older children, encouraging different kinds of rules, from open peeking, to the specific rules suggested by the game-makers. As parents we can take a certain amount of cheating lightly. Nevertheless we must be ready to explain the benefits of playing the game by the rules, namely the special satisfaction one gets from winning fairly.

Is cheating wrong? Why? Second attempt

It depends. If we are taking unfair advantage when breaking the rules, by peeking for example, then we are cheating; it is wrong, because it is unfair, and must be discouraged. If, however, the cheating has been mutually agreed by the players in the game, then it is probably acceptable. Even here, however, this can be complicated by the problem of competition. So it is still wrong to agree to break the rules, if there are overriding rules laid down by the sport authorities to ensure general consistency. The famous cheating scandals in world-class bridge (ice-skating is another example) in recent years involved collusion amongst players (and sometimes referees) to mutually break the rules. If, however, individuals, or groups have cheated in this way, it may still be harmful to the entire sport or activity, and to the thousands who compete, adhering to the official rules. The famous tennis playing Williams sisters (Serena and Venus) were encouraged by their father (their coach when they were very young) to play against very competitive men who were likely to cheat, by calling balls in that were out and vice versa. Mr Williams in a recent interview on CNN defended this practice as preparing his girls for the real world.

Stealing

Stealing is like cheating; a matter of getting away with something, getting something for nothing. It may start with taking gum or candy from the corner store without paying, a common occurrence with many children, as we know. Children willing to do this, understand the thrill involved. As parents, this must be acknowledged, and talked about. Also children can be told that adults may have done this, or something similar, when younger.

Saint Augustine, in his Parable of the Pears, relates an incident which occurred as an adolescent, which he regretted to his dying day. He stole some pears, a fruit that he didn't particularly like. Perhaps the thrill of doing it (getting away with it) was sufficient motivation; more likely, peer pressure had its effect.

Philosophers have been puzzling over this passage in Augustine for a thousand years, particularly because Augustine tells us that the event of his pear stealing is crucial for understanding virtue, vice, sin and his ethical system [13] One small lesson we can learn as parents is to discuss frankly and openly, as Augustine did, the temptations in life. We can talk to our children about how they may be tempted to take something which doesn't belong to them: In addition to the thrill of the act, mentioned above, there is the immediate gratification of possessing the stolen object. What is the down side of stealing? This is the responsibility of parents to make known to children. As with cheating, one can point out that, sooner or later, one will get caught. More importantly, even if one never gets caught, there is the issue of unfairness. "Would one want someone to steal something from you?" we might offer (a good application of The Golden Rule). Next there is the satisfaction of having earned the desired object, obviously absent when it has been stolen. Working for something, saving money for it, and paying for it with one's savings, can have its own rewards, which can counterbalance the thrill of stealing it. Finally, with cheating, stealing, and self-serving forms of lying, there is the issue of trust and confidence. Someone who cheats more than once, or all the time, or steals a lot will lose the trust of those around them. Do we not cherish the trust of friends, family and neighbors more than the stolen candy, or the game we won by cheating?

Keeping Promises

"What a fool Honesty is! and Trust, is sworn brother a very simple gentleman." (William Shakespeare "The Winter's Tale," Act IV, Scene iv.

Promises are the intention to do something, usually for someone else, but occasionally for oneself. Typically, we say "I promise" which indicates this intention, creates an expectation that we will do it, and is equivalent to the legal contract. The promises that we make, and teach our children to make, are not, of course, legally binding. They do, however, create a moral obligation. The key ingredient involved in this moral obligation is trust. If we do not keep our promises then we will not inspire trust and confidence in others. What makes all of this even more complicated is that there are sometimes occasions where breaking the promise is the right thing to do. One such example involves making a promise not to reveal a secret, yet by not revealing, it may lead to real harm. A more comprehensive discussion of these matters will appear in Chapter 11 of this book.

The failure to keep a promise can be seen as a kind of lie. Many educators and philosophers discuss promise keeping and promise breaking in just this way.[14] In the movie "Lies My Father Told Me," based on the book of the same name, the "Lies" are promises made by the father to the child and not kept. Most children, even up to age 9, will see the breaking of promises as a kind of lie. Despite this, we have to try to disentangle those parts of promising which are forms of lying, and those that are not. If we promise our child to take them to the park and have no intention of doing so, then this is very much like a lie. If however, we mean to take them to the park and make the effort, but unforeseen events stymie us, we have in no way lied; we have just not been able to keep our promise, perhaps because of bad luck. It is important when making a promise to a child to be as precise as possible about time and duration. Therefore, if we say "I promise to take you to the circus" it is better to state when we have in mind. Is it today? Sometime this week? This month? This year? It is important to try to get these nuances across to our children when they are still very young. As stated elsewhere in this book, by the age of five, they are capable of a very sophisticated morality, and can certainly handle these distinctions.

The role of judgment: A review

There are very few rules about honesty, or at least very few simple organizing rules that tell the story. We do want this moral virtue in our children, and so it is an important moral value to discuss. However, the injunction "be honest" or even "tell the truth, don't lie, don't cheat" won't do the job. Or at least in a short-hand form we can use these slogans, but we still have work left to do: Judgment on our part (and our children as they develop it along with us) will allow us to look at every case and situation, bearing in mind some of these nuances discussed above. We will have to determine whether it was a case of lying or cheating, whether we think this is an example of good or bad lying or cheating, what the intentions were, and how much harm might be involved to the actor, or to others. We have to see in what way this particular situation is like, or unlike, others in which we have discouraged lying or cheating (for ourselves or our children), or, on the other hand, encouraged it. As discussed in Chapter 2, we can make use of all the stratagems at our disposal to make our best appraisal. Above all, it will be actively dialoguing, debating and discussing with our child, as well as with other people whose views we respect. As applied here, we should consult 2 or 3 friends about the issue, if needed, and involve 2 or 3 friends of our child as well, asking what they think about this particular act of lying or cheating, whether they think it is right or wrong, and why.

4
Politeness

Why be polite?

"Be polite," we say to our children. "Don't be rude" is also common. Why should they be polite? Why do we want them not to be rude? But, again, we have to first ask: What do we mean by "politeness" or "rudeness"?

What is "politeness"?

For the Oxford dictionary (and for many parents), politeness (or respect) means a kind of deference (as in saluting a superior officer in the army). When we talk of respect or politeness in this sense, we might really have in mind obedience, even blind obedience. If this is so, then we should rather avoid politeness altogether. In the southern U.S., this kind of politeness or respect was tantamount to racism as one expected a certain kind of talk from Blacks to Whites and vice-versa. A recent seminar on politeness[1] had several women objecting to the speaker's justification of politeness and etiquette on the grounds that it has often been equivalent to subjecting women to discrimination, humiliation or even justifying violence. Politeness (or some forms of etiquette) may be a guise for sexism or racism.

On the other hand, perhaps all we want from our children is that they say "please" and "thank you" when appropriate. We want them to abide by these conventions. However, even here, there are problems. For the rituals and conventions of politeness are notoriously cultural, and vary from people to people, country to country. So we have to consider these and other dangers of politeness.

Cultural considerations of politeness

In some cultures, burping is the way to show appreciation of a meal, in others a (respectful) silence. In some societies, the quiet student is considered polite, in others, it is the one who verbalizes more. Swearing is considered impolite by some, but not by others. Furthermore, what constitute a "swear word" (or blasphemy) differs from culture to culture, group to group. For some, the taboo words have a sexual connotation (the F word, for example), for others, it is some reference to bodily functions, for still others, the prohibited terms refer to religion. In all these cases, what has become taboo, prohibited or a swear word is connected to what people find "disgusting."[2] So we have to be careful about that form of politeness we wish to uphold as a moral value, and accept that different forms and nuances acceptable to some, may be unacceptable to others.

Two forms of politeness, which can be considered more appropriate, because they appear universally across cultures, are gratitude and greetings. How to show gratitude, however, may vary widely from culture

61

to culture. For example, in some cultures, burping is the way to show appreciation of a meal, in others a (respectful) silence. Non-verbal demonstration of gratitude (hugs, kisses, touching) are more acceptable in some cultures than in others.

Greetings also have a cultural aspect. Thus in Japan certain greeting rituals involve different kinds of bows; in different countries (Greece and Italy for example) and in large parts of the southern United States, certain forms of hand shakes and salutes are considered appropriate with different kinds of people and in different circumstances. Apparently a large part of the original reason for the hand shake and salute rituals was to demonstrate to a possible enemy that one did not bear a weapon (my left handed grand-daughter, Hannah, reminds me that all of this only applies to right-handers; for all we know the "sinister," in Latin meaning left handed, have a knife or gun in their left hand, even while bowing, shaking hands or saluting). What is important in regard to greetings, as in regard to gratitude, is to underplay the cultural aspect and emphasize the universal one.

Gratitude

We have stated that in all societies, and all cultures, some forms of showing gratitude or appreciation to other people, is important, whatever the specific form it may take in any given culture.

We can ask our children to display gratitude, and even explain that a smile (or a burp) might not be enough, that the verbal expression will help show the person who did something for them how appreciative they really are. Furthermore, we might even insist that this not be a grumbling, unfelt gratitude but one that is genuinely felt. This entire area has been discussed extensively by philosophers and psychologists.[3] The philosophers have emphasized the importance of gratitude as a moral virtue, the key to our treating other people as free, dignified and morally responsible individuals.[4]. The psychologists have shown how gratitude has important benefit for mental health and well-being (feeling it and expressing it).[5]

Dangers of gratitude

One important danger which may arise in showing gratitude has to do with the use of physical gestures. Many parents and grandparents see it as entirely appropriate to ask children to give a little kiss (on the cheek?) to an aunt (or whoever) has bestowed a gift (whether the gift is desired, or liked.) One might say "it is the thought that counts" (but how much thought did the aunt give, if it is a gift that the child hates?). In any case, many children (particularly girls) have argued that they have bad memories about these enforced kisses, which often create conflicts when they become teenagers or preteens. Because they have been socialized to accept that physical affection as a sign of gratitude is acceptable (even demanded) they have to re-confront this issue (as teenagers) in situations of possible sexual innuendo. The case of "Lisa"[6] depicts a girl who, after a date with a boy, does not give him a kiss, and he tells her she is rude (compounded by his expectations after he paid for the movie). Lively discussion on this situation in my moral education and philosophy classes have revealed to me that my granddaughters, even at ages 4 and 5 are right when they argue that they should not be *required* to show affection, particularly physical affection. But what if one is not in the mood even to say "please" or "thank you," as my grandchildren have also raised as an argument with me? We will suggest that one should not be forced to utter the words but allowed on occasion to just offer a smile. Children

should be encouraged, however, to try to use the words "thank you," because they make people feel better, in addition to the smile, or silent gratitude. We should explain this to our children as early as possible. In other words, when encouraging "thank you," provide the reason for saying it: It feels good for the one who says it, and for the other person.

There are other dangers of expressing too much gratitude. For some children this may lead to passivity, lack of initiative and interfere with a justified or appropriate pride in their own achievement. Too much gratitude can lead to the loss of the distinction between what can be controlled and what may be due to uncontrolled external factors. Gratitude comes in different forms: we may be grateful to our parents or friends, we may be grateful to God (if we believe in God), or even grateful for pure luck (for a further discussion see Chapter 11). All these forms of gratitude are external, and do not attribute success to ones own effort and ability. A large body of psychological research has shown that this external (locus of control) is a particular danger for girls, which can lead to under achievement.[7] For stories and questions about gratitude appropriate for very young children, see Appendix I.

Greetings

Children should be taught to regularly use everyday greetings like "Hello" and "Goodbye" (and even "how are you?") when meeting a person or leaving a situation.[8] This rudimentary politeness applies to telephone conversations as well. In addition to the initial "hello," it is reasonable to expect a child to at least utter one friendly sentence, especially to a person that they know. *Children who do not get into the habit of greeting others will be seen as sullen, and may become unpopular and shunned by possible friends and classmates. Parents and teachers should be ready to explain to children that conventional greetings have a use, even as pure conventions.* Even very young children can understand that they will make others happier by adhering to these conventions. Although the conventions, as such, do not have the status of moral rules, they still retain a certain importance for getting along in society. As we noted in our discussion of different forms of values in Chapter 1, very young children (2 or 3 years of age) can see the point of conventional rules as well as moral ones.[9]

Why be polite? Second attempt

Now we can answer, it depends on what we mean. If it is linked to deference and obedience, then "politeness" is not to be encouraged; if linked to consideration of others, and the expression of gratitude and greetings, then it is to be encouraged. Above all, we must be ready to explain how and why it is appropriate, taking into account the actual case before us. Wanting the right kind of politeness can be put another way: We do not want our children to be rude to others. Examples of rudeness would certainly include interrupting others who are talking, or jumping into line ahead of others ("jumping the queue" they say in England). These good manners can be modelled by adults, and justified to children in terms of fairness, as well as a form of the Golden Rule (for example: "if you are talking, or if you are in line, would you like it if somebody interrupts you or jumps ahead!"). Of course, interrupting or jumping ahead for an emergency is justified. So, once again, we must make use of the Golden Rule, amended by judgment. Another example of rudeness often displayed by some adults, concerns tardiness. For some, punctuality is seen as a relatively unimportant virtue. It is, however, an example of rudeness, and some scholars have seen it as a kind of theft (we are stealing a person's time, which might be more valuable to them than possessions).[10]

Consideration, respect for others, a form of the Golden Rule (in modern form)

We do want children to respect the property, space, and privacy of other children, including their siblings, and their parents, teachers and other adults. As mentioned before, we also want them to understand respecting the right of unimpeded speech ("Don't interrupt" is a common plea, we all know). As with all moral values, it is incumbent upon us to explain why these are good rules, and behaviors. The Golden Rule is appropriate here because we can show, via examples, and modelling, how we are expecting the kind of adherence to respect which they would like in return. But of course the Biblical Golden Rule only tells. "Do unto others . . ." This must be amended. People are different, with different needs, temperaments, desires, and backgrounds, and contexts and situations vary. So here is the amended golden rule: "Do onto others . . . taking into consideration the differences and similarities between them and you, and between situations." In other words, the Golden Rule plus JUDGMENT!!

Swearing, cursing, blasphemy: "dirty words"

One has to watch oneself. Parents are models for their children. Saying one thing and doing another is often the case in regard to swearing or cursing. We will tell our children "don't swear" or "don't curse," yet often children will gleefully point out that their parents have used a "bad" word. There is also the entire matter of peer pressure. We discussed this matter with the example of Saint Augustine in Chapter 3 concerning the theft of the pears. Many adults remember using their first swear word, because people around them were doing it. Swearing occurs often on T.V., so that our children are exposed to it. We know that part of the attraction for children to say forbidden words, is the thrill associated with doing something which is "naughty." Although we will try as parents not to swear in front of our children, we know that cursing seems to help a bit when we are in pain or frustrated. Everyone understands how saying a curse word may be needed when we bang our finger with a hammer. Therefore, we should not overreact about swearing with young children. Rather, we should try to explain to the best of our ability how the use of certain words may be offensive to others. That some language may hurt some people is a legitimate consideration for deciding not to use specific words with specific people. Even here the issue is more complicated because of a cultural consideration. In English, the taboo words are typically associated with sexuality and bodily function (think of the "F" word or the "S" word). In French, the words people try to avoid are associated with religion. There are some words which are more than rude to a specific culture; they are hurtful in a more important, universal way. Here I am referring to racist or sexist language. Some philosophers of education have pointed out that this kind of language should be treated as a form of violence.[11] We agree with this group as opposed to another set who argue that racist and sexist language may be rude, but even rude language must be protected by the right to freedom of expression. We believe that this latter group has gone too far in the direction of political correctness. Tolerance of different points of view is a very important value; however, tolerance must have its limits.

Burping, flatulence, nose-picking: "disgusting behavior"

One hundred years ago, these questions were not discussed, certainly not with children. At the beginning of the twenty first century, we are ready to talk about even these things. A recent popular children's book is entitled "Walter the Farting Dog".[12] At a recent meeting of psychologists, philosophers and educators with the Dalai Lama in Tibet, these topics were also discussed![13]

As parents, we have to be prepared to say something about these things to our children. It is not enough to simply order them to say "excuse me" after they burp or flatulate. Some children may ask us why we are telling them this; others may not ask but be wondering just the same. There are a set of reasons which we can offer. As with all other matters, we have to prepare ourselves by thinking about them. We can tell our children that there are questions of health involved; this is certainly appropriate in explaining why they should use a Kleenex or go to the toilet. We can also add the dimension of privacy; independently of any health consideration most societies encourage these kinds of activities to be done in private. We can, in this respect, once again, invoke the idea of "convention" and the expectations that society has. We should tell our children, even our very young children, that many people will find a public display of these behaviors disgusting or offensive. The issue of disgust is both universal and complex.

The role of judgment: A review

In Chapter 2, discussing honesty, we emphasized trust as crucial in our relationships. We noted that one had to be careful to treat every situation case by case because too much trust can also be wrong. In this chapter the same point must be made about politeness: *Too much politeness, or respect might be as wrong as too little.* For example, we want to show gratitude in an appropriate way, but not too much gratitude, especially if it involves unacceptable forms of behavior, such as being forced to kiss the aunt who gave us a gift, or kiss one's date who paid for the movie. Another example involves avoiding politeness in circumstances where it may be dangerous. Children need to learn to discriminate between the behavior called for with strangers, which is often very different than that with family and friends.

On the surface, different situations may seem alike, but are relevantly different. One example which was discussed above concerns expressing gratitude and voicing greetings. We should encourage our children to greet others, almost all the time, and even if not in the mood. This would include common courtesy on the telephone. Therefore, we might very much urge our children, and at very early ages, when answering the telephone to say hello, and respond to a few simple questions. Children who just bang down the receiver are aptly considered rude. Greetings then are different than gratitude expressions since the latter can have substitutes, like a smile, or even at times a happy silence.

In regard to all of the issues discussed in this chapter, we have urged parents to offer explanations for the "polite" behavior which we are teaching. Here yet again, we obviously must use our judgment on how much detail to provide to our child when offering the rationale and explanations. We will, naturally, go into greater detail with our nine-year old, than with our six year old, and in turn with our three year old. Although the amount of detail will differ, the need for dialogue and discussion must begin at the very earliest of ages.

5
Responsibility

What is "responsibility"?

We want our children to be responsible. What do we mean by this? Responsibility is a complicated concept with moral, legal and psychological components.[1] For the purposes of this chapter, there is one main question to ask; namely, what is the value we want as parents and teachers to impart to our young children. To answer, we will sum up much of the philosophical and legal literature in the following way. *Responsibility is: "answering for what we do."* We can see this in the roots of the word ("respondere," "to answer"). To account for our acts is what we have in mind: we want our children to understand that they are the authors of what they do, that when they do things that are bad, it is appropriate to blame them (they are blameworthy), and when they do good things, they may deserve credit or praise (they are praiseworthy). We want them to understand that some things are done by them, sometimes by other people, and sometimes the causes are natural, or unknown. At the very earliest ages, we identify our children by giving them a name, and then using this name when referring to their space, their possessions or their body (Mary's room, Mary's teddy-bear, Mary's nose), as well as to what action she did (Mary is walking, Mary is kissing, Mary is throwing a tantrum, Mary hurt her finger). We are reminding her that it is not daddy, or her brother who is walking, kissing, throwing a tantrum or whose finger is hurt. Personal identity and autonomy, two components of responsibility, make an appearance in very early childhood. The child, even before speaking, is very aware of his accomplishments (walking is a great example), and we (and the child) are proud of this developmental milestone.[2] The two-year-old, as every parent and early educator knows, insists on doing things for himself, and will persevere at a task for a very long time to get it done. It is often frustrating that the young child will refuse assistance for putting on his clothes. As good parents, we have learned to balance our wish to have our child have this important early autonomy, but also help him when it is needed, for his safety, or even because we are in a rush and can't afford the luxury of waiting for him to put on his own shoes. We, of course, have to exercise our judgment in balancing the competing values, in this case, autonomy versus safety.

Autonomy

Everytime we do something for a child which he can do himself, we harm the development of his autonomy and self-esteem

The notion of autonomy originates in political contexts; it prefers to independence and self-government. In regard to the individual, the notion of autonomy has had two main strands in philosophical writings. The first is associated mainly with Emanuel Kant and sees autonomy as control of desires and impulses (more on this in Chapter 8). The second interpretation comes from Jean Piaget and refers to the ability of a child to make decisions for himself and be responsible.[3] Educators want to foster this kind of autonomy in children. One of the instruments used in our investigation of this form of autonomy can be found in the appendices at the back of the book. We ask children to choose what to do in a dilemma involving, for example, loyalty to a friend or reporting to an authority. The measure of moral autonomy is their ability to stick to their decision yet, nevertheless, be open to arguments of others.

"I didn't do it!"

Before we get to the more complicated issues of moral responsibility – blame and praise, punishment and reward – we have to be ready to deal with the question of causality. All questions of wrong-doing, whether in the law or in morality, begin with the issue of causal responsibility.[4] If we are dealing with some good event, the question of who is (causally) responsible is also relevant. Whose (beautiful) painting is this? We want to know which child did it, or perhaps which group of children helped create it. Of course, there are some events which are not due to human agency, but we attribute the causes to nature, God, accident or luck.[5] These are not easy issues, but we must, as parents and teachers, be prepared to say something about them to our children, and therefore should have reflected a bit about these concepts. At the very least, let us accept the principle that no questions of blame (or praise) will be made until the issue of causality is discussed, and (hopefully) settled. In doing this, we will know that we are at least following a universal model of responsibility which appears in virtually every culture.[6]

"I didn't mean to do it. It wasn't my fault"

Once having established that some act (or even the omission, which is also a kind of act) was due to a specific actor (let us simplify things and leave collective responsibility aside), we proceed to the question of blame, assuming that the behavior is "bad" (i.e. prohibited, against clearly established rules, harmful to oneself or others). Let us say our child has taken some cookies before dinner (against explicit rules), eaten a whole bunch of them, and when asked about it, says "I didn't do it" The facts being clear (he *did* do it), we get to issues of blame. We can determine that this is a case where our child is blameworthy, and explain why we think so (we will also be angry, disappointed and a bit sad; we return to a discussion of the emotions in Chapter 7). Blameworthiness is the crucial element in moral responsibility; it is the judgment that our child has done something wrong, and we must express this, and why it is so. The conditions of blameworthiness are that our child acted freely (that is, could have acted otherwise, chose this course, and it was clearly against standards or rules which had been previously set, discussed, and explained and the child meant to do it – there is clear intention). So one will say, for example: "You acted badly in taking the cookies, when it was explained that it is better to have them after dinner, that this rule is because of your health." "You lied here to try not to own up to what you did, an example (also previously discussed) of not justified lying."

In the cookie case, the child cannot say "it was not my fault, I didn't mean it," although this can be an excuse or justification for other acts which as parents we may have found blameworthy. So if, to take a second example, our child has taken away her brother's comics, she may plead that she didn't know they were his, or thought that she had been given permission to use them and so on. Here parents have to, exactly as in a court of law, seriously consider the excuse, and judge each case on its merits. Perhaps there is some ambiguity about the rule, or its application. Maybe the child is a little bit to blame, or even not at all. Of course, a child might say, in response to either the cookie example, or the comic-snitching one, "I was very hungry, and couldn't wait for supper, or "I needed to look at those comics for my homework, or I had no books to read." These are justifications not of the "I didn't mean to" variety, but at a more sophisticated level. Once again, sometimes they are acceptable, sometimes not. Parents will be the judge, but, like judges on the bench, have to make their ruling clear, the parent to the child, like the judge to the defendant.

It must be made clear that everything said so far pertains to an act freely chosen by the child, where it is the case that the child might have done otherwise (we are ignoring a great deal of philosophical debate on whether freedom is really possible.[7] In this book we assume that it is). For the purpose of the present discussion let us assume freedom. See, however, the discussion in Chapter 8 on taking responsibility even in the absence of freedom or control. Acts, furthermore, include omissions. So, for example, if we have asked our child to put away a glass, having explained why this is important, and the child fails to do so, we still attribute causal responsibility to the child, assuming the facts are clear, and the child is blameworthy for the negligence or carelessness. If someone trips on the glass, and hurts themselves, the consequences are clear. Even if no one trips, it is possible that someone might have done so. Here again parenting is like the law, with the parallel cases being a drunk driver exceeding the speed limit, and injuring a pedestrian. This person is blameworthy, but so is the same person (or another one) who drives drunk, exceeds the speed limit, but (perhaps through luck) does not injure anybody. The second person might have injured someone and he is equally to blame.[8]

Carelessness, negligence and foreseeability

Very young children understand that things may be their fault even though it was entirely unintentional. As parents, we may legitimately be angry if we have asked them to take care, and they do not. This grey area of blameworthiness was entirely neglected in Jean Piaget's classical theory and research. However, here as elsewhere it is clear that Piaget underestimated the ability of the child. In 2006, *there can be no doubt that children as young as three years of age, fully understand issues of carelessness and negligence. Furthermore, the key ingredient in assessing blameworthiness, both for children and adults is that of foreseeability.*[9] The question we want to ask in regard to our children's behavior is an exact parallel to the question asked in a law court, namely, is it reasonable for the person to have foreseen the consequences of their act? It should be noted that there is no parallel for foreseeability or negligence in regard to praiseworthy, good acts.[10] In general praise and blame are not symmetrical notions; they have entirely separate logics. As compared to blame and punishment, praise and reward have been neglected by psychologists. This is perhaps understandable because the law concerns itself with negative behavior. Similarly, parents are often confronted with acts needing discipline. Responsibility, however, is a wide notion as we mentioned earlier. Educators should be concerned with both praise and blame, both of which are important components of responsibility.

Punishment

Notice that the question about whether the drunk driver, or the child, should be punished (what kind of punishment, and how severe) is a separate issue from that of blameworthiness. It is, in fact, the third level of responsibility, following causal and moral. Whether or not to punish, and how, is a separate issue from blame. It may be the case that having told the child that he has done wrong (the words: "That was bad" along with "I am sad, disappointed and angry") uttered by a loving parent may be sufficient punishment. Some would say that blame (verbally transmitted) is itself a kind of punishment. Of course, we know that actual punishment of the drunk drivers are needed, either as retribution, or more importantly deterrents. In the Scandinavian countries, drunk drivers go to prison, whether or not they have injured anybody. There are fewer drunk drivers there than in North America!! With children, we may decide that there is a suitable consequence, as going to one's room, being deprived of television and so on. I am leaving out physical punishment (spanking) as almost always unacceptable. Here, too, I am aware that this is controversial (the Canadian Supreme Court has recently made its ruling).[11] I will say no more about punishment, since this is handled well by other parenting books.[12] I will just emphasize that whatever punishment, if any, one judges relevant to mete out, one should explain why it is being done, even if one has done this before, and thinks that it is obvious. These explanations should be offered at the very earliest ages. Let us not forget that even the child who cannot yet speak will understand a great deal.

"I am sorry"

Repentence, remorse, and regret, mentioned by Linus in the cartoon on the next page are all important. All of these are somewhat different, and are not only important developmental moral virtues, but also moral emotions. All of these are relevant to our deciding whether a person (and to what degree) should be blamed, and then ultimately punished. Of course, the key with our children (again like in the law) is whether we believe an apology, whether it is sincere. This is not easy, for parent or law court judge. Judges on the bench use their experience with criminals. Parents and early childhood educators are usually in a pretty good position to know their own children. In any case, one can decide to be compassionate, to forgive, to be merciful, giving our children the benefit of the doubt, at least the first few times the transgression occurs. Like the judge who wants to temper justice with mercy, we should do at least that much for our

young children. There is an added benefit. Forgiveness and compassion are, in their own right, the kind of moral virtues and moral emotions we want to model for our children and hope that they will make use of.[13]

It is important to stress that the kind of forgiveness we want to encourage in moral education is not necessarily tied to deep repentance and contrition. As Patricia White suggests, the kind of forgiveness we want to talk to children about is more of the variety "that's okay, no big deal."[14] In preschool, at home, and in life generally, there are many opportunities for this garden-variety kind of forgiveness. Furthermore, forgiveness is tied inextricably to apology.[15] If an adult or a child bumps into somebody, however accidentally, it is important to say "I'm sorry," "pardon me" or "excuse me." When playing a sport involving a partner such as doubles tennis, it is important when goofing up a shot to say "sorry;" one's partner will normally say "forget it." Parents and coaches should not only teach the behavior, but explain why the words are helpful to the other person. We have to add that the apology has to be meant and felt. As one educator has put it, saying "I am sorry, but . . ." is not good enough.[16] When it comes to a genuine apology, with the accompanying forgiveness, there are no "buts." A second point to emphasize is that the words have to be said in a way that makes the other person convinced one means it and feels it. Saying for example, "sorry, sorry, sorry, sorry" in a sarcastic or sullen tone, is worse than no apology at all; the other child will not be fooled. Another kind of cop-out, which adults use, and children readily grasp, is to say "I am sorry that you are upset." This has the advantage to the speaker of not admitting any wrong-doing; it is more an expression of sorrow. This may sometimes work for a temporary making-up between partners who agree to disagree. It is not, however, a real apology. Finally, *we should not neglect the obligation for parents, and other educators, to apologize to children.* It has been reported that a majority of people in a recent sampling, in a North American context, remembered never having their parents apologize to them for anything.[17]

There are a few other points to make about the interplay between apology and forgiveness. When apologizing one wants to be as specific as possible about what one did or didn't do, therefore, an "I'm sorry, for whatever I did" does not do the job. Although, as we have discussed above, it is sometimes very difficult to apologize, because we would be admitting that we were totally wrong, and we can accept only part of the blame for a situation. In a conflict, it is rare that either person is entirely to blame. Even if one doesn't believe one is entirely wrong, one can still confess to being partly wrong. These considerations will help the other person to forgive.

There is a saying in French, which is best translated as "to understand all is to forgive all." There is however, a corresponding English motto, which says "to understand all is to forgive nothing." These two slogans reflect an important aspect about forgiveness. It is generally true that if we can find an explanation for what a person has done, that may have slighted or hurt us, we are more likely to forgive him. This is exemplified in the common-place occurrence of bumping into somebody by accident and saying "sorry." The words are important, and signify that it was an accident. The second person will very likely say "don't worry, no problem" or something of the sort. On the other hand, looking for psychological explanations for every bit of behavior in order to diminish responsibility will not work. Whatever explanations there may be for any kind of behavior, there are good reasons to treat the other person in terms of moral responsibility, including the dynamics of apology and forgiveness.[18]

Two other considerations about apology. One should look the person in the eye, just as in the case of greetings and gratitude. Children can learn to do this rather easily; it is a sign of *meaning* the apology (or the gratitude or greeting). The second element to remember about apology is that it is appropriate even if one feels one could not have done otherwise. The important thing is to acknowledge that one hurt the person, to be genuinely contrite, and to wish one had been capable of making a different choice.

To further illustrate the complicated dynamics of apology and forgiveness here are two quotes from *Time Magazine* (October 2004, just before the presidential election in the U.S.):

> I had forgotten that Mrs. Bush had worked as a school teacher and a librarian, and there couldn't be a more important job," (Theresa Heinz Kerry, Wife of presidential candidate John Kerry, apologizing for saying in an interview that she didn't know whether First Lady Laura Bush had ever held a real job.)

> She apologized, but she didn't even really need to apologize. I know how tough it is, and actually, I know those trick questions. (Laura Bush, accepting Theresa Heinz Kerry's apology.)

Praise and reward

Praiseworthiness is not the opposite of blameworthiness. We often lump together praise and blame, partly because we have unreflectively accepted the Skinnerian psychological vocabulary of positive and negative reinforcements.[19] However, if we go beyond conditioning and ask ourselves questions of moral responsibility, the questions of when a person should be praised are not symmetrical to questions of blameworthiness. There are many good things that we, and our children, do in the course of a day. It is not only inappropriate to praise all these acts, it can be dangerous. Much research has shown that preschool children motivated to paint, draw, and build will become less motivated when the teacher starts praising too much.[20] Attribution theory has an explanation for this in terms of internal and external states of locus of control.[21] Therefore, one has to be careful to praise those acts which are really beyond the normally expected. The second important asymmetry concerns negligence and carelessness. With blame, as discussed above, failure to do something may be very highly blameworthy, although not completely intentional. One may even want to punish negligence or carelessness very much. With good acts, there is no parallel to this. One cannot be praised for a "negligent" or "careless" act which turns out good. It will simply be seen as an accident. So, if one falls into the water and one's belt hooks onto a drowning person, that would be a negligent good act. It would not, however, be praiseworthy, particularly if one didn't make any effort (perhaps out of cowardice or laziness) to help the person.

Finally, rewards are a separate matter, just as punishments are. Whether, and how to give stickers or money to our children for a good deed is a different question as to whether they are deserving of praise.

Obedience

The responsible child, like the responsible citizen, is not one who obeys blindly, not rules, not laws, not even the orders given by a parent. We want to emphasize that it is responsibility which involves reflection and awareness, where the rules have been explained and justified. There may be bad rules, as there are bad laws, and we want our children to be capable of telling the difference. Of course, as emphasized, there are the exceptions where we must be paternalistic, for the safety and protection of the child. We may not have time to explain or justify a rule about not taking one's tricycle on the street as our two year old is about to do it. However, as Piaget stresses, these are inevitable obstacles to autonomy and responsibility. What we are adding to Piaget's notion is that we begin as early as possible to help the child towards a higher moral responsibility. Unlike Piaget we do not want to wait for certain rigid ages (defined by stage) but insist that we do this as early as two years of age. Piaget is surely right to talk about the importance of moving from seeing rules as rigid, coming from an authority (God and adult), to a point where one sees them as open to discussion, justified, and decided upon by the group. He is right, also, to tell us that rules of games are like this, and so are the important moral rules. He is wrong, however, to think that only older children (in fact adolescents) are capable of the formal thought which can give them the higher autonomy and responsibility. In 2006, *we know that by the age of 5, the child is capable of a very sophisticated morality.[22] We also know there is much in the way of dialogue and explanation which has to begin before age 5 (from 2 onwards).*

Moral judgments of other's acts

Piaget, in his book *Moral Judgment of the Child* (1932), the Bible for all psychologists and philosophers who wish to think about responsibility, not only asks about judging one's own acts, but also those of others. Part of our job as parents is not only reacting to the acts of our children (good or bad), but helping them learn to judge the acts of others. The model of responsibility which we model for our children in talking about what they do, is also the same model they can apply to the acts of others. They will learn – with us – about the complexities of blame and praise, intentions and consequences, gratitude and resentment, apology and forgiveness, punishment and reward, and all the other complexities of the world of responsibility. We will also want our children to begin to judge us, using these complicated notions, concepts and criteria. If they are angry at us, or blame us, or even want to punish us, we can hope that they will want to apply the same model we apply to them, and they in turn use with their friends and classmates.

The role of judgment: A review

In regard to the question of autonomy discussed in the first section, parents must judge how much autonomy is the right amount to provide to their children. We want to encourage, for example, our children at very young ages (as early as 3 years old) to inform their friends by themselves if they will not attend a party to which they were invited. We want also to allow our children to take some risks in regard to physical activity and not smother them with over-protection. On the other hand, there is also the danger of children sometimes becoming "*too* responsible." There are some children who are burdened with making decisions which their parents cannot or will not do. The phenomenon of a seven-year-old, for example, acting more responsibly than one or both of his parents, is often portrayed in contemporary films, books and TV shows. We must judge how much risk for our children is appropriate, how much responsibility does not become too big a burden and what balance between dependence and independence is justified in different situations or contexts.

One other example where judgment is needed is in the case of blame and praise. To what degree is praise, for example, helpful or harmful? As we have seen in the text above, sometimes it is the one and sometimes it is the other. As usual, we have the very general guidelines or rules of thumb to help us; however, again as usual, there is no substitute for good judgment.

Interlude

A time to keep silent, and a time to speak

We have looked at the core values of honesty, politeness and responsibility, and will now turn to feelings in part III. Before doing this, however, there is one matter, which arises from all the chapters on values, and also constitutes a bridge to the next section. This is the issue of how to explain to our children when to keep silent and when to speak. With honesty, we discussed keeping quiet and not speaking what one believed, or not all of it, perhaps showing tact. In the politeness chapter, in regard to gratitude and its expression, we also raised the question of keeping silence vs. speaking. Finally in the responsibility chapter, in dealing with the question of apology, we stressed the importance of how and when to encourage verbal expression, and when not.

In regard to both politeness (gratitude and greeting), as well as apology, our main point can be summed up this way: When we ask our children to say "thank you," "hello/good-bye, or "I am sorry," they have to mean it when they say it. We can now add that "meaning" it is tantamount to "feeling" it. Therefore, a "thank you" said grumpily and without a smile, or an "I am sorry" accompanied by facial and bodily signs indicating that one is not thankful or sorry, are often worse than no expressions of gratitude or apology at all. So what to tell our children in the face of all this? First of all, educators should not insist that children say "sorry," "thank you," or "hello," without having provided the justification for expressing apology, gratitude and greetings. As always, the amount of detail in the explanation will vary with the age of the child. For example, we can discuss with our nine-year-old why these conventional verbal expressions are necessary, how they are linked to people's expectations, and one should try to not needlessly offend people by failing to utter the appropriate words. One can go further, and explain that not being in a good mood should not stop one from responding appropriately. This is not to encourage a faked or pseudo politeness, because one hopes one is saying "hello, how are you" to a relative, classmate, or especially a friend, because one feels it. One may be sad, angry, distracted by some event, nevertheless, one should still greet a person one knows. As adults, we all understand that a person in extreme grief will not perhaps want to engage in a long discussion with a friend or colleague. We still appreciate, however, them greeting us; and they will probably benefit from the reciprocal greeting.

This kind of complex consideration can be understood by children as young as five years old. From ages 2-5, we will obviously only offer skeletal explanations. For example, we can say "thank you means I am happy about the gift you gave me or I am happy you were thinking of me, whether or not I really like the gift." From ages 0-2, we will restrict ourselves most of the time to teaching the words "thank you, hello, etc." Even at these very early ages, however, we should accompany our teaching of the words with the appropriate non-verbal expression.

Simply insisting on "proper behavior" is almost always a mistake. If children are not given explanations or justifications when they are very young, the outwardly polite child will sooner or later turn into the surly rude teenager we all want to avoid. Some parents may object to the recommendation that we always offer explanations. They may think that very young children must just get into the habit of using appropriate words of gratitude, greeting and apology. They may insist that they want to prepare their children with required social skills, fitting in with their teachers and classmates and with society as a whole. Didn't Aristotle, or some other philosopher/psychologist, insist on instilling proper behaviors first, and only providing explanations later? Leaving Aristotle to the footnotes,[1] our answer is as follows: Instilling a habit of saying "sorry" or "thank you," without the appropriate accompanying feelings and some understanding of the appropriate situation, will not achieve the desired goal of getting our children to have social skills, and fit in. Young children are just as adept at picking up the discrepancy between a verbal expression, and an inconsistent non-verbal one as are adults. Just like adults and school-aged children, very young children make use of facial expressions as the primary cue of whether the verbal component is meant, or faked. As Shakespeare stated "there's daggers in men's smiles" (*Macbeth* Act III, scene iii). Children can, as Shakespeare indicates, detect phony smiles. A contemporary example of phoniness is at the corner grocery/convenience store, where the clerk says: "Have a good day" or sometimes "Have a good one," without a smile, or eye contact. Even worse, sometimes the words are uttered with a scowl or frown. It is definitely better to have no greeting at all than an unfriendly one. We must try to teach this to our young children.

Recent research has shown that children 2-5 years of age will also make use of the nonverbal over the verbal, where there is any discrepancy.[2] What is important to emphasize is that the children who are trained to say the words, without necessarily meaning or feeling them, will be the most unpopular with their classmates and friends. It is certainly okay to remind one's child to say thank you, hello, goodbye and so on, when they forget. At day care for example, if the educator says goodbye and the child does not respond, it is appropriate to urge one's child to respond. This will indicate to the child that a friendly greeting is important and also has the benefit of showing we care about the feelings of the nursery teacher. Although reminders in this sense are often a good idea, they should not replace an initial attempt to explain to one's young child why greetings or expressions of gratitude are important to others. In fact, we can remind our child not only about the greeting, but why the greeting is a good idea. We should add that one should try to receive people with a cheerful expression. In an interesting discussion of this matter, the *Talmud* (the main body of rabbinical commentary on the bible and ethics), asks whether one is expected to greet someone cheerfully when one is in a bad mood. The *Talmud*'s answer is yes; the fact that you are feeling unhappy does not entitle you to inflict your bad mood on others. True, at any given moment you might be unable to control what you are *feeling,* but that does not mean you cannot control how you *act.*[3] We want to teach children that, just as they would prefer to be greeted by someone in a cheerful, pleasant manner, so should they greet others.

By insisting that children be genuine in their messages, both verbal and nonverbal, we still want to leave a place for pretending, play acting and, make-believe. If our children are good actors they will be able to feign sadness or anger, and enjoy doing it. Our role as parents is to point out that sometimes there is a time for play-acting but sometimes it is the genuine emotion which is required.

There is one more advantage to insisting that words be accompanied by their associated feelings. Children will thus be keeping true to themselves; authenticity and genuineness are good qualities in themselves. We can refer back to the cartoon at the beginning of this interlude section. Lucy cannot bring herself to say the words "I like you Charlie Brown." Schultz, as usual, has captured an important feature of our interpersonal life. We can all identify with Lucy, who feels that by saying words she does not mean, she will be betraying something fundamental within her. In Lucy's case, the words were "I like you." Every adult, and every child as well, will have their own personal examples. Perhaps the most common of these concerns apologies once again. To say "I am sorry," meaning it as a real apology will inevitably be admitting that one was wrong. Many novels and plays have depicted this dilemma, whereby we chose not to apologize, because this would betray our convictions.[4]

We can sum up the main point about apology in this way: To apologize it is necessary to say "I am sorry" (or the equivalent). Saying the words, however, is not sufficient; the apology has to be meant. Likewise with greetings and gratitude: saying the words is necessary but not sufficient. Furthermore, there is also the possibility of adding a hug or little kiss to the word, and the smile, although this demonstration of affection should never be required (see preface and the discussion to hug or not to hug in Chapter 11).

In order to illustrate the main point of this section, namely that if you say it, mean it, I have lumped together greetings, gratitude and apologies. While there are similarities between these themes, there are also differences which are not being discussed here.[5] Another theme which will be discussed in the next part of the book concerns pride and humility. Although that theme is in many ways different from the values discussed up to now, the issue of keeping silent or speaking is central there as well. Both feeling and expressing one's pride, we will argue, is to be generally encouraged; there will, however, be circumstances where the appropriate moral emotion will be humility.

There are a number of other areas in which the antinomy "keep silent or speak" has to be resolved. We might want to prepare ourselves for talking about these issues with our children. The slogan "a child should be seen and not heard" was prevalent when I was a youngster. We recommend that this particular slogan be abolished. Children have a right to speak, as much as adults; the question is when. The following is a list of situations, in no particular order, where deciding between silence and speech may be difficult. In general the choice will be in favor of speaking:

1. We want to impart to our children the importance of speaking up and speaking out. We want children to intervene when they see a bully, or some form of violence, to themselves, or to others. If they have a point of view, we want them to express it, and we hope that if they hear an abusive remark (or a racist/sexist one) they will have the courage to say something about it. Contrary to some educators/philosophers, racist or sexist remarks are not mere "rudeness;" they should not be ignored on the grounds of political correctness.[6] As adults, we know that we often must decide to speak out, or keep our silence. We can only try to model the best behavior we can for our children, and help them develop their judgment about this. We know, unfortunately, that it is not always right to speak out, and that one has to choose one's moments of intervention carefully. Sometimes, the fine line between being a Good Samaritan and a busybody is hard to draw. However, this is the messiness of life, and we have to look at each situation as it arises.

2. If my friend has just lost a loved one, it is appropriate to say "my condolences." However, if we haven't seen them for a while, and only just found out about the loss, and were told that they had a hard time getting past a bad depression due to grief, do we still say "I'm sorry," although there is a good chance of this making them feel badly? These are not easy questions. Where one cannot decide to speak or keep silent, it is usually better to opt for speaking. In the case of condolence, speaking is generally less likely to lead to harm than saying nothing. In cases of grief we should take the risk of making the person think about their sadness; chances are even if they prefer not to hear condolences from you at the time, they will appreciate the feelings behind the words. For children, the loss may be of an animal. How should they react when a friend's dog, rabbit or hamster has died? This example is discussed in Chapter 6 (section on empathy) and in the appendix J.

3. Let us turn to a somewhat less serious (some might call it frivolous) subject, just discussed on a sports radio talk show! Should one mention that someone has lettuce in their teeth, or food on their face? Is it better to risk embarrassing them, or to endure the discomfort of looking at them throughout the meal? Might they not be upset and embarrassed to find out about their lettuce or smudge, or fly undone, and resent no one mentioning it." What kind of relationship makes it more appropriate to speak up rather than maintain silence? Should we be more prone to be honest with a friend, less so with a fellow employee, or not at all with a complete stranger? And how to go about it? A discrete whisper, a verbal hint, a nonverbal miming? The callers in to the talk show had many and conflicting opinions. Some insist on always speaking up, others on always maintaining their silence.

4. Should we speak openly about sexual preferences? At what age, in what way, and at what opportunity? We know that silence may be dictated by circumstance. Questions relating to gays

and lesbians will inevitably crop up for children. How to talk about these delicate matters will be the subject in a later chapter.

5. Jealousy and envy, disgust, shame and guilt are all important moral emotions. The challenge of how to talk about these topics is the subject matter of Chapter 8.

6. It is better to speak of one's feelings to others, to voice one's doubts, to express one's wishes and share one's emotions. In general, it is healthier in most relationships to communicate these things, rather than keeping silent. This is true in marital relations,[7] relations between friends, and certainly in therapeutic contexts. Keeping things quiet in situations of conflict usually leads to worse problems. What we are guessing about another's feelings and thoughts can be a lot worse than their real feelings and thoughts. In the counselling groups for violent men, led by my collaborator Cynthia Martiny, the crucial ingredient for therapeutic breakthrough is the expression of emotion, often with tears, accompanied by a verbal expression of an awareness of the importance of the moment. This same combination of verbal and nonverbal expression is typical in other forms of psychotherapy as well, both in groups and with individuals.[8]

7. Adults have learned to talk about certain situations which involve self sacrifice or resistance to temptation. Watching ones weight, or trying to give up cigarettes may plausibly require the strategy of talking about this with friends and family. In clinical practice, we encourage people to talk about their struggle with an addiction and enlist others as motivators and reminders. Another example, less dramatic but closer to home at the moment, involves writing a book. One talks about this with friends and family partly as a means of keeping to the task and resisting distractions. Whether talking about book writing or control of intake of food and drugs, one has to try not to talk too much about these things, at the risk of becoming boring and a nuisance to people around them. Here, as in most things only good judgment will help.

8. It is important to acknowledge flaws to oneself, but also openly to others. In adult life it is almost always a good idea to admit that one has difficulty with some task or competency. If a person uses English as a second language, it is important for that person (or a friend, or colleague) to articulate that they may have difficulty with vocabulary or structure. We want to teach children to speak up in these kinds of contexts.

9. In cases of charity, as when giving money to a beggar or pan-handler, it is important to do it in the right way. Children must be taught that sharing with a mean expression is often worse than no sharing at all. One should normally speak to the person one is helping with a few words of consolation or sympathy. Even if one has no money to give, one can at least speak to a poor person in a kind, encouraging manner (such as by saying "I hope your situation improves").[9]

10. We want to encourage children to speak up in class. Participation, usually verbal, is evaluated positively. It is true that a student can be an active listener for a while; nevertheless, at some point teachers and professors will expect verbal communication.

11. An issue that is present for many adults, but certainly important for children, is whether or not to be polite and keep silent, or risk rudeness by expressing a dislike for a particular food when you are a guest at someone's house. Parents often tell their children it is polite to eat what is being served to you and not say anything. What may happen as a consequence of this advice

to keep silent are any of the following: one eats the food and suffers the indigestion or at the very least the displeasure of distaste; one's host assumes that one likes the food, so she will prepare it on future occasions to please you (you may be stuck for years), or one ultimately struggles with the discomfort of fakery over a relatively trivial matter. In general, it would seem better advice to speak up and advise our children to speak up in a pleasant matter, and risk offending the host. In any case, a good host should anticipate this situation by asking the invitee (including children), in advance, whether they like the particular food being prepared. An added challenge is how to guide a child who may have a shy disposition and who has difficulty expressing preferences.

In the previous list where the choice between speaking or keeping silent may be a close one, we want to argue that speaking should take precedence. To be fair, there are contexts where silence is often the better route. Here is that list:

1. It is better not to speak unless one has something to say. Here is a story that Rabbi Telushkin uses to make this point, which is worth repeating here.[10]

A new member of Parliament once solicited the advice of Benjamin Disraeli, the nineteenth century British Prime Minister, on whether he should speak up on a controversial issue.

"Do you have anything to say that has not already been said?" Disraeli asked him.

"No," the man conceded. "I just want the people whom I represent, and the members of Parliament to know that I participated in the debate."

Disraeli answered, "It is better to remain silent and have people say, 'I wonder what he is thinking,' than to speak up and have people say, 'I wonder why he spoke.'"

2. One should not say everything that one thinks or feels. Children must be taught that words can wound or hurt others. Being outspoken can sometimes be good. We must, however, be mindful of others feelings. In stressing that angry words should be avoided, we must still remember to point out that the worst kind of verbal violence is never as bad as any form of physical violence.

3. Silence is better than speech most of the time when we are appreciating the beauty of nature or music or just another person's company. Talk may interfere with people's enjoying the moment. The expression "Silence is Golden" has its roots in these kinds of contexts.

4. In meditation and prayer, silence is usually recommended. The most extreme cases, of course, are the vows of silence adopted in certain Monasteries.

5. There is the recommended quiet time which nursery school teachers and parents find important and convenient. Maria Montessori was particularly insistent on periods of silence and meditation in her *Casi Del Bambini.*[11]

6. Silence is in order when we want to take care not to cause other people to lie. This kind of situation is also described in Rabbi Telushkin's book.[12] To quote: "If you see people whispering to each other, and you want to know what they are saying, control your curiosity and don't ask them, lest you make liars out of them. If they wanted you to know, they would have told you. Since it is clear that they don't want to share their secret with you, they will lie to you."

7. When a friend shares a confidence with you, asking you not to repeat it, we have another excellent example where keeping silence is usually the right thing to do. The keeping of

secrets and related issues of trust and loyalty are certainly matters that we want to discuss with our young children. There are, of course, sometimes limits to secret keeping and contrary prevailing reasons to disclose the confidence.

8. There is the tactful or discrete silence called for as when for example my wife says"am I getting fat?" Many times the right thing to do is to be diplomatic, tell only part of the truth, or find a way of understating the case. All of these stratagems are usually meant to avoid hurting the other person. A child may be asked by another child "Is my dress pretty?" This is the parallel to the adult example already mentioned.

9. During public concerts, movies or lectures, the audience is often begged to refrain from speaking or making noise (turn off those cell phones).

10. It is important to respect another's turn to speak; not interrupting is an important lesson to share with young children. It is a form of politeness or courtesy whose justification can be formulated with a form of the golden rule. "Would you like to be constantly interrupted?"

In helping children decide whether to speak or to keep silent, we often are confronted by an antinomy, that is to say, two contradictory or inconsistent messages. Here are a few examples:

1. We sometimes say to children, or to each other: "If you can't say anything nice, don't say anything at all." This slogan captures the notion of showing some tact, not to hurt someone's feelings. The other side of the antinomy is summed up in the phrase "a friend must at all times be honest with a friend." As we have seen in previously there are times when we need to be told the truth. One philosopher has said that everyone needs at least one friend to be brutally and completely honest.[13]

2. On the one hand we offer "don't be a busy body," suggesting that we keep quiet, even when curious about what is going on, or tempted to intervene in a situation. The other side of this antinomy is covered in the fact that we urge people to be good Samaritans. We want people, including children, to help in situations where they can offer something, even if it is not their duty or obligation. Research has shown that children by the age of 5 understand perfectly the concept of blameworthiness and praiseworthiness in these kinds of situations.[14]

3. The antinomy about expressing feelings can be seen by looking at number 6 in the first list above and number 2 in the second list. The first counsel stresses the importance of talking about feelings; the second stresses the importance of not doing so.

This entire area is an excellent illustration of the importance of developing good judgment. It is clear there is no set of rules to cover the choices that we want to help our children make. We can formulate some kind of rules of thumb or guidelines such as: "don't say cruel things," "better to keep quiet than harm another" or "speak up to stop cruelty." We will still have to interpret and apply these rules, like any others, in light of the context and circumstances. We cannot escape having to make use of our judgment.

Part III
Feelings

Chapter 6 will examine what we mean by a caring child. Kindness, sharing and cooperation are all values to be looked at. Underlying these moral acts will be the important accompanying feelings. Two important emotions for morality are discussed, compassion and empathy. What is empathy, and why do we choose it rather than compassion as the key emotion? We will show how empathy can be developed, and how empathy and good judgment must be combined.

Chapter 7 looks at the development and education of the emotions. What do children know about the basic emotions, and those called "mixed"? Should we retain the distinction between positive and negative emotions? How can our children be helped to better comprehend their emotions?

Chapter 8 looks at emotions and morality. Feelings are central to moral values, particularly in regard to the issues of control and responsibility. In discussing virtues, vices, and moderation, the key role will be played by judgment. What are "moral" emotions? We will look in detail at shame, jealousy and pride.

6
Caring

We want our children to behave kindly to others, to share, in the sense of being generous with their possessions and toys, but also in the sense of sharing, playing together, and cooperating with others. We want to model the appropriate behaviors, of course. However, it is not just behavior; it is the feeling, which goes along with it which must be modelled, and which we must foster in our children. Sharing has to be done in the right way, it has to be meant.[1] Cooperation can be a good thing, but can have its downside as well. Before considering sharing, generosity and cooperation as such, let's begin with the feelings.

In recent years, psychologists and educators have introduced an Ethics of Caring.[2] Moral education programs, dissatisfied with an emphasis on reasoning and moral dilemmas, have insisted on teachers providing a perspective which has been called "relational ethics."[3] The focus here is on natural caring, and on situations involving relations with other human beings. Instead of striving away from affection and toward behaving always out of duty, one consciously moves towards obligations based on affection and caring. Initially, this was seen as a facet of the feminist movement, with the caring orientation being associated with women as opposed to the justice orientation with men.[4] We can state unequivocally that there is no evidence that males or females fall more into one orientation than the other.[5] If parents and early childhood educators decide to follow this new tendency in moral education of talking about caring as well as justice, we can confidently do it with both boys and girls. Here is an example of one of these new "caring" situations discussed in schools:

> Nicole/Jason has been invited by her/his friend Janice/Eric to come with her/him for dinner after school on Friday. The next day another friend Pam/Danny invites Nicole/Jason on the same Friday to see their favorite rock band as she/he has tickets for two good seats. What do you think Nicole/Jason should do and why?

This is a good example of a topic, which we can readily transpose, and should, to discuss with much younger children. We want our three and four year olds to begin thinking about the issues involved and develop the kind of caring we would like to see.

Kindness

Children are already naturally kind, not cruel. Researchers have documented kind behaviors at very young ages, with 6 month old children helping other children in distress, sometimes bringing their own mother over to the hurt child.[6] This early "sympathy" is the root of more developed empathy as well as developing kindness. Closely linked to this is "motor mimicry." The picture on the next page is an example of this motor mimicry.. Recent research has shown that motor mimicry is wired into the brain of babies; it is innate and part of the neural structure.[7] It has also been shown that newborns as young as eighteen hours are perfectly capable of reproducing mouth and face movements displayed by the adults they are facing.[8] Three-month-old babies of depressed mothers can mirror their mother's moods while playing with them, displaying more feeling of anger and sadness, and much less spontaneous curiosity and interest, compared to infants whose mothers were not depressed.[9]

Kindness is as natural to children as is babbling. Just as babbling (early sounds) will develop into full-blown language, so rudimentary sympathy will develop into a more general kindness. In both cases, educators have a role to play. With language, parents will talk to their children in their first language or first languages, and the child will, by the age of two, be a sophisticated speaker of one or more tongues. In regard to kindness, similarly, the role of parents is to continue to provide appropriate input. What is needed is an awareness of what's going on in the environment. Adults can point out opportunities for kindness and niceness. If a child has a pet at home, this will provide good early examples of being kind, nice, and gentle. At the very least, one can read stories illustrating animals or children being nice and kind to one another, with the appropriate approving comments. One should be alert for opportunities to perform deeds of kindness. For example, if one sees a frail person in the street carrying a package that seems too heavy for the person to manage, or one may come across an acquaintance who seems upset or distracted, and is in need of someone to speak with, both adults and children may be tempted to ignore these people and continue to do whatever it is they are doing. We can all try, however, to practice "offering one's time and one's heart." One can understand why kindness is considered the highest type of giving, even greater than charity. Charity is done with one's money, while kindness may be done with money or one's person. Charity is given only to the poor, while kindness may be done for anyone.[10] As Anne Frank says in her famous diary "give of yourself . . . you can always give something even if it is only kindness."[11]

Many children's stories have plenty of examples of cruelty as well. Here, of course, educators can make disapproving comments, where appropriate. There will be examples of play-fights between animals, as well as acts of aggression and violence within species (lion vs lion) or between species (lion vs hyena, or lion eating zebra). Whether it is a book or a movie like *Lion King* or *Jungle Book,* there are ample opportunities to accompany one's young child, and make appropriate comments.

Very young children may on occasion bite or pull the hair of an adult or of another child. These are not examples of cruelty or aggression; nevertheless, parents will gently discourage this behavior with a nonverbal gesture and a verbal comment. This will begin at very young ages (even a child of a few months old). We may also have examples of aggressive behavior at home or at preschool. Educators will, of course, may want to make use of whatever discipline or control is needed in such cases. However, one should always offer an explanation of why hitting, pushing, or spitting at another child is wrong. Generally speaking, boys will be more active and there will be more acts of aggression than for girls.[12] There may be a few aggressive or hyperactive children whose problems have a neurological base.[13] From ages 0 to 5, it is rare to have children in need of medication for their aggression or hyperactivity. In any case, a clinical psychologist or psychiatrist should be consulted if there is any doubt. The vast majority of children exhibiting aggression or hyperactivity in early childhood will be cured with a gentle soothing environment, such as a good day care centre.[14] In our own research, on children 2-4 years old diagnosed as "hyperactive," we found that most of them had needs which were not being met by their parents. The mothers were stressed or themselves hyperactive, and not able to provide proper care. Medication with these "normal active" children increased the symptoms of irritability, aggression and hyperactivity; the combination of therapy with these parents along with the care of the preschool eradicated all symptoms within two months.[15] *A good nursery school environment is the appropriate cure, not Ritalin!*

Three out of the thirty-five children were genuine hyperactives with a neurological base and responded to appropriate medication as mentioned. Follow-up longitudinal studies tracking these children from their preschool years into their life as teenagers and young adults demonstrated the importance of clearly diagnosing true hyperactivity as opposed to the reactive sort. The early indications that we found at age two and three were good predictors of whether or not these children would exhibit psychological problems later on in life.[16]

To our surprise, we have learned that pediatricians are still prescribing Ritalin for preschool children.[17] Educators are the first line of defence of children; they should be aware of this practice, and take measures to ensure more appropriate interventions.

There is a form of cruelty, which children will exhibit, usually in the form of teasing. We will unfortunately see this occurring even during the preschool years. This behavior is almost always due either to jealousy or to ignorance. Jealousy is a complicated moral emotion and will be discussed further. One step that we can certainly take is to point out to children how teasing is cruel, and may make the other child feel very badly. Most children may not be aware that "making fun" of a child who is handicapped or overweight may be a very mean thing to do. We should always try to explain why this kind of behavior is wrong. Here, as in other matters, a version of the golden rule can work: How would you feel if someone said something like that to you?

Sometimes teasing can be done as a joke. Adults, or children may say "I was only teasing," by which they mean "I was only joking." Telling the difference between a joke, and something said seriously is difficult at any age. Many adults that I know have adopted non-verbal codes to signify to the other person that what was said was meant as a joke. For some people, the sign is a little laugh. Some of my friends and I have used another gesture, namely raising one's hand in the air. The raised hand means "Don't be insulted, or misled, I was making a joke." It is not a bad idea to discuss some of these nuances with children.

All children, as we have said, are naturally kind. We might still wonder whether some children are naturally kinder than others. We do often say that some children have a particularly "kind heart." We may notice that these children will more spontaneously help an injured animal, or assist a friend who stumbles. Why it seems to be easier for some, and less easy for others, is in part due to temperament, and in part due to early upbringing.

Compassion

Simply stated, compassion is a painful emotion occasioned by the awareness of another person's undeserved misfortune.[18] When speaking about compassion, we are talking about an emotion, which goes beyond the rudimentary behaviors, where infants react to another's distress. Those very early reactions are sometimes called "sympathy;" the emotion of compassion is thus partly based on sympathy. Explained differently, we are dealing with questions of value and judgment when we talk about compassion. This is, in fact, one way that emotions are a special subset of feelings. Many philosophers have argued that the emotion of compassion is the central one in regard to ethical deliberation.[19] There is, of course, another group of philosophers who dispute the role of compassion in the moral life; in fact, some see all feelings (including emotions) as obstacles to moral reasoning and moral judgment. This is a complicated debate, and as usual, we will indicate some of the sources in the footnotes.[20] We will merely state here that our position is that people's emotions are central to moral education; children's ability to obey rules, even supplemented by "a good will" will not be enough.

There are other candidates for the role of the key moral emotion. One of these is "pity."[21] Although this is an important part of caring which we want to see in our children, it does not do the job as well as compassion. This is because the word has come to have nuances of condescension and superiority to the sufferer. Another term, which we prefer to use, rather than compassion is "empathy."

Empathy

Empathy designates an imaginative reconstruction of another person's experience. Our reason for preferring to talk of the development of empathy rather than compassion is that empathy is not restricted to situations where the other person is in distress. We have to help our child develop the ability to understand, feel, and reflect on the joy of others, as well as their sadness. When we empathise with another person's joy, it makes it possible not to feel jealous or envious.

One reason offered by some philosophers, educators and psychologists not to talk about empathy is because they think a person can be very empathic, but use the empathy to harm or manipulate the other person."[22] For us, the truly empathic person (whether adult or child, psycho-therapist, teacher or friend), will necessarily consider the needs of the other as well as their own needs. For us, empathy is not only a competence or technique, involving verbal and non verbal components, cognitive and affective ones. Empathy, for us, is a moral notion.[23] *We consider it impossible for a clinical psychologist, counsellor, psychiatrists or teacher to be truly empathic, and yet consider their own needs ahead of the needs of their client or student.* Even in situations where one uses empathy for one's advantage, it will not be for the purpose of harming another. In the game of poker for example, a player tries to "get into the other person's head," making use of the cognitive aspects of empathy. This is self-serving, since it will help one win. Furthermore, it is an example of reading the thoughts and feelings of another. Although it may work for ones own needs, it cannot be counted as Machiavellian, or manipulative.

Empathy, in a nutshell, is the ability to get into another person's shoes.[24] It is the capacity to understand, reflect upon, and decode another's thoughts and feelings. It is not simply "sympathy" as when we begin to cry seeing another cry (as the very young baby can do). In older children and adults, including professional therapists and counsellors, empathy has to be distinguished from projection, and "emotional contagion."[25.] As a therapist, I must have the skill to see the point of view of my client, to read his thoughts, feelings, and perspectives, but maintain my own sense of self, identity, and not lose my own perspective. With children, we have to help them on each of the multifaceted strands of empathy. We must get them to practice seeing different points of view from their own, a skill which has been shown to be crucial to their moral judgment and moral behavior.[26] Children can apply forms of the Golden Rule much better if they have the requisite cognitive empathy. They will be more disposed to share and cooperate if they have a more developed affective empathy, being able to read and understand the emotions of others (of course they must as a prerequisite learn to identify, label, and comprehend their own emotions. Finally, if they are trying to do the right thing, just as for us adults, it is a prerequisite to genuinely care. This last moral strand of empathy is the most elusive.

The development of empathy

Empathy can be developed in three steps. These parallel the training of empathy with therapists and counsellors. First of all, since there is an inevitable affective component to empathy, one must help in the recognition and labelling of one's own emotions. The second step involves increasing the sensitivity to the feelings of others. This can be done via story-telling, which includes open discussion about the feelings and thoughts of the characters (animals or humans). One also refers to one's own experiences in real life. So parents talk of their own feelings in similar situations and contexts. Finally, there is the third step of suggesting strategies for coping with another's feelings.

So here is an example: Older sister (3 and a half) is playing with a puzzle. Brother (1 and a half) snatches a piece. Sister grabs object, continues playing, ignoring the screaming and crying of the brother. One can show one's daughter that there are strategies for dealing with the brother like letting him hold the piece, or giving him another. One can tune into another's feelings. But why should a 4 year old care? We are trying to get our child, even at this early age, to be more aware of the consequences of what they do. They can foresee that not only will the brother be upset, but mother and father as well. So it is a good strategy to tune into the other's feelings, and it will also lead to increased self-worth. We are imparting values. After all, if one's child acts imperviously to the feelings of others in pre-school, this will not be the good child we hope to help develop.

To summarize, our development of empathy in children parallels the three steps used to train counsellors. These are emotion recognition, awareness of others, and focusing on strategies and consequences. From only five days after birth you can begin to help our children to develop empathy. During this period of 0-2 years old, even before the child talks well enough for the verbal strategies mentioned, there are useful things to do. One of these is the mimicking of expressions game. The game is played by you imitating their facial expressions and vice versa. Another fun thing is to hum along with the child, mimicking their noises and sounds. What we are doing with these non-verbal interactions is validating their feelings and our own. We are exhibiting inter-subjectivity, one of the first traces of empathy. These games can be used from the earliest infancy. At about 8 months, the games can become more complicated because the child can understand sufficiently so that you can add verbal communication to the nonverbal. In other words you can use the words: "you are sad," "I am sad," etc, at the same time as the relevant facial expressions appear.

To take an example, a very young child tries to bite or pull your hair. Instead of simply disciplining (shouting or punishing) we can gently take the child's hand and say "make nice." Note that the soothing tones we use, along with our words and gestures, are already imparting values. Notice the difference between simple training (as for one's cat or dog), and this rudimentary moral education, where we actually begin talking to the child. For the first several months of life you are simply talking. By one year of age, however, children will certainly understand a great deal. Therefore one should always attempt to provide explanations. For example: "Biting or pulling hair hurts." Between the ages of one and two, one can certainly begin to introduce all of the topics to be discussed in this book. For example, the delicate questions in regard to the body can be introduced at this very early age. We can talk about hugging, kissing, touching, etc. to one's 2-year-old, preparing the ground work for the later conversations.

As we stated before, empathy is much more than a response to the distress of another. Dramatic play of children, perhaps playfulness at all age levels, has an empathic component. Each player looks at the other or others to judge the seriousness with which the rules of the game or fantasy are being followed, and the extent to which the signals that are being sent are being picked up by the participant. There is also an empathic component in humor. Much children's literature and folklore are replete with examples of empathy.

It is of interest to note that here again Jean Piaget underestimated young children's capabilities (see the discussion in the introduction). For Piaget, children are only capable of empathy at ages eight or nine because they do not have the requisite cognitive capacities.[27]

Sharing

Sharing toys and possessions with other children is generally something we want to encourage even at the earliest ages. Whether at home or at day-care, we can use various stratagems to teach this behavior. Very young children, even before they speak, will follow the action of cutting a piece of cake in two, or dividing a group of ten candies into two sets of five. They can even help do the cutting of the cake or the dividing of the candies. When they are a little older (two and a half years onwards) one can add the following: one child cuts the cake, and the other child chooses the piece they want. We are, with these practices, introducing our children to the idea of fairness, a form of what philosophers call "distributive justice.:

We want to talk to our children about why sharing is a good thing; how it will make others feel happier, as well as making the sharer feel happier as well. One should also make a point, at home or at the nursery, of talking about public places, group space and toys and objects to be used by more than one child. Just as we have already emphasized the importance of personal identity and privacy by saying "Mary's nose" or "Mary's doll" so do we want to introduce phrases like "this truck is ours" or " this room belongs to Mary and John." In the same way, just as we say "This is my time," "this is your time," we can sometime say "This is together time."

One of the Jewish traditions in training for Tzedaka (charity) is to encourage children celebrating their Bar Mitzvah or Bat Mitzvah to give away ten percent of the money they receive in gifts. Clearly we can start at a much earlier age, setting aside a sum of money offering some choices to the child "keep or share, and how much" and even discuss and decide where to give or donate some of the money (for example, poor children in a nearby community, or any where else in the world).

We also want to stress that sharing must be done in the right way. As the philosopher Maimonides explains:

> whoever gives charity to a poor man illmanneredly and with downcast looks has lost all the merit of his action even though he gives him a thousand gold pieces. He should treat him with good grace and with joy and should sympathize with him and his plight . . . he should speak to him with words of consultation and sympathy.[28]

Cooperation: Why is cooperation a good thing?
A time to throw stones, and a time to gather stones together.(Ecclesiastes 3:5)

A time to tear apart, and a time to sew together.

(Ecclesiastes 3:7)

Why do we want our children to cooperate? As usual, we have to begin by asking what "cooperation" means.

What is "cooperation"?

Research has shown that many very young children understand cooperation to mean obedience.[29] They have heard the word "cooperate" and perhaps their parents (or teachers) have really wanted to say "Obey, follow the rules." If this is indeed what is meant, then it is not the kind of moral value worth pursuing. There is, however, another sense to cooperation which is linked to sharing, working with others, interdependence, and group or team work. When this strand of meaning is in play, we are in the realm of an important moral value.

Why is cooperation a good thing?

Once again we can turn to Piaget, who not only considered cooperation good, but an essential moral value in the child's development. Others have emphasized cooperation as a means to an end-perhaps better results in math or language – and still others as an antidote to too much competition. Piaget, along with other philosophers, educators, and psychologists, sees cooperation as an end in itself.[30] For Piaget, cooperation was defined as a kind of mutual respect, and was the essence of the higher form of responsibility and autonomy. Unfortunately, as noted, Piaget thought that full cooperation could only bloom in very late childhood, and early adolescence. Here, as in other things, Piaget has been shown to be wrong.[31] So, although we accept that cooperation is a moral value in Piaget's sense, we amend his view, here as elsewhere,[32] by noting that cooperation can be fostered and achieved in its highest forms at very early ages.

Can cooperation be bad?

There are a number of dangers to be mentioned in regard to cooperation, particularly in its popular strand in the schools which emphasize team-work, shared projects, under the model of "cooperative learning."[33] Although there are undeniably benefits of this kind of work for academic success, and improved relations between ethic and racial groups, there is also a downside. In the first place much of this kind of cooperation is linked to results, and the groups are often involved in forms of competitiveness (with other groups) which often seems the opposite of true cooperation, as outlined here.[34] In the school setting, there is also the worry among many that too much group or team work of this kind will not prepare the student for "real" life, where genuine competition is the norm, and preparing exams or term papers with others is often considered a form of cheating.[35] In regard to very young children (2 to 5), there has been a tendency to overemphasize working with others, often to the detriment of autonomous work, and also solitary play.[36] Clearly a balance is needed, because there are important benefits for the young child, as for the older child and adult, to work and play alone, as much as to work and play with others.[37] One other advantage to solitary play is that it allows the child self-soothing, often an important ingredient where the caregivers have not been adequate in responding to emotional need.[38] As parents, we have to be aware of this, and use our judgment on how much or how little of each kind of play or work is the right amount for our child.

If children are involved in making a get-well card for a parent or teacher, they can work individually, or together. If together, they can share roles, discuss the different parts of the task, communicate about their project and so on. There are clear advantages to cooperation, with proven benefits to cognitive and emotional development. The key component to the cognitive dimension is improved skills at communication, both linguistic and non-verbal. The concept which encompasses both this cognitive dimension as well as the relevant emotional development is called "empathy."

The role of judgment: A review

We have already noted that too much play with others might be bad, similarly too much play (or work) alone might be bad too. We have to use our developing judgment (ours and our children's) to determine what is best. Besides cooperation in regard to work and play, we also hope for our child to develop empathy, and learn to share. We want our children to be generous, and share their possessions, space and skills. Generosity, however, like every other moral virtue, can be too extreme.[39] A child who gives everything away (like the corresponding adult) is as bad as one who never shares at all. Too much or too little is to be avoided. Our judgment will be called into play, therefore, to determine what the happy balance is, where the moderation lies. We will want to teach our children that the moral value of generosity is, as Aristotle said 2500 years ago, a happy medium between two extremes.[40] As Aristotle also told us, this "mean" cannot be calculated mathematically, only judgment can help us find it. There will be few rules to help, and those that exist will have to be interpreted case by case.

We have to encourage both work and play despite the Montessori insistence (against Froebel and his kindergarten concept) that work in daycares should take priority. Another antinomy we have discussed concerns playing together with others and playing alone. There is a time and place for both, and we must judge how much or how little to encourage with any given child.

Another important role for judgment emerges from the discussion on the development of empathy. As we have seen, the challenge is to extend a child's empathy and his compassion to as wide a group as possible. We do not want children to begin to exclude others because of irrelevant considerations. Skin color is never relevant in a decision to whom one will be caring and empathic. Here good judgment is needed to assure that empathy will become universal. It is judgment which allows us to separate out those differences which are relevant, and those which are not. The other component of judgment which will help in this context is imagination. Boys can try to imagine how things feel like to girls; White children can attempt to see things as Blacks do; affluent children can try to understand how things look to less fortunate ones.

Sometimes it is the perspective of others which is different, sometimes their beliefs, and sometimes their needs. In regard to perspective and beliefs, the exercises on cognitive empathy are of use.[41] These can most profitably be combined with the exercises in judgment which allow better discriminations. In regard to needs, one may similarly make use of a combination of judgment and empathy skills. To return to an example of sharing, we may ask a child how to share a chocolate bar in the fairest way with ten children. Some may give a mathematical answer, dividing the bar in to ten pieces. A sensitivity to the needs of others will lead some to see that the best distribution may be different. One child may be quite satisfied with a smaller piece, another may be allergic to chocolate, and a third may not want any at the time. By the age of five, children are quite sophisticated at the nuances of these situations. They can readily grasp the idea that it may be best to give some children more chocolate, and some children perhaps a substitute rather than any chocolate at all.

7
Understanding Emotions

A time to weep, and a time to laugh
A time to mourn, and a time to dance

(Ecclesiastes 3:4)

A time to love, and a time to hate

(Ecclesiastes 3:8)

What are "emotions"?

Emotions are the special subset of feelings that most concern us in moral education. The world of feelings (the "affective" world) is, of course, much wider. It includes pain and pleasure, motivation, appetites (like thirst and hunger), attitudes and dispositions. The most common way many people have seen the role of feelings in regard to moral values is as an obstacle and an impediment. Plato and Kant are the main representatives of this view whereby the passions (our impulses, and desires) are to be mastered in order for us to be good, and do the right thing.[1] One philosopher who rejected this view of feelings was Plato's favorite student, Aristotle. For Aristotle, feelings were not in opposition to morals; they were the very essence of it. We will follow Aristotle in this, as do many philosophers writing today about emotion.[2]

There are other feelings, which have been made relevant by philosophers to morality, including pain and pleasure, attitudes, desires, appetites, passions and motivation. The most common way of making these feelings relevant to moral reasoning were as elements in human moral psychology.[3] Moral knowledge was seeing what is right; these various feelings would provide the apparatus for doing what was right.[4] Feelings took the place of "the will" as the favorite explanation of what was needed to get children, as well as adults, to do the thing which they knew should be done. Feelings "pushed us;" like all motives, they helped us do the right thing in the face of temptation. In other words, some feelings pushed us to do the wrong thing, others the right one.

In contrast to these two philosophical perspectives, which either see feelings as impediments to morality, or as a kind of "motivator," there is a growing modern consensus supporting the Aristotelian view that feelings are at the very heart of morality. As Sharon Bailin states in discussing education:

> The opposition between intuition and rationality rests on a misleading opposition between reason and emotion. Reason and emotion are not necessarily one to another, but, in fact, closely intertwined . . .[5]

Another educator makes the same point in a somewhat different way. Kieran Egan, in his book on imagination and education, details a number of errors he believes have been commit-

95

ted by contemporary educational practice with young children. These include the failure to recognize the importance of fantasy, the underestimation of young children's capacities of understanding of profound abstract concepts such as love, hate, and oppression, and the neglect of
the affective dimension.[6] Margaret Somerville, Professor of Law and Medicine at McGill
University, and expert on the making of ethical decisions, agrees with Bailin and Egan:

> I believe that intuition and emotion are our primary decision making mechanisms . . . Some
> people say 'Don't trust them, they are not rational.' Rather, I would say, 'Don't trust them if
> they are *only* rational.'[7]

Emotions are central to values; they are often the same as certain virtues and vices, for example, jealousy, pity, pride and shame. What are "emotions"? One way of seeing what emotions are, is to
say what they are not. They are not just desires, impulses, or motives; the things which may push
us to action. They are also different than hunger and thirst, our two main appetites. Hunger is
always about food, thirst always about drink. In contrast, emotions like love can have as object
any number of people, or by extension, pets, books, music and so on. Nor can emotions be
reduced to desires and passions, including sexual desire. Emotions are not pleasure and pain,
although, of course, they may involve both these sensations. Having said what emotions are *not*,
let us try a positive description.

The best way of summing up a vast amount of philosophical and psychological literature
of the last thirty years[8] is to say: "Emotions are about something in the world." If we ask ourselves what we naturally call emotions, we would give quite a long list which would include fear,
anger, joy, sorrow, grief, jealousy, pity, shame, guilt, pride, hope, wonder, love, hate, and the like.
What sort of criterion underlies this selection? The connection is that all these emotions are
forms of cognition; they are sometimes called "appraisals." All emotions involve seeing situations under certain aspects which are agreeable or disagreeable and beneficial or harmful in a
variety of dimensions. To feel fear is, for instance, to see a situation as dangerous. To feel pride
is to see with pleasure something as mine, or as something that I have had a hand in bringing
about. In a recent comprehensive book, Martha Nussbaum argues that emotions should be
understood as "geological upheavals of thought." *Emotions are judgments in which people
acknowledge the great importance, for their own flourishing, of things that they do not fully control —
and acknowledge thereby, their neediness before the world and its events.*[9] Nussbaum credits the
Stoics for the essence of this view that emotions are judgments.

For the purpose of the present book, we accept the cognitivist analysis of emotion which
is sketched above. The essential point to our view, which follows Aristotle and Nussbaum, is
that emotions are a form of judgment. It is only fair, however, to mention that there is an
opposing group of philosophers who insist that emotions should be primarily defined not in
terms of cognition, but rather in terms of physiological changes.[10]

There is no consensus about whether emotions are uniquely human, or whether other animals have emotions as well. The Stoics, as Nussbaum points out, were convinced that no animal could have any emotion. Nussbaum herself, along with a philosopher/ dog- owner called
George Pitcher[11] argue forcefully that some animals display grief, anger and love. The only
emotion about which there seems to be a universal agreement between philosophers and psychologists is the emotion of fear. Every creature seems to have fear built into whatever brain it
possesses. It is no doubt for this reason that most of the recent exciting research on the phys-

iology of emotion has concentrated on the emotion of fear.[12] In our view, disgust is probably uniquely human, as are emotions like hope, shame, and pride. This is because there are elements of thought involved of a kind only humans are capable of. Among other concepts necessary to these emotions are a consciousness of time, of past and future, something only people seem to be capable of. Pride is about things we have judged to have done in the past which we consider due to certain effort, and as an accomplishment.[13] Shame relates to an ideal of ourselves which we have, and feel less than perfect about.[14] Hope involves expectations about the future, along with certain associated fears.

How are emotions different than moods?

Nussbaum suggests a conceptual distinction between emotions and moods. On her analysis,[15] the former have an object, the latter do not. Although she grants that both emotions and moods are "upheavals," Nussbaum does not accept that what they have in common is of sufficient importance to warrant retaining an umbrella term like "affect" as some have suggested.[16] The emotions are invariably related to some event which is important in the person's life. All our emotions, Nussbaum argues, have an object in a similar way. Joy, sadness, hope, fear, anxiety, shame, guilt, disgust and grief all are about something (Of course this "something" may be real or imagined). Moods, on the other hand, are objectless in Nussbaum's account. Depression (at least "endogenous" depression), euphoria, elation, gloom, and equanimity are the moods she mentions; they all lack even the vaguest of objects, according to Nussbaum.[17] Although she admits that in practice it is sometimes hard to distinguish an emotion with a very vague object from a mood with no object, she nevertheless maintains that the basic conceptual distinction is sound.[18]

Nussbaum also reminds us of Lucretius's point that we may have some emotion (about something) but we are not aware of it. We may, for instance, have a general fear without an object (a mood?) but this may really be about death (therefore an emotion). Lucretius's point, of course, has a more modern form with Freud's unconscious[19] and the latest neurological consensus about the human emotional brain.[20]

These "background emotions," as she calls them, are, as mentioned, unconscious; they are neither moods nor specific emotions.[21] Although she examines Lucretius's example of the fear of death, there are others she does not discuss or acknowledge. One of these "background" emotions would be the important and very pervasive fear of depression.[22] In addition, there are universal fears (phobias) of snakes, spiders, heights, storms, darkness, blood, large carnivores, strangers, confinement, deep water and social scrutiny.[23] The general heaviness (or weight in the chest) described by Lucretius, may or may not be linked to a fear of death. The unconscious is too complex for this kind of generalization. In fact, the fear of death people do have (for example in regard to fear of flying phobias) is more plausibly interpreted as a fear of loss of self. Many of those afraid to fly will willingly be sedated, or ask to be otherwise "knocked out" and then do not fear the imagined disaster quite so much. This counts as some kind of evidence in favour of the "fear of loss of self" interpretation, rather than the "fear of death" explanation. Fear of depression, as mentioned, is also a crucial unconscious background emotion, and is related to one's sense of self. This too is not discussed by either Lucretius nor Nussbaum.

Nussbaum maintains that her analysis is valid, insofar as it is faithful to the "phenomena."[24] We accept her criterion which is in keeping with the Aristotelian perspective which we share. In several areas of our lived experience, however, her analysis fails by this very criterion.[25] One of these is the field of psychopathology, particularly the condition of clinical depression. We have argued elsewhere that Nussbaum's analysis has to be modified to consider that emotions and moods, although different, are often causally related.[26] Let us briefly look at two sets of emotions/moods. The first is sadness (an emotion) and depression (a mood). The second set will be fear (an emotion) and anxiety (a mood).

Sadness and depression

Sadness is one of the basic emotions, and every child will very soon know what it is like to be sad. As with other emotions, educators will help the child identify sadness, label it where appropriate, and trace the causes of sadness, and its manifestations. A child may be sad because of some event that has occurred or through sympathy or empathy with another person, animal, or storybook character (see Chapter 6). *Often, sadness may be confused with fear or anger; part of the job of parents and other educators is to help young children sort this out.* It is important to be aware of the distinction between sadness, which is common, and clinical depression, which may sometimes occur in children. Both sadness and depression have common features; they are, however, distinguishable in certain ways. It is important for educators to think about this matter, because a decision on whether to involve a clinical psychologist or psychiatrist will sometimes have to be made by them. We can summarize the gist of Nussbaum's analysis, with which we largely agree, in the following way: "Endogenous" depression (caused by our internal chemistry) is to be clinically treated; it is a mood. Sadness is a "reactive" depression, about some event in the real or imagined world; it is an emotion. This is okay as far as it goes, although we, and others, have suggested certain modifications. Our main suggestion of modification is to join emotions and moods together under an umbrella term like affect. This suggestion is supported by Stocker and others.[27] The principle reason for our modification is that emotions and moods are often intertwined. If a child, for example, is in a good mood this may lead to an emotion of joy, and less sadness in certain situations. Music is an excellent vehicle for influencing both moods and emotions.

Although Nussbaum uses "endogenous depression" as an example of a mood,[28] as opposed to reactive depression, (an emotion) she herself gives a personal account of the relationship between her grief about her mother death, and her subsequent depression.[29] She does not tell us whether this depression was severe, treated by medications, or long-lasting. In any case, those are the important considerations, rather than the less helpful distinction between "endogenous" and other. The point here is that her borrowed distinction between endogenous depression and reactive (emotional) depression is not only difficult to determine in practice, as Nussbaum acknowledges,[30] but also is a distinction which raises general doubts. Those who work with the diagnosis and treatment of depression have largely given up this distinction between depressions due entirely to inner chemistry, and depressions due entirely to outer conditions such as stress, frustration and grief.[31] Paralleling the old nature-nurture debate, there is a growing consensus that both the environment and the brain interact in a complex way.[32] It is not only, as Nussbaum states, that both kinds of depression can be treated by either medications or forms of psychotherapy. It is also the case that one must treat serious depression[33] as a combination of outside and inside factors from initial diagnosis onwards.

Nussbaum has relied heavily on Seligman's important work on learned helplessness, which constitutes her main source for the distinction she makes between "endogenous" depression (one of her example "moods") and sadness or "reactive" depression (an emotion). However, more recent work, both with animals and humans, have gone beyond Seligman. One important post-Seligman distinction in psychopathology is that between helplessness and hopelessness. It is the latter which is more related to the extreme forms of depression clinicians must contend with.[34]

Fear and Anxiety

Fred Rogers died in 2004 leaving hundreds of television episodes of Mr Roger's Neighborhood. One of his specialities was dealing with children's fears as encapsulated by his famous reassuring song "We can never go down the drain." Mr Rogers, as he was known to adult and child alike, never talked down to children and talked about their fears openly and honestly. He encouraged children to verbalize their fears and anxieties.

Fear is one of the common, basic emotions. All children will experience being afraid, as will every living creature. Fear is a universal reaction to a situation which any animal, including man, sees as threatening. It has two main behavioral manifestations; fight or flight. In addition, there is well-documented research evidence of accompanying physiological components.[35] Fear has been the most studied of all the emotions, both by psychologists and philosophers interested in the meaning of feelings. For example, among the latter group we have William James who postulated about one hundred years ago that we are afraid because we run, rather than what his opponents, and most people thought, which is that we run because we are afraid.[36] It is of interest that in the recent debates about emotion, James' view has been given credence because of the discoveries about the body and the brain. We now know that people are often fearful in certain situations because they notice that their body has reacted in a certain way. There are many examples of children's phobias (fears) which we can treat clinically, using what is known about the interaction between feelings, thoughts, and bodily manifestations. For purposes of illustration, we will use an example from clinical practice with adults.

For example, a person suffering from fear of flying, will notice that he is sweating, that his heart is thumping, and that he is reacting to every small noise. These physiological signs will trigger extreme fear, even panic independently of any event which has occurred in the real, or in the imagined world. Successful control of this kind of fear is based upon the recognition that William James had been partly right in his analysis.

Anxiety, like depression, is a mood rather than an emotion. Educators should be aware of clinical anxiety; it will manifest itself in a very general kind of worry, about nothing in particular, or about everything rather than about a specific situation in the world. If there is any doubt that the young child may be experiencing general anxiety, then a clinician should be consulted, as in the case of clinical depression discussed above.

What should we know about temperament?

The tendency toward a melancholy or upbeat temperament – like that toward timidity or boldness emerges within the first year of life, a fact that strongly suggests it is genetically determined.[37] In infants, ten months of age, researchers have found that the activity level of the frontal lobes predicted whether they would cry when their mothers left the room.[38] In this research, the correlation was virtually 100%: every infant who cried had more brain activity on the right side, while those that did not cry had more activity on the left.

Even if some basic dimensions of temperament are laid down from birth, or very nearly from birth, temperament is not destiny, as Goleman said.[39] Those with a morose pattern are not doomed to go through life brooding and crotchety; not all fearful infants grow up hanging back from life. The emotional lessons of childhood can have a profound impact on temperament, either amplifying or muting an innate pre-disposition. The great plasticity of the brain in childhood means that experiences during the pre-school years can have a lasting impact on the sculpting of neural pathways for the rest of life.

One good example concerns the timid child, whose natural timidness at the outset can be lost by the time he is about five years old. The parents or caregivers (in this research, mainly mothers) play a major role in whether an innately timid child grows bolder with time or continues to shy away from novelty and becomes upset by challenge. Those mothers who were too protective, picking their infants up and holding them when they fretted or cried, longer than other mothers, made their children more timid. In contrast, those mothers who reversed their children's timidity set firm limits, putting "gentle pressure on their child to be more outgoing."[40] Although the temperamental trait of timidity is slightly harder to change than others, the consensus in 2005 is that" no human quality is beyond change."[41]

Temperament may be best viewed as a general term referring to the *how* of behavior. We can contrast it with ability, which is concerned with the *what* and *how well* of behavior, and for motivation, which accounts for *why* a person does what he is doing. Two children may dress themselves with equal skilfulness or ride a bicycle with the same dexterity and have the same motives for engaging in these activities. Yet, these two children may differ significantly with regard to the quickness with which they move, the ease with which they approach a new physical environment, social situation or task, the intensity in character of their mood expression, and the effort required by others to distract them when they are absorbed in an activity. These last categories are all examples of temperament.[42] One of the categories which has been most studied is activity level which has shown significant differences between males and females right from birth,[43] with boys being more active than girls (science confirms what parents/educators have known for a long time).

Furthermore, how we judge and reason morally cannot be divorced from our "temperament,"[44] that is to say the kind of person we are, whether we are (generally) virtuous and also exhibit the specific moral virtues of temperance, generosity, courage, "mildness," and the rest. This Aristotelian focus on temperament is generally ignored by Nussbaum. One example of this facet of Aristotle's analysis which we want, in contrast, to emphasize, appears in his discussion of "akrasia" (weakness of will) in Book VII (1150b 20-30). He distinguishes two kinds of weakness of will, one called "impetuousness" the other "weakness:"

> The weak person deliberates, but then his feeling makes him abandon the result of his deliberation; but the impetuous person is led on by his feelings because he has not deliberated . . . Quick-tempered and ardent people are most prone to be impetuous types.

Another example, this time in the discussion of the virtues, has Aristotle classify different kinds of people in regard to anger. His four types (irascible, choleric, bitter, and irritable) remain, despite our greater knowledge of brain chemistry and physiology, still remarkably accurate as a general portrayal of different temperaments, and how they impact on the manifestations of anger. We still mark out those we call "irascible" in English because of their "hot temper, and being easily provoked" (Webster's) from others whose relationship to anger is generally of a different kind. Aristotle compares these different temperaments to the difference between individuals who are ticklish or not. Can anger be controlled? Further discussion on this is needed.

Are there universal basic emotions? How many?

The consensus about the universality of emotions is tied to the issue of facial expression. In the first psychological research on emotion in the modern era, the emphasis was on four of these basic universal emotions; namely, anger, fear, joy (happiness), and sadness.[45] Subsequently, two other emotions were added to the list; specifically surprise and disgust. (See appendix L) Some philosophers, like Nussbaum, have questioned the legitimacy of this list, claiming that facial expressions are not universal, but may have a cultural component. This issue remains an open one; further research is needed.

What are "mixed" emotions?

There are complex emotions like "longing" which are a blend of the primary emotions of happiness and sadness.[46] The emotion of hope is another example of a complex one which embodies some joy and some fear. A third example concerns the emotions of frustration and disappointment, (a mixture of sadness and anger) something that children will begin to comprehend between the ages of two and five. Children by the age of five or six can discuss complex emotions of this sort, as well as others like shame, guilt, jealousy, and pride.

There is another sense in which emotions are mixed, which is more fundamental. Children often confuse anger, sadness, and fear, even up to five years of age. In our research project on the prevention of violence, we tested 5-year-old's ability to recognize the four basic emotions. Most children had trouble disentangling anger from fear, fear from sadness, and sadness from anger. It is important to stress that this kind of confusion can last for a very long time, and can have serious consequences in adult life. Work with violent men centres upon this same kind of confusion concerning the basic emotions. Successful therapeutic intervention is partly based upon them becoming aware of some of their confusion of sadness and fear with anger. It is clearly an important task for early childhood education to begin helping children understand this area of mixed emotions.

Should we talk of positive and negative emotions?

Philosophers and psychologists do not agree on this issue. Some, like Nussbaum and Stocker do recognize that some emotions like wonder, awe, joy, hope, and love are positive ones whereas jealousy and shame can be seen as negative. On the other side, Robert Solomon has argued that we abolish all talk of the distinction between positive and negative emotions.[47] He and others want to stress that all emotions have a role to play in the moral life. This same debate ranges psychologists like Paul Ekman, against others like Daniel Goleman concerning so called destructive and healing emotions.[48] For the former, an emotion like jealousy will always exist; the job of educators will be to make children aware of it. For the latter, with the support of the Dalai Lama, jealousy is an emotion to be completely eradicated.[49] Our view is that there are some emotions which are painful, or at least unpleasant; others are pleasant. Among the unpleasant ones, we would put hate and disgust; among the pleasant ones we will list wonder and love. (yes, some kinds of love are painful at times too) A brief word about how to talk to young children about these four emotions.

Hate

Hate is a very strong word; it signifies a desire for the other person to suffer greatly, even to die. Children, even very young children will say "I hate you," when they are angry or frustrated. We should always take the opportunity to help them identify their feeling of sadness or anger or frustration or fear. Furthermore, it must be explained that this does not mean that they truly "hate."

Disgust

At about the age of two, usually along with toilet training, the emotion of disgust will appear. As noted above, disgust seems to have universal facial expressions, and is often listed as one of the basic emotions. Children, of course, may not use the word "disgust" but will substitute some term like "yucky," which they will have picked up from adults or elsewhere. In general, what is found disgusting relates to bodily functions, particularly excretions such as, urine, vomit, excrement, and phlegm (with children we will more likely say "pee," "puke," "poo" and "snot").[50] There are theories about the origin of this emotion, mostly related to a human being's desire to distance himself from the other animals. It is important that we talk about the use of the word "disgusting," discouraging a child from using it to describe another person. Nussbaum has suggested that the emotion of disgust may be one of the main impediments to universal compassion. The gist of her argument is that children learn to apply disgust to other groups of people, eventually leading to prejudice, hate, and violence. Two of Nussbaums's other impediments to compassion, love, and morality are shame and pride, two moral emotions which she suggests are primarily human.

Wonder

The emotion of wonder is a kind of delight at the world. The young infant has an incipient kind of wonder at parts of the world that are not related to its own states. These parts of the world include persons and parts of persons, toward whom wonder and gratitude may be profoundly interwoven. It has been suggested by Nussbaum and others that wonder plays an important part in the development of a child's capacity for love and compassion. Wonder, Nussbaum suggests, is a striking exception to all the other emotions in the sense that it is "non-eudaimonistic." This means that wonder can be concerned with others, without a relationship to one's own goals and plans. All other emotions are "eudaimonistic" which means that they have some reference to one's own important goals and projects.

In the Philosophy for Children approach, whose orientation we adopt in this book, the key emotion is wonder. Children are naturally curious about the world and about the meaning of words to describe it. The introduction of philosophical discussions in the classroom was intended in large part to satisfy the needs of a child "wondering at the world." In this book, we have provided exercises and materials to cater to this emotion that can be used by parents and early childhood educators in the same manner as the Philosophy for Children approach in the classroom.

Love

A child will talk about loving his parents, his friends, an animal, a doll, some candy and any other item he may choose as an object. The use of the word "love" is no different than "like" (in French the same word"aimer" is used for both loving and liking.). At an earlier period of development, during early infancy long before there is any verbal competence, there is a kind of rudimentary love associated with gratitude, which is an awareness that others are there to help in its attempt to live. From the infant to the comprehending 1-year-old, followed by the speaking 2-year-old, we eventually arrive at the stage where we must begin to talk about "love" in somewhat more detail. From ages 3 to 5, we want to begin to distinguish between "loving" and "liking" (in French "aimer" and "bien aimer"). The other obligation is to distinguish different kinds of love, primarily love between parents and child, (particularly between mother and infant), love between friends, and romantic love typically between parents (for the preschool child we can usually ignore, for the time being, romantic love between other partners other than parents). The Greeks were more inventive and had three words for the different kinds of love;

namely, "*agapé*," "*philia*," and "*eros*." We can watch a movie like "Love Actually" together with our children. The dozen or so main characters display the emotion of love in all it's sundry forms.

One necessary condition for love is missing the beloved person. Children can readily understand that if they miss a person very much in their absence, this will be a sign of love. Conversely, if one does not miss a person, this is a good sign that there is no love. Love, of course, involves many other factors in addition to missing a person. That is why the condition of "missing" is necessary but not sufficient.

The development of emotion: What do children understand?

After quite a long period of neglect, the emotions have recently reappeared as an important focus of investigation within psychology. During psychology's first historical period (1860 till 1913), the theories and researchers of Williams James were predominant, these views later to be contested by Cannon. During the "scientific" era – 1913 to the present – emotions were largely ignored, first because of behaviorist ideology, and later by the emphasis on cognitive process. The last quarter century marks this renewed interest in emotion. Paradoxically, much of the recent debates about the meaning and definition of emotion restates the earlier James vs. Cannon disputes often captured by two encapsulations: "Do we fear something because we flee from it?" (James) or "Do we flee from it because we fear it?" (Cannon) Of course, the debate is now colored by neurological information about the emotional brain unknown to James and Cannon, as well as a growing body of scientific research with animals, as well as young children. In any case, there is still major controversy, between those who emphasize the motivational aspects of emotion, and those who stress its cognitive components. For Nico Frijda, emotions are defined as "changes in action readiness" whereas Nussbaum defines them as: "judgments of value." For Frijda, emotions push us, for Nussbaum they pull us. Of course, these theorists, and other philosophers and psychologists concerned with how best to conceptualize emotion, all acknowledge the multifaceted complexity of emotions; the difference between theories lies in the choice of the *sine qua non* (necessary) feature which each sees as essential to his/her preferred definition of emotion.[50]

Developmental research on emotion has yielded the (surprising?) discovery of the confusion manifested by even older children and adults regarding the identification of the so-called basic emotions of anger, sadness, fear and joy, not to mention more complex ones like hope, guilt, shame, pride, and longing. Children from 3 years onwards begin to feel, understand and label many of the emotions; they continue, however, to develop their comprehension and articulation of their own emotions, and through empathy, in others. Empathy for us is a complex concept with verbal and non-verbal components. Contrary to the exclusive trigger of empathy by the so-called "negative" emotions, we include in our orientation the noticing and reflecting of all emotions of the other person, including the "positive" ones. In fact, as we have mentioned, there are those who strongly suggest abandoning all talk of polarity and valence, including the positive/negative dimension of emotions.

Although some have recently claimed that children before age 5 have mastered the recognition and prediction of emotions in others, as well as the correct labelling of emotions in themselves and others, our clinical experience tells us, and research data confirms, that children, as well as adults, mislabel and confuse even the basic emotions. The first important developmental period is early childhood, (ages 2 to 5) then the crucial stages from ages 5 to 9 and 9 to 11. Although Paul Harris claims that there is no significant change after age 11 concerning emotion, in our view, development continues throughout life. Paralleling the psychological research on emotion, there has been a renewed awakening to the importance of emotions in moral development and moral education. The affective facet was largely ignored by the focus on reasoning from the 1960s. Of course, the cognitive strand, inspired by Piaget, was itself a necessary reaction to the earlier behaviorist reductionism of morality to the paradigm of resistance to extinction in situations of temptation. It is understandable that the focus on moral reasoning left emotions out, since a long philosophical tradition has put reasons and emotions in opposition to one another. This opposition is linked more to the perception of emotions as "motivators" (pushing us), and like desire or impulses, often in conflict with our reason (Kant, Plato). If, however, emotions are conceptualized as closer to judgments (Aristotle), then it is easier to see their central role in the moral life. Aristotle, in fact, saw the emotions as essential to moral reasoning. For example, for him anger is linked to many of our moral choices: he reminds us that one must know how to be angry "at the right things and towards the right people, and also in the right way, at the right time and for the right length of time" (NE 1126b). It is all a matter of good judgment (1128c). Even within these new strands of interest in emotion, both in psychology and in education, there is yet a more recent advance; namely, awareness of the need to start at the very earliest ages. Of course, the rudiments of fear, anxiety, anger, love are present, as Winnicott and Bowlby, have stressed, from the earliest days of infancy, because of the presence, and sometimes absence of the nurturer/caregiver. More relevantly to the concerns of parents, children from around age 2 onwards begin to put words to some of these emotions, and very soon (by around 3 years of age) others like disgust, surprise, hope, guilt, shame, jealousy, envy, love and hate begin to appear.

The education of emotions: How can we help children to better understand?

Although developmental work on emotion is relatively recent, its results parallel the large body of clinical work which has reached a similar conclusion; namely, that many adults, not only adolescents and young children, are confused about their own emotions, and those of others - particularly anger, sadness and fear. *Furthermore, this lack of clarity about emotion is perhaps the single most important ingredient in explaining some instances of violence and abuse, as well as marking the way for clinical interventions.* Part of the impetus for looking at very young children's emotions, and helping them to clarify their meaning, causes, and consequences, is the hope that one can contribute to the prevention of later manifestations of violence, abuse, incest, and bullying. These problems have caught the attention of not only the public, but also psychologists, social workers, teachers, and therapists who must deal with these phenomena. There is an increasing demand to start to work on the emotions while children are much younger. In fact some intervention programs have been recently developed to help educate young children, along with their parents about emotions. One of these programs has shown some success in helping children understand and articulate certain specific emotions like pride and shame. Another program (SMILE) was successful in improving the understanding of the emotions in typically developing 9-year-olds by means of classroom instructions. Fransisco Pons, one of the collaborators on our project on the prevention of violence, recommends that similar efforts be made with younger children in the classroom. One of our just-completed research projects has in fact, shown significant impact of philosophical discussions on 5 year-old children's understanding of the four basic emotions – fear, anger, joy, and sadness as well as their ability to recognize the emotions in others. This last study also showed significant results even after one year for these 5 year-olds exposed to the Philosophy for Children approach as compared to controls on one measure of empathy (perspective-taking), and their judgment in regard to situations involving conflict and violence. We have included some of the material in the Appendices of this book. Others, using the same P4C approach, have shown that working with children from 3 to 5 can increase their self-confidence and self-esteem. Despite the evidence of some progress concerning emotions – recognition in our project, it is important to point out how limited this progress was. A large number of children continue to confuse anger, sadness, and fear in post-test, and a certain number even are mixed up about "joy." Although parents, teachers and researchers often take it for granted that children of 5 years old have gained a basic mastery of the primary emotions ("glad, mad and sad"), children (and many adults) display more confusion than is generally believed, not only about the range of nuanced emotions, like disgust but even about the basic "primary" ones like joy, fear, anger and sadness. One can see why Izard suggests intervening from birth. Our present project, on the prevention of violence, begins working with children as of age 3 (see Appendix B for more details).

A number of results with the preschool child show that children's sensitivity to emotion is a good index of their relationship with peers and adults. For example, some have looked at the relationship between pre-school children's accuracy on an emotion attribution task and their popularity amongst peers. Children with a better understanding of the external causes of emotion proved to be more popular with peers, even when the effects of age and gender were controlled. In a study of "hard-to-manage" children, aged 3 and 4 years, researchers found a significant, negative relation between emotion understanding and behavioral problems (anti-social behavior; aggressiveness; restricted empathy; and limited pro-social behavior). Similarly, the same group found a significant, positive relation between 4-year-old's understanding of emotion and the quality of their play with a close friend (good co-operation, efficient communication). In a longitudinal studies of children aged 4 and 5 years, researchers have shown that accuracy in identifying facial expressions of emotion was correlated with popularity one or two years later, even when initial popularity was taken into account.

8

Emotions and Morality

Virtues, vices and moderation in the 21st century version

As we have seen, all our moral decisions are linked to some feeling, as Aristotle noted 2500 years ago. Anger and fear will always exist; the question is how to express it in the right way, to the right person, and at the right time. The key point is that one must show the emotion, but not too much and not too little. Aristotle applied his idea to all the emotions, including what we have called the "negative" emotions, as well as the "positive" ones. This list of moral emotions the Greeks called "virtues."

What is a "virtue"? Let us just stay that a virtue is an admirable or desirable state of character. Virtues have been interpreted as things that are pleasing to self and others, or as things that are good in themselves, or as action tendencies that are aimed toward an independently justified set of values.[1] We will suggest the following definition in line with the modern philosophical consensus,[2] which sees virtue as a trait:

A virtue is a human excellence whose possession tends to enable, facilitate, promote, express, honor, and appreciate a value.

As we mentioned, Aristotle offered us a neat list of virtues which include courage, temperance, liberality, magnificence, pride, good temperament, friendliness, truthfulness, wittiness, shame (a "quasi -virtue"), justice, plus the various virtues of practical reasoning and intellectual life. His entire *Ethics* is essentially the fleshing out of his list. Aristotle's teacher Plato was also a virtue ethicist (as was his teacher Socrates), who also provided us with a concise little list of virtues in *The Republic*: wisdom, courage, temperance, and justice. Saint Thomas Aquinas, Aristotle's eventual medieval pupil, gave us a series of lists, in particular his list of cardinal and theological virtues: prudence, fortitude, temperance, justice, and faith, hope, and charity. If we compare Aristotle and Aquinas' lists, it is of interest to note that at least two of Aristotle's virtues, namely magnificence and pride, are absent from Aquinas' list. Later lists, including some representing a number of religious orientations replaced magnificence and pride with their opposite, namely humility.[3] On many of these same lists, pride was classified as a vice and a sin. The pride-humility debate offers an interesting application for using our judgment. What should educators in the 21st century say to children about this matter? We will return to this question in a following section.

As Robert Solomon reminds us in his recent book on Nietzsche,[4] we must make sure not to be overly ethnocentric or narrow. Nietzsche himself offered us two short lists of virtues, one in *Daybreak;* "honesty, courage, generosity, and politeness;" the other, Beyond Good and Evil; "courage, insight, sympathy, and solitude." As Solomon states, we should not be surprised that Nietzsche's two lists are not consistent with each other, or with what he says elsewhere in his work, for he penned them at different times, and no doubt in different moods. Here are a few of some of the other lists of virtues from different parts of the world: Confucius provided several lists, the most common mentioning *jen, li, yi, xiao, an, chung,* and *shu.* (humanity, ritual engagement, appropriateness, filial piety, tranquillity, loyalty, and respect). From the Upanishads, we get a different list: equanimity, compassion, self-control, wisdom-wakefulness, diligence, openness to one's higher self and contentment – self-acceptance.

Given this hodgepodge of virtues, many of which refer to moods as well as emotions and are often inconsistent with one another, we must concentrate not on the specific content of the virtues and vices, but on the spirit of Aristotle's analysis.

Moral virtue for Aristotle revolves around his concept of the "mean." Virtue is "a mean between two vices, one of excess, one of deficiency" (1107a). To discover courage, for example, implies avoiding both cowardice and foolhardiness. For courage, the key emotion is, of course, fear;[5] this fear is essential for one to be courageous because the person without fear is simply foolhardy. We must recognize, and acknowledge this fear; nevertheless, we make a decision about what to do in difficult circumstances despite our fear. Only then would we consider it a courageous act. Modernizing Aristotle's account a bit further, let us take some difficult 20th century decisions people have had to make which involve some degree of risk as well as some intensity of fear. The example can be very serious as when deciding whether to fight in a war, a decision which had to be made by many people in Canada when there was no conscription at the beginning of the Second World War, or by many Americans during the time of the Vietnam conflict despite conscription. A somewhat less serious case is that of a person who must decide whether or not to fly on an airplane after the 9/11 terror attack in New York (or in slightly different scenarios, choose to send their children, or encourage other loved ones and friends to fly). Those who decided to fight fascism, those who went to fight, in Vietnam, (or in some cases refused to fight and left the U.S. or went to prison) and those who decide to get on an airplane (or send others on the airplane) all exhibit courage – albeit in different ways. One is ready to risk injury and death, another to face exile or prison, and those in the airplane examples to perhaps confront anxiety, terror and even panic. Every difficult moral decision is inescapably a personal one. Aristotle says: "virtue is the mean relative to us" (1107), and insists that he is not talking of an arithmetic mean, or a mathematical calculation.[6] Whatever general principles or moral rules are invoked, a decision often has to be made by one person at a specific time. Each individual will factor into his choice as many details deemed important. In the case of confronting one's fears, for example, these details will include information about the situation, an evaluation of the risks or consequences stemming from whatever decision is made (to fight or not to fight, to fly or not to fly), and whatever personal information is available to the individual concerning themselves (age, background, responsibility to others, personality character quirks etc.).

Controlling emotions: Anger, fear and joy

What is it we want to tell children about controlling their emotions? The short answer is that they should not try to control their feelings, but rather control the behavior or expression of these feelings. In talking about fears, it is important to acknowledge and recognize what makes one afraid, and in which circumstances. The examples of fear discussed in the previous section, taken from modern everyday life, and clinical practice with adults, are relevant to the life of the young child as well. Other negative emotions such as sadness and anger can also be controlled in a similar indirect way. Concerning anger particularly, there has been a great deal of research and discussion about the best way to handle, manage, regulate or control anger.[7] The consensus is, as mentioned, that one not try to control the feeling of anger, but rather exhibit the kind of behavior which is acceptable or appropriate.[8]

Do we need to understand our emotions in order to control them?

Comprehending one's fears is the first, and the most necessary step towards controlling them. This is true for controlling sadness, anger, and any of the other emotions. Of course, there are other methods which have been successful in controlling various emotions which involve the use of drugs, or surgery.[9] Most of this research work has concentrated on the emotion of fear, and has been done with rats.[10] It is already the case that human beings may directly control their fears with the use of medications. In these cases, one does not need any kind of comprehension of emotion in order to control them. However, regarding children, and *education* of the emotions, we will insist that understanding is always the first priority.

Responsibility for emotions and moods - even without control

In talking about any emotion or mood with young children, a higher priority than regulation or control, concerns responsibility. The key to responsibility, as discussed in chapter 5, is accountability; it is *taking* responsibility, leaving one open to the possibility of blame or praise. Emotions are part of the fabric of moral responsibility. As educators, we want to stress that children are the authors of their feelings, and must be accountable for them, just as they are accountable for their actions. The expression of their emotions and moods through behavior, verbal or nonverbal, can often be blameworthy. We will always want to point out to children that whatever feelings they may have are theirs, even if not controllable nor blameworthy.

Everything we have said thus far applies not only to emotions like fear, anger, and sadness, but to others as well. Even a positive emotion like joy sometimes has to be controlled, as, for example, when a child is over-exuberant about some achievement to the point of making others uncomfortable. Or example, in sports, we may have the baseball player who, after hitting a home run, celebrates too much, perhaps annoying the opponents. In N.F.L. football, there is actually a penalty for "taunting" when the referee considers that the celebration after a touchdown is too close to an opponent, and might have been meant as teasing.

We have been discussing the basic emotions and their relevance to morality. We must be ready to say something, as well, to young children about what have been called the moral emotions. The four we will discuss are shame, jealousy, pride and trust.

Shame

Shame is often confused with guilt, and, in fact, in common parlance the two words are sometimes used as synonyms, as in "look what you did, aren't you ashamed of yourself?" However, as an emotion, shame is more primitive, and is quite different than guilt. One way to explain this is to point out that shame does not have to have anything to do with a wrong act. One can have the emotion of shame in regard to some lack of achievement or lack of success, or about tones body and one would not talk of guilt. Guilt, in contrast, is related to some act one feels is wrong, and where one may not be punished by an authority, but has a form of internalized punishment. It is the feeling of guilt, the conscience, and the "superego." Another way to make the point is to remind ourselves that many animals show guilt, that is behavior showing they somehow know they have done wrong, even where there is no punishment. Shame is an emotion which does not, at least in any obvious way, occur in dogs, or other animals. What then is shame?

Shame is an emotion where one feels one has not lived up to expectations or ideals. Its roots, according to the same group mentioned above (Nussbaum, Bowlby, Klein, and Winnicott) are in very early childhood, and are connected with feelings of helplessness and dependence. Here again, it may be helpful to sketch the story, which educators can bear in mind, when talking to children.

When an infant realizes that it is dependent on others, he will experience a primitive and rudimentary emotion of shame. This emotion of shame is coupled with helplessness. Shame involves the realization that one is weak and inadequate in some way in which one expects oneself to be adequate. Its reflex is to hide from the eyes of those who will see one's deficiency, to cover it. (Notice the Garden of Eden story where Adam and Eve become aware of their nakedness). If the infant expects to control the world, as to some extent all infants do, it will have shame, as well as anger, at its own inability to control.

Educators should be careful about using the expression "shame on you" or "aren't you ashamed of yourself?" *There is much evidence that too much feelings of shame can lead to low self-esteem, and even depression.*[11] Some philosophers and psychologists have seen shame (and not necessarily guilt) as a threat to all possibility of morality, and to a creative inner life.[12] On the other hand, *we must stress that too much guilt can be oppressive, and there can be too much focus on remorse and reparation, which can be unhealthily self-tormenting.* On the other side, shame of a specific and limited sort, can be constructive, motivating a pursuit of valuable ideals. Many have pointed out that shame and pride are connected. We will discuss pride and humility in a section following. First, however, we will turn to another moral emotion which is also connected to shame; namely, jealousy. If a child is not stricken by annihilating shame at his imperfection, he will have less need for envy and jealousy, emotions that express the desire for omnipotent control of the sources of good. The function of morality (this comes from Winnicott primarily) is to perform the holding function of a loving mother (we can stipulate that the "mother" can sometimes be a father or other caregiver). Rather than making a forbidding and stifling demand for perfection, morality, in Winnicott's sense, holds the child in his imperfection. Morality is telling a child that the world contains possibilities of forgiveness and mercy, and that he is loved as a person of interest and worth in his own right. He does not have to fear that his imperfection will cause the world's destruction.

Jealousy

As stated in the previous chapter, we accept the analysis of philosophers like Nussbaum, and psychologists like Winnicott and Bowlby[13] that jealousy is an inevitable part of the emotional development of the human child. Jealousy, may, indeed, be a destructive emotion, as Goleman, Ekman, and many others have pointed out,[14] but we do not agree with this latter group that it can be eradicated. *If then, jealousy, is part of life, our task in education is to talk about it, acknowledge its existence, clarify it, and help young children to anticipate the consequences of the emotion.* So, just as it is our task to say "you are angry, you are sad, you are happy, you are a little bit happy and sad," as we have sketched above, so must we say, "you are jealous," and because you are jealous, you are angry and/or sad" etc. A parent about to give birth to a younger sibling might consider not only saying the usual "you will soon have a cute little brother to play with." One might also say something like "when your little brother arrives, this will take a lot of time and you may feel a little sad and a little angry." It is perhaps helpful to understand something of the roots of jealousy. Here is an account, as told by Bowlby, Winnicott, Klein, and Nussbaum:[15]

> In the life of the infant, if things go well, the child's emotions evolve in relation to an environment which is relatively stable, which provides space for the development of wonder and joy, as well as stable love and gratitude. But of course, no such environment is completely stable. Caretakers must come and go, support the child and allow him to fend for himself, so that, he will learn how to get around in the world. The infant is always inhabiting a world that is both safe and dangerous, both able and unable to rely on receiving nourishment and security from his caretakers.

> Before long, the child recognizes that the very same objects, who love and care for him, also go away at times and attend to other projects, heedless to his demands. He realizes that he depends on caretakers or parents, who are not in his control. This means that love and anger come to be directed to one and the same source. Thus love, anxiety, anger, and sometimes hatred, come to be aroused by one and the same person. This anger is itself ambivalent, for it is mixed up with the wish of love to incorporate and possess the needed object, and the anger itself may be used as a device of control.

In consequence, next to anger we now have on our hands the emotion of jealousy, the wish to possess the good object more completely by getting rid of competing influences. The emotion of jealousy is a judgment (yes, it is a bit strange to talk about an infant having "judgment") that it is very bad that there should be these competing influences and that it would be very good for them to vanish from the earth (As we have seen in Chapter 7, this is the essence of "hate," namely the wish that the other person disappear or die).

A close cousin of jealousy is envy. Jealousy, as we have seen, has the caretaker as its focus; envy takes as its focus the competing objects who for a time enjoy the caretaker's favor – especially other siblings, and the lover or spouse of the primary caretaker – or their love for one another, if both caretakers are primary. In envy, the child judges that it would be a good thing for him to displace the competing objects from their favourite position.

In talking to young children, we should probably use the word "jealous" to refer to their feelings. They will quite readily understand the emotion we are talking about. Young children grasp the Cinderella story with the jealous or envious step-sisters. The child will normally be at a stage (two years plus) where psychiatrists have placed the Oedipus complex. Notice that this complex is not defined in terms of the familiar sexual drama that Freud portrayed, and that has become part of popular culture. Rather, it is a stage of insecurity and emotions connected with the desire to possess and control. There are many literary descriptions of this stage, ranging from the biblical examples (Cain and Abel, Jacob and Esau, Joseph and his brothers) to modern novels such as those by Marcel Proust.[16] It is interesting to note that Proust tells us that it is only toward literary characters that one can have love without jealousy and envy. Proust's narrator can love real people without jealousy only when they are asleep.

As we have mentioned, we side with Nussbaum, Bowlby, Winnicott and Proust in thinking that there will always be jealousy. What we must do in talking to children about this is to

identify the emotion and point out the consequences of behavior which can be based on jealousy, envy, extreme anger, and even hate.

Pride

Joke: Once you have managed to resist six deadly sins, it is really hard not to be full of
pride.

In talking about jealousy and shame, we suggested treating them as necessary evils, as moral
emotions which exist and may very well interfere with the development of the values we wish
to see in our children. In the case of pride, we are dealing with a different situation. For some,
pride is a sin, (some say the worst sin), and humility occurs prominently in the list of moral
virtues of many esteemed educators and religious traditions.[17] Despite this strong opposition

to pride in some quarters, we will argue that pride is an important virtue, which is important to encourage in our children. We want to avoid certain excesses, certainly; we need, however, to likewise avoid excesses of humility.

What we need is an understanding of the positive features of pride, and where it can turn into arrogance, brashness, boastfulness and an insensitivity to other's feelings. By the same token, humility can be a virtue, yet one must separate it from meekness, lack of confidence, and various false projections of oneself.

Pride in oneself, and pride in others, is a *prima facie* good thing. There is ample psychological evidence that pride in accomplishment is tied to good self-concept, self-esteem, and this, in turn, is one of the best predictors of success.[18] We have already discussed the importance of developing autonomy in the young child (see Chapter 5). We are assuming a realistic evaluation of one's abilities and achievements. Obviously, one can have misplaced pride, in oneself, or others, where one overestimates abilities or talent. Parents may very well have a natural pride in their children, (this, too, is usually not a bad thing), although the "apple of our eye" may sometimes lead parents astray to think they have the next Mozart, Shakespeare, Picasso or Babe Ruth as soon as they see their child play his first piece on the piano, act out his own drama, draw his first picture or hit his first baseball. Encouraging proper or appropriate pride, means avoiding overconfidence, overestimation of one's talents or abilities, or those of others, or a too smug attitude, culminating in the arrogance of a "know-it-all," or the snobbish stance that one is better than everyone else. These last examples of arrogant pride are, of course, the last kind of thing we want our children to become.

Humility, of course, has its place. We do not want, as adults, to be smug or self-satisfied with what we may have accomplished. As the saying goes: "If you are sitting on your laurels you are wearing them in the wrong place." One needs motivation to continue learning and getting better at whatever we enjoy working at or playing at. In the same way, we want our children to be motivated to continue progressing and developing their talents. (Of course, sometimes, we may err as parents, teachers, or coaches by pushing the child too far or too fast to work at their gymnastics, piano, or hockey.)

The 5th century B.C. philosopher Socrates, as portrayed by Plato and others as one of the wisest of men, embodied humility as a virtue in the sense that he was aware of how much he did not know or understand. He reminded himself, and stated often to others, how ignorant he felt he was, in compared to whatever knowledge he possessed. This attitude is one which we would want to impart to our children. It seems to us a good counterbalance to the virtue of pride, which we also must include, as we have said, as an important moral value. Many religious traditions have espoused something like this kind of Socratic humility. It is the kind of humility which is tied to a wonder at the complexity and marvels of the world. The great 12th century Jewish philosopher, Maimonides, argued for humility in this sense. (Paradoxically, he was called upon to defend himself for arrogance, and lack of humility, because he attempted to explain portions of the Bible's Old Testament, and to reconcile religious faith and science). Great scientists often expressed the same kind of humility as we find in the religious traditions. Albert Einstein, for example, perhaps the greatest scientist of the 20th century, was clear about how much he, and anyone, did not know about the mysteries of the universe.

Our position, in brief, is that educators must try to instil proper pride, and proper humility of the sort described above. Encouraging "proper" or appropriate humility means avoiding self-effacement or "meekness," (a term often used in religious contexts as a synonym for humility). This is a genuine danger, which can lead to poor self-esteem, and lack of motivation for success as we mentioned above. Research has shown this danger to be particularly acute for girls.[19] This is the main reason we consider humility overrated as a virtue. The following story is told by Rabbi Joseph Telushkin:

> My grandfather, Rabbi Nissen Telushkin, of blessed memory, told me of a man he knew who, as a highly respected member of the community, was entitled by Jewish tradition to occupy a prominent seat at the front of the synagogue. Instead, he chose to sit at an undistinguished seat at the back row. But my grandfather soon noticed that the man's eyes were constantly darting about to see if people were noticing how humble a seat he took for himself. My grandfather told him "It would be better to sit in the front of the synagogue and think you should be sitting in the back, than to sit in the back and think the whole time you should be sitting in the front."[20]

This story illustrates false humility. Sometimes people understand that humility is considered an important virtue. But what matters more to them than being humble is that people perceive them as being humble. Because of this concern they loose their humility. *When we are sorting things through with young children, we will want to bear in mind that even if humility is a virtue, false humility is not.*

If we accept that pride can be a virtue, there remains another complication. To what degree is it appropriate and proper to speak of one's pride? Is it ever right to tell others of one's achievements and accomplishments? What do we want to say about this to young children? Perhaps having a certain amount of pride, in oneself, and others, is okay. *Voicing* the pride, however, may seem to many as unacceptable. This issue is part of the antinomy discussed earlier in the book about when to keep silent and when to speak. To sort out some of the issues, the biblical story of Joseph and his brothers can be useful. For those who do not know, or may have forgotten the story, here are the highlights: (The great novelist Thomas Mann took four volumes to describe this, for those who would like a longer version).[21]

> Jacob had twelve sons, the 11th being Joseph, the 12th Benjamin (these last two with Rachel, the others with other wives). Joseph was smart, cute, and very much liked by his parents, and particularly his father. The ten older brothers, were very unhappy (jealous!) about the situation, They were particularly offended when little Joseph (about 3 or 4 years of age) reported to them about his vivid dreams. These dreams invariably involved the theme of Joseph being rich and famous, and the 10 older brothers being less rich, less famous, and usually Joseph's servants. Joseph was thrown into a pit by the brothers, who decided to kill him. They relented at the last moment, because of the pleadings of one brother, and sold him as slave into Egypt. There, we have a series of dramatic events, which include his getting thrown into prison for the crime of flirting with the wife of another man (not clear if he was guilty). His talents as dream interpreter and economic manager are recognized by the prison warden (who also becomes his friend and buddy), and by others, including finally the Pharoh (Joseph becomes his friend and buddy too). Joseph becomes the most powerful person in Egypt next to Pharoh. The ten brothers find themselves needing grain because of the famine which Joseph foresaw, they come to Egypt from Israel Joseph recognizes them, there is a reconciliation, some apology, some forgiveness, and a tearful reuniting with younger brother Benjamin.

The theme of the sin of pride can be seen at various points in the story. Jacob is very proud of his son Joseph, a bright, friendly, intelligent boy, with a very handsome appearance. (He is proud of himself and his wife Rachel, because this birth was unexpected, and deemed somewhat of a miracle because of the very advanced ages of the couple) Joseph is proud of himself, and saw nothing wrong with talking of his talents and charms, not to mention his dreams, with the older brothers. He was thrown into the pit, and sold into Egypt. Many commentators have argued that one moral of the story was that Joseph paid for his arrogance.[22] Being thrown into a pit to die, or even sold as slave to Egypt, has always appeared to me as a very high price to pay, even if we accept that Joseph committed a huge sin (arrogant boastful pride). Our question is, how was Joseph to understand about the difference between proper pride, and the arrogant sort which could cause such jealousy and hate in his older brothers? Certainly his parents didn't make him aware of it. Perhaps if there is any fault, it is that the parents had too much pride in this son, and were insufficiently sensitive to the feelings of the others. For our 21st century purposes, we can apply the lesson that we should talk about these matters to our young children.

There is also another side to the Joseph story which one does not find in the typical Bible commentators. We can find the positive virtuous side of pride as well. Joseph continued throughout his life to accomplish great things. (We get to follow him until his early to mid thirties) He was good at interpreting dreams, and not shy about saying so. He was an excellent manager, and could figure out quite quickly how many sets of grain to put in storage. He talked of this, and one can see that talking of it was appropriate. If he hadn't told his jailer of his skills, if he hadn't volunteered that was good at dream interpretation or mathematics at the right time to the right people, none of the good stuff would have happened. Instead of becoming rich, famous, and powerful, he might have rotted in jail. His suggestions that it all ended well, and might have been part of God's plan have to be tempered by the fact that he had to take action, often speaking up, at every step of the way. So perhaps one can see the story as embodying the motto. "God helps those who help themselves."

We find some of the major concepts of our book in the Joseph story, particularly the development of good judgment and empathy. Just as Joseph had to learn to steer a course between legitimate recognition of his own talents and achievements (proper pride), and the boastfulness and arrogance which so infuriated his older brothers, we have to learn the same middle course. We have to develop the kind of judgment Joseph did not have as a child, but exhibited more of as an adult. Joseph was also portrayed as being very empathic throughout his life, able to "read people," and reflect and respond to their feelings and thoughts. His empathy was conjoined with increasing good judgment, as he learned to choose which situations and contexts were relevantly different than others. He continued to be friendly with everyone, from jailer to prisoner to King; he learnt, in addition, that one might phrase what one said differently, depending to whom one was talking. There were times to speak, and times to keep silent. This is one of the hard lessons we have to help our children learn.

What is it, then, that we want to teach our young children about pride and humility? We want to impart to them that pride is a good thing, and that it is okay to voice their pride. We want the pride in ourselves, or pride in others to be appropriate, proper pride. Above all, we want to avoid putting others down; in celebrating our achievements, or the achievements of another, we want to avoid gloating, boasting, and taunting.

Concerning humility, we want to encourage the proper sort, that is the humility which is associated with wonder and awe. We want to teach our children to look for something good in everybody; they will be sure to find things to be proud of in every other child. At the same time, we want to teach them to avoid the phony or false humility, which is associated with meekness and low self-esteem.

Trust

Trust is a moral virtue and a moral emotion which is crucial for morality. It has been said that "whatever matters to human beings, trust is the atmosphere in which it thrives"[23] Trust can be defined as relying on another's good will, in having confidence in the other. In discussing promise keeping previously we pointed out that the element of trust was crucial. It has to be stressed however, that the kind of trust we want to talk to young children about goes beyond the trust involved in promise keeping or contracts. Trust for a young child is almost always associated with a person who has some power; what people have called asymmetrical relationship. The most important thing educators must be aware of in regard to trust is that there can be not enough of it, but also sometimes too much. Unlike shame and jealousy, but more like pride, trust needs to be appropriate, and felt to the right degree.

Part IV
The Most Difficult Subjects

Children will inevitably ask us questions about delicate issues, including marriage, divorce and separation (Chapter 9), illness (Chapter 10), "touching" (Chapter 11) and God, religion, and other beliefs, including Santa Claus and the Tooth Fairy (Chapter 12).

The general advice of Chapter 2 on judgment is here applied to these sensitive areas. All the tricks for the development of good judgment, both in our children and ourselves will have to kick in. (see last section of Chapter 2). Perhaps the most important of these will be debate, dialogue and discussion (suggestion 9) and consulting other judges (suggestion 10). As we stressed, parents have to be ready to take the risk of talking and explaining moral choices to their children; they must be ready to admit to uncertainty.

Chapter 3 on honesty is also relevant in regard to these most difficult topics. Perhaps the most important of those suggestions is to avoid dishonesty, unless there is a good reason for it. Children will sense the phoniness, if one tries to pretend at a definite answer, when one doesn't have one. Much better to admit that one isn't sure, or one is still thinking about the topic, than to give a dogmatic or definite answer. Not only will this not create the stability and security one might aim for. There will often be long-range negative consequences. Children fed half-baked answers, or a faked certainty, will suffer later because of what Chopra calls "The Grip of Illusion." Many of us were told things at ages 3 or 4, and have taken a lifetime to cope with overcoming the perceived and felt fakery. Nowhere is this more the case than in regard to the topics of the next 4 chapters!

9

Separation

Separation anxiety?

The earliest kind of separation occurs in early infancy, when the caregiver is absent. As we have seen (Chapter 7), emotions are present at very early ages. Loneliness, fear, sadness and anger are all intermingled in cases of separation, and then some joy and relief at finding there is still a caregiver or substitute there. At home, then at preschool, separation anxiety is a major concern for caregivers and parents, and how to cope with it is a difficult thing to learn. One needs intelligent sensitive educators who can recognize the gamut of emotions the child will feel and how sadness may even become depression, anger, followed by relief and acceptance. Notice that this series of emotions parallels the series people experience during mourning.

For some children the separation anxiety may to some degree be an act, as for example, when a child throws a tantrum in front of his parent, and then is happy and playful until his other parent returns, at which point he throws another tantrum. But the emotions are often genuine, because there is the sense of loss, the fear that the parent will not return and the confusion about new people in his life. These emotions are often experienced by children ages 2 to 4, attending day care or nursery school for the first time. Parents should be aware that their 2-year-old is likely feeling many of the above emotions (we can call them negative ones, for they may be causing suffering), and one should talk to him about them. One can help the child also by not simply putting him on the school bus and saying "have fun." One can talk a bit about the more negative emotions he may feel including fear, anxiety and loneliness. Sometimes, there may be a longer separation, where one or both parents are absent, perhaps for a week or so. One should anticipate the appearance of many of the same emotions listed above, and talk about them with the child. As concerns age, the earlier the better, but certainly begin with a 2-year old. Here, as usual, *our children understand much more than we think!*

Families and divorce in the 21st century.

Divorce was a topic not talked about in front of children when people of my age (I am 63 in 2006) were growing up. Young parents today are much more willing to discuss these things with their children. They may however not be sure how to talk about the issue. There are a number of guidelines we can offer. If it is possible for both parents to talk to the child together, this is always a good idea. In any case, at least one person should explain that there will be a break-up, and that the parents will be living separately. It should be made clear where the child will be staying, and what the visiting arrangements are. One should certainly try to avoid bad-mouthing the ex-spouse, always a temptation, when there has been conflict leading to the marital separation. Children as young as two years old will sense that something is amiss, if only by tuning into the emotional atmosphere. It is always a mistake to try to hide from the child what is obvious. If the child asks, as he is prone to do, especially at age 3-5: "Do you still love daddy?" one has to be prepared for some kind of answer. A simple "yes" will not do; yet a tirade listing all the faults of the ex-partner is not appropriate either. One may be angry at one's ex-spouse, and on the whole it is better to admit it, when asked by the child, because he will sense it anyway, and it will make it worse when he sees you clearly lying or faking. In these circumstances, it is particularly important to be aware of the need for the child to maintain a feeling of trust.

One need not go into gory details about the reasons for the break up. Above all, do not use your children in the place of a therapist or adult friend if you need to vent feelings! So to the question "do you still love daddy?" the best kind of answer will be an honest one, in sufficient detail for the child. These cases are perfect examples of telling the truth, but not the whole truth. One might very well say "Feelings change sometimes, and the kind of love daddy and I had before we don't have now." One can make this clearer by using examples in the child's own life, where he may have loved an animal or a doll, but then stopped loving it as much, or even at all. Caregivers should always be aware of divorce occurring, and be prepared to talk about these things in the same way as the parents do, that is, honestly, openly, and with enough appropriate detail so that the child can grasp what is happening.

A preoccupation of the young child will be for his own security; he will want to be assured that he is not to be abandoned. What can one say about whether the parent, or parents still love him? Will this love perhaps end? We cannot, of course, give absolute guarantees, because the child will already have worked out that there is rarely unconditional love. One can, however, restate one's love for the child, and remind him of the existence of others who love him as well. If there are aunts, uncles, grandparents, and close friends who are in a loving relationship with the child, it is an excellent idea to mention these other people. In this way, even if one cannot reassure the child with an absolute certainty (there is hardly ever that kind of certainty about anything!) of one person's love, one can make it clear that there is very likely always to be some adults to care, protect, and love him.

Death

There is the most final kind of separation when a person dies. Here, too, many of the emotions discussed before will occur. Unlike the way things were when I was growing up when no one talked to children about death, these days young parents are ready to talk about it much like they will talk about divorce. Much of the same suggestions made above about how to talk about separation through divorce will be applicable in the case of death. One wants to talk honestly and focus on the feelings that the child will have, inevitably including fear, sadness and maybe some anger. It is not necessary to wait for the death of a relative or a pet, although, of course, these events will provide the catalyst for this discussion. It is very common for a child to see a dead bird or a squirrel while on a walk, and starting at the age of about three will begin to question about dying. There are movies, like Bambi, and many stories, which provide another stimulus for this discussion. We have to be careful with cartoon characters, who fall off cliffs, and are neither injured nor die. Parents want to be present as often as possible during television or video watching; they certainly should stress the distinction between make-believe and reality.

Piaget contended that children between three and five have an "animistic" concept attributing life and consciousness to anything that exhibits activity, usefulness or a function.[1] More recent research on children's concepts of life and death show that the pre-school child has a much more sophisticated idea about these things than Piaget thought.[2] The young child has developed an understanding of three general death-related concepts, namely irreversibility (death is final), universality (death comes to all) and inevitability (death is due to the cessation of internal bodily functions). We have created materials, which help young children between three and five, begin to discriminate between living and non-living entities (see appendix D). In one example, children will learn to see that the hammer, an inanimate object is different than the three other living objects. In a second example, they learn to choose the Peacock, the only living creature, as different than the three inanimate objects. Five year olds who were exposed to discussions about the butterfly (see Appendix A for this episode) for about a year, significantly improved their ability to make the relevant distinctions. It makes sense that our discussions would have this effect. Children talked about how tearing the wings of the butterfly is different than tearing paper, and then again than tearing their own doll. They begin to understand not only about life and death, but about pain and suffering. The paper does not feel pain at all and cannot die; the butterfly may very well feel pain and certainly die. Finally, the doll may not feel pain or die, but the child may feel something like loss or grief when the doll is torn.

10
Illness

"Am I sick because I was bad?"

Illness will involve certain emotions, and almost always questions related to blame, and responsibility. Am I at fault for being sick? Was I bad? These are not rare or crazy questions, only voiced by disturbed children. It is perfectly normal for the preschool child to wonder in this way, since there are some similarities between a situation when he is sick, and situations when he was punished. In both illness and punishment, one may be isolated, often told to stay in one's room; one is told to take medicine which may be bitter, and therefore seem as though one is being punished; in both cases, one is usually not allowed to play with other children. *A large part of the discussion which we should have about illness is to make it clear that sickness is not a punishment, and that it is not the child's fault.* Most illness cannot be prevented, and is certainly not causally connected to some "bad" behavior. As usual, it becomes a bit more complicated, because there are things which we can sometimes do to prevent getting ill. These will include proper nutrition, and certain habits like washing hands and blowing one's nose. Therefore, it is possible that the cold that one's child picked up may be due to not washing their hands for example, and therefore perhaps controllable after all. Even if this is so, we must try to be very clear that questions of blame worthiness do not apply to questions of illness. We have to note at this point that Piaget underestimated, once again, the capacity of young children of three or four years old, to understand these nuances, because of what he said was "imminent justice thinking."[1]

There will be fears about sickness as well. Will I die? Will my friend or animal or parent die? Frank discussion is needed at the level of the child's age, and in relation to the questions and concerns. These queries are usually voiced at age 3 or 4; sometimes, however, one has to be sensitive to nonverbal indications, such as frowns, tears, and other signs of worry on the face. Fears that are genuine have to be separated from those that are not. Books about sick animals, hospitals, and doctors can be very helpful.

Mental Illness

Discussing physical illness is a touchy enough job, but talking about mental illness may be even harder. In the past, there was complete silence on this topic. Even today, there are still powerful taboos about it. Children will be confronted with examples of clinical depression, mood problems, or disturbed behavior of children at preschool or on the street. This may include extreme aggression, or very inappropriate behaviors. *We want to find a way to explain that the child or adult has a kind of sickness about his "mind"* (one can say "in his head" for the very young child who may not understand the word "mind"). We can add that there is a sickness about his thoughts or feelings, and that he may need help from a special kind of doctor.

There will be ample situations in everyday life that will provide the opportunity to engage a child in a discussion about mental illness, as well as other handicaps. These will include chance meetings on the street with homeless people, beggars, people with physical handicaps, and those exhibiting odd and eccentric behavior. We do not want to look at any person with embarrassment, or pity. We do want to acknowledge the child's queries (verbal or non-verbal, via a questioning look) frankly and honestly. We can accept that a deformity may be difficult to look at, and create some discomfort.

All of these things should be talked about, including questions of luck and gratitude. Gratitude is relevant as an emotion and an attitude as we are aware that we are lucky to have the use of our eyes, ears and limbs. Of course, we will want to make clear that people with handicaps also may feel gratitude and luck for their abilities, skills, achievements and everything they possess. As we have discussed, pride is an important emotion to be encouraged in its appropriate manifestation. Pride is universal, and all people, whether handicapped or not, will feel pride as well as gratitude.

11
Touching

A time to embrace, and a time to refrain from embracing

(Ecclesiastes 3:5)

The body

We have created materials in the spirit of Philosophy for Children (P$_4$C) for use with very young children (see appendix A for one episode). We have experimented with these stories with children from three to five years old.[1] In the novelettes, children discuss themes such as the body, its boundaries, and what can be considered as violations of privacy. As in the usual practice of philosophical discussions in the classroom, the stories stimulate a dialogue and questions about the thoughts and feelings of the children. For example, when is it uncomfortable to be touched by another, or to touch another? On the one hand we need, because of the newly dangerous world we live in, to make children aware of boundaries, but we must also keep them open to showing and receiving affection. Hugs and embraces are an important part of life. One objective in all this is to distinguish between people in their lives – friends, family, strangers and so on. They, of course, will sort it all out on their own in time, but it is a good idea to help them by talking about it.

Friends, family, and strangers

In order to help children determine who is a stranger, the best way to approach it is to try to make clear who is family and what is a friend. In the 21st century, defining family is not as easy as it was years ago. We can often start with mummy and daddy, adding sisters and brothers if there are any. However, we know that often the situation requires saying something about a mother alone, a live-in partner, a boyfriend, half-sisters, ex-spouses and even these days, two Mummies or two Daddies. What is important is to explain honestly, and in a way that the young child will understand, who these various family members are. From three years of age onwards, children will be curious about these matters, and will ask questions about relations and relationships.

What is a friend? Philosophers have been discussing this for a long time. Let us sum up for purposes of talking to our young children. A friend is someone they like, who likes them, that they have special feelings for, whom they want to help (yes, they should want to help everyone, but they have the right to choose some special friend). There is the question of trust and loyalty, along with the telling of secrets, and sharing jokes, possessions, and time together. They may want to play with different children, but will often choose a few, or maybe even one. *By the age of five, they will understand the notion of friendship, and its moral dimension, in about as sophisti-*

125

cated a way as an adult. As with most topics, we continue to learn as adults throughout life abut these matters. We can be clarifying things for ourselves as we are helping our children to become clearer about them.

Two of the philosophers who have discussed friendship are Aristotle and Nietzche. They both believed in the following: "No one would choose to live without friends." We agree with them, and consider this dictum quite appropriate to tell our children. Another consideration by both of these philosophers concerns the relationship between friendship and love. They, like most of us, understand that there are different forms of love. The Greeks had three words for love: agape, eros, and philia. The last form of love, philia, is also translated as friendship. The story is even more complicated, as usual, because Aristotle, and many others, have delineated different sorts of friendship. The most common is the friendship of mutual advantage, where so-called friends are actually "using" one another. There is a second sort of friendship, the friendship of mutual enjoyment. Here two friends are not "using" one another but the friendship lasts as long as it is "fun." (This aspect is often heard where romantic love is involved). The third and "highest" is the friendship of mutual inspiration. Inspiration is aimed at the future, and the friendship consists primarily in each inspiring the other to perfect himself, and be the best that he or she can be. Another aspect of friendship, which we would want to add to this philosophical analysis, concerns honesty. *One definition of a good friend, is that we can trust them "to tell it like it is."* We would go so far as to say that every person needs this kind of a friend. As educators, we can attempt to think about all this, and then find the appropriate vocabulary to share it with the children.

Violence: abuse, incest, harassment, and bullying.

In Chapter 3 (honesty) we talked about secrets, including the dilemmas used in our research on moral autonomy (see Appendix I) Should a child keep a secret, if he has promised a friend,

160   *"He followed me home. Call my lawyer."*

or tell an authority when he is asked? One of the key aspects here, as in issues of lying, is the possibility of harm. In all of the cases of violence mentioned in the section title, the crucial ingredient is whether the child is feeling uncomfortable, either with the physical touching in cases of abuse or incest, or is uncomfortable with the words and gestures of a bully. We want to make clear that in all these cases where they are uncomfortable, they are to speak up. At the same time as we get this message across, we must also avoid discouraging appropriate hugs. The recent expulsion of a five year old boy from kindergarten because he kissed a girl represents the other extreme, which should be avoided. When to hug, and when not to hug, is a difficult and controversial matter even for adults. One context where this issue is hotly debated concerns what is appropriate in psychotherapy.[2] The fact that this is a tough issue does not, however, mean that we can afford to avoid it with children. To the contrary, with all the difficult and delicate issues discussed in this book, the earlier the better!

The key, as always will be good judgment. We have to help our young children judge when it is appropriate to trust, and when not. On the whole, they will trust people close to them, including family and friends; as we have seen, we want to help them distinguish family from strangers. Of course, abuse can sometimes occur close to home as we know, and may involve family or friends.

12

Beliefs

God

Sooner or later, our child will ask: "What happens to Fluffy when he dies?" (Fluffy may be the pet cat, hamster, or dog, or a story-book character.) We should give our answer according to our beliefs, which may include reference to God or Animal Heaven. We will make the assumption that 99.99% of us have some doubts about the existence or nature of afterlife. The .01% who have absolute certainty about these things are unlikely to be reading this book. Our orientation, as we state in the title, and discuss in detail in the introduction and Chapter 1, is that we are dealing with education, not indoctrination. Whatever place parents make for introducing religious traditions, rituals and practices, this should be separated from discussing beliefs about the ultimate nature of the universe with children.

In answering the child's question about Fluffy, *it is recommended that we phrase our answer to offer consolation to our child, but admit some doubt or uncertainty.* So, one might say: "Fluffy may be in animal heaven, that's what I believe": that is appropriate for a two year old. For three years old onwards, one can and should offer a bit more detail. (The child has begun to grasp the concept of death, as we have seen in Chapter 9). We could say, "We buried Fluffy's body in the backyard, but I believe his soul, that is his mind, feelings, thoughts will be in a place called heaven." With five year olds, it will not be out of place to add "Many people believe something like this," and anytime from five years onwards, we can use our judgment to mention that not everybody believes as we do. Children from three to five years of age will enjoy talking about the mind and the brain; for example, whether machines (robots, computers) can think or have feelings.

Santa Claus, the Tooth Fairy, Mickey Mouse: Keeping the Magic

Is Santa Claus *really* real? Children will inevitably begin to wonder about this, and eventually ask the question. We must prepare ourselves to talk about the real and the imaginary. We can confidently recommend not disabusing our child of belief in Santa Claus, the Tooth Fairy, and Disney characters for the first three years of life. In any case, they are unlikely to be questioning it, and it is all fun. From three years onwards, there will be doubts in their minds, but we can allow a certain ambiguity about magic. This can apply to matters other than cartoon characters, or mythical creatures. For example, I used a remote device to honk the horn in my car (useful for all of us who lose our cars in parking lots). My granddaughter Rachel noticed it, and we "talked" to the car, which was saying "hello." I wondered how long she would believe this, and whether I should tell her it was make-believe. I even worried that she would discover that I had tricked her, and be upset. Talking about this matter with my two daughters, and the two older grandchildren, the consensus was that Rachel would begin to doubt the magic on her own, but that it was better to let her believe it for as long as she wanted to. Sure enough, at age five, she asked once, whether she could make the car talk. I asked what she meant. She wasn't sure. But several weeks later, she noticed the remote, used it herself, and was now happy that the magic had a "scientific" root. This little personal story encapsulates all the features we need. Keep the magic. Be honest about the boundaries of reality and fantasy. Allow the questioning of the child to dictate how much detail to give. By age eight or nine, the belief in Santa Claus can still be there, as it is for adults. It may be that Santa Claus is the embodiment of the mystery and wonder of the world, that not everything can be explained scientifically. Watching the movie *Miracle on 34ᵗʰ Street* together with one's children is probably the best way of handling the Santa Claus situation. We can all come up with similar scenarios to deal with Disney and other cartoon characters. The bottom line is to encourage imagination, yet be aware of the necessity to demarcate reality from fiction when needed. One time to make it clear that it is "just make-believe" concerns T.V. violence. Very young children are exposed to the Road Runner, Bugs Bunny and other characters who are hitting, bopping, and throwing each other off cliffs. Let us accompany our children as much as we can, as they watch the cartoons, and be ready to remind them that this is "pretend."

Certainty and Doubt

The development of judgment, which is one of the main topics of this book, deals with an uncertain world. With the exception of fanatics, we will all have some doubts about fundamental questions, about the nature of the universe, and about the best way to behave in the world. The greatest and wisest religious thinkers (Maimonidies, Augustine, Buddha, Confucius) all had doubts, as did the greatest scientists, from Galileo to Einstein. It is only natural that all the rest of us should have doubts too.

Although we have our doubts and uncertainties, which we must honestly admit to our children, we can also profess a degree of certainty. This certainty, a reasonable confidence and practical sureness about things, is also important to get across to children. We can be quite certain ("morally certain," "for all practical purposes" certain) that the sun will rise tomorrow, and we should be happy for our children to have the same confidence and trust in the expected stability of things. This kind of certainty is not an absolute certainty, but it is good enough. What is important is that we do not have to fake a degree of certainty about things which we do not feel. In discussing values and feelings, as we have stressed throughout this book, it is always a good idea to admit one is not sure about a matter, when this is the case. One might always tell a child that one will think more about the situation, talk to other parents or educators, and encourage them to think about the matter some more, and talk to others as well.

The last word

In the Schultz cartoon we have an important philosophical idea, namely that one person's opinion may be the right one, even if a great majority hold the opposite opinion. It is worth quoting this principle from the philosopher John Stuart Mill, in his book *On Liberty*.

> If all mankind minus one were of one opinion, and only one person were of the contrary opinion, mankind would be no more justified in silencing that one person, than he, if he had

the power, would be justified in silencing all mankind. For we can never be sure that the opinion we are stifling is false opinion. And even if we were sure, stifling it would still be evil.

In helping to develop the judgment of young children, we will contribute to their moral autonomy, and to their ability to think for themselves. Everything Cynthia and I have offered in this book represents our best judgment. As such, it is in the spirit of the last section about certainty and doubt. Advice in this book, like advice in our clinical practice, or in university courses, represents our best effort, based on experience, knowledge, and discussions with others. In the case of the specific values in each of the chapters of the book, we talked to each other, but also discussed as much as possible with parents, other educators, and our children and grandchildren. In the final analysis, I take responsibility for the beliefs and convictions of this book.[1] We do not hold absolute beliefs, but we stand behind the suggestions we have made. We are morally certain of the following:

We want caring/thinking children.

Developing good judgment and empathy are the key ingredients.

One must begin to talk about feelings and values with the very youngest children.

Notes

Introduction

[1]Some of my publications concerning moral education:

Daniel, M.-F., Schleifer, M. (dir.) (1996). *La coopération dans la classe/Cooperation in the Classroom.* Montréal: Éditions Logiques, 303 p.

Caron, A., Schleifer, M., Dupuy-Walker, L., Brunel, M.-L., Lebuis, P. (1987). *L'éducation morale en milieu scolaire: Analyse de situations et perspectives.* Montréal: Fides, 135 p.

Schleifer, M., Daniel, M.-F., Lafortune, L. et Pallascio, R. (1999). Concepts of Cooperation in the Classroom. *Païdeusis,* vol. 12, n° 2, p. 45-56.

Schleifer, M., Lebuis, P. (1991). Éducation morale, formation fondamentale et philosophie. *Arrimages,* (7-8), p. 9-16.

Schleifer, M., Lebuis, P., Caron, A. (1987). The effect of the Pixie program on logical and moral reasoning. *Thinking, VII*(2), p. 12-16.

Schleifer, M. (1976). Moral education and indoctrination. *Ethics, 86*(2), p. 154-163.

Conference Papers (available on request) E-mail: schleifer.michael@uqam.ca

Schleifer, M. (1999). The Training of Character in School/La formation du caractère à l'école. Annual Meeting of the Canadian Society for Studies in Education (CSEE), Sherbrooke, June.

Schleifer, M. (1974). Moral education and indoctrination. Annual Meeting of the Canadian Association of Philosophy, Toronto, May.

Schleifer, M. (1978). Le comportement moral de l'enfant. Annual Meeting of the Canadian Society for Studies in Education (CSEE), London, June.

Schleifer, M., Lipman, M., Caron, A. (1992). Educating for violence reduction and peace development. Second World Conference on Violence. Montréal, July.

Schleifer, M., Daniel, M.-F. (1992). A community of inquiry in the classroom: its effect on children's ethnic tolerance. Association of moral education, Toronto, November.

Schleifer, M. (1993). Cooperation in education: a moral perspective. Annual Meeting of the Canadian Society for Studies in Education (CSEE), Ottawa, June.

[2]Some of my publications concerning emotions:

Schleifer, M., Daniel, M.-F., Peyronnet, E. et Lecompte, S. (2003). The Impact of philosophical discussions on moral autonomy, judgment, empathy and the recognition of emotion in five year olds. *Thinking,* vol. 16, no 4, pp. 1-19.

Schleifer, M. (2004). Moods, Emotions and Morality. Annual Meeting of the American Philosophical Association, Pacific Division, Pasadena, California, March.

Daniel, M.F., Schleifer, M., Perronet, E., Quesnel, M., (2003). Emotion and psychological dialogue. European Association for Research on Learning and Instruction (EARLI). 10th Biennial Conference Padova, Italy - August.

[3]We are using the word "education" as distinct from socialization, training or indoctrination. This reflects a large consensus among philosophers of education. See further P.A. White (1972). Socialization

133

and education. In *A critique of current educational aims,* pp. 111-129, International Library or the Philosophy of Education. General Editor R.S. Peters. See also:

Schleifer, M. (1976). Moral education and indoctrination. *Ethics, 86*(2), p. 154-163.

Olivier Reboul. *Endoctrinement* (1980). Presses Universitaires de France.

Olivier Reboul (1971) *La Philosophie de l'éducation.* Presses Universitaires de France.

Richard Peters (1966). *Ethics and Education.* Routledge and Kegan Paul.

[4]Coles, R. (1997). *The Moral Intelligence of Children.* New York: Random House, 217 p. This excellent book emphasises dialogue, with educators learning from our kids, as they learn from us. Coles also reminds us that we recognize a "good" kid, even if we can't quite put into words what "goodness" is. This is reminiscent of the well known quote by the philosopher William James: The best thing education can aspire to accomplish, is this: that it should help you to know a good man when you see him. From his article What Education Can Be: Education for Judgment: In Lipman, M. 1993. *Thinking Children and Education.* Iowa: Kendall Publications, p. 701. See also Burba, M.. *Building Noral Intelligence* (2001).

[5]Lipman, M. (1995). Caring As Thinking. *Inquiry.* Autumn, vol. XV. Also available on the Internet: www.shss.montclair.edu-inquiry

Bernstein, J. (2003) Caring Thinking. *Thinking.* Vol 16, no.3, pp. 16-25.

[6]The rudiments of fear, anxiety, anger, love are present, as Winnicott and Bowlby (see References) have stressed, from the earliest days of infancy, because of the presence, and sometimes absence of the nurturer/caregiver. The development of emotion is discussed in Chapter 7 of the present book.

[7]Gohier, C., Schleifer, M. (ed.) (1993). *La question de l'identité. Qui suis-je? Qui est l'autre?* Montréal: Éditions Logiques, 264 pages. English Version, *The Question of Identity available* on request. See particularly chapter 3, pages 61-94 by Jean-Claude Brief.

[8]Dr Benjamin Spock's child rearing book *Baby and Child Care* first published in 1946 and the latest edition the eighth in 2004. The internet versions are of course handled by Dr Spock's successors under the name the "Dr Spock Company," primarily Dr. Robert Needleman. For a discussion of Spock's place in the history of parenting advice books, see Anne Hulbert (2004) *Raising America: Experts, Parents, and A Century of Advice About Children.* Vintage Books. Hulbert stresses the fact that all of the advice books were written by men. As she states: "Since many of the experts were long on opinion but short on scientific research, they often based their theories on the childhood they knew best – their own. Equally fascinating are these men's own experiences as parents. Too often, their advice failed to translate from the page to the nursery, and their wives and children suffered accordingly."

A recent successor book to Dr Spock is by Lu Hanessian entitled, *Let the Baby Drive: Navigating the Road of New Motherhood.* Like Spock before her she tells mothers that they are the experts and "to trust their intuition and the babies instincts."

[9]Some of my publications concerning pre-schoolers (2 to 5):

Schleifer, M., Campbell, S., Weiss, G., Perlman, T. (1977). A two-year follow-up of hyperactive preschoolers. *American Journal of Orthopsychiatry, 47,* p. 149-162.

Schleifer, M., Weiss, G., Cohen, N., Elman, M., Cveijic, H., Kruger, E. (1975). Hyperactivity in preschoolers and the effect of methyphinidate. *American Journal of Orthopsychiatry, 45,* p. 38-50.

Markovits, H., Schleifer, M., Fortier, L. (1989). The development of elementary deductive reasoning. *Developmental Psychology, 25*(5), p. 787-793.

Fortier, L., Markovits, H., Schleifer, M., Surette, K. (1987). Résolution des syllogismes chez les jeunes enfants: un effet de "matching." *Société québécoise pour la recherche en psychologie,* Québec, octobre.

Schleifer, M., Campbell, S. (1976). Predictions from infant and preschool data: hyperactive-normal comparisons. Annual Meeting of the American Association of Psychology.

Schleifer, M., Daniel, M.-F., Peyronnet, E. et Lecompte, S. (2003). The Impact of philosophical discussions on moral autonomy, judgment, empathy and the recognition of emotion in five year olds. *Thinking*, vol. 16, no 4, pp. 1-19.

[10]Some of my publications on school children (5 to 12):

Daniel, M.-F., Lafortune, L., Pallascio, R. et Schleifer, M. (1999/2000). Philosophical reflection and cooperative practice, in an elementary school. *Revue canadienne de l'Éducation*. vol. 24 n° 4, p. 426-440.

Daniel, M.-F., Lafortune, L., Pallascio, R. et Schleifer, M. (2000). The Developmental Dynamics of Community of Philosophical Inquiry, in: an Elementary School Mathematics Classroom. *Thinking*, vol. 15, n° 1, p. 2-9.

Lafortune, L., Daniel, M.-F., Pallascio, R. et Schleifer, M. (1999). Evolution of Pupil's Attitudes to Mathematics When Using a Philosophical Approach, *Analytic Teaching*, vol. 20, n° 1, p. 33-44.

Schleifer, M., Daniel, M.-F., Lafortune, L. et Pallascio, R. (1999). Concepts of Cooperation in the Classroom. *Païdeusis*, vol. 12, n° 2, p. 45-56.

Schleifer, M., Neveu, F., Mayer, M. et Poissant, H. (1999). Arguing with Government. *Thinking*, vol. 14, n° 3, p. 33-39.

Garnier, C., Schleifer, M., Carbonneau, F. et Sykes, P. (1998). La coopération existe-t-elle dans les classes de philosophie pour enfants. *Canadian Journal of Education/Revue canadienne de l'éducation*, vol. 23, n°4, p. 373-389.

Daniel, M.-F., Lafortune, L., Schleifer, M. et Pallascio, R. (1998). La philosophie pour enfants: une approche coopérative significative dans l'apprentissage des mathématiques, in *Revue Pédagogique Résonnance*, n° 2, October, p. 13-16.

Poissant, H., Schleifer, M. et Neveu, F. (1998). L'évaluation des habilités métacognitives chez des élèves du primaire en situation de production de texte, *Journal of Educational Thought/Revue de la pensée éducative*, vol. 32, n° 2, p. 119-138.

Schleifer, M., Courtemanche, L. (1996). The effect of "philosophy for children" on language ability. *Thinking*. vol. 12 n° 4, p. 31-32.

Schleifer, M., Poirier, G. (1996). The effect of philosophical discussions in the classroom on respect for others and non-stereotypic attitudes. *Thinking*. vol. 12, n° 4, p. 32-34.

Schleifer, M., Lebuis, P., Caron, A. (1987). The effect of the Pixie program on logical and moral reasoning. *Thinking*, VII(2), p. 12-16.

Shultz, T.-R., Schleifer, M., Jaggi, C. (1987). Assigning vicarious responsibility. *European Journal of Social Psychology*, XVII, p. 377-380.

Shultz, T.-R., Wright, K., Schleifer, M. (1986). Assignment of moral responsibility and punishment. *Child Development, 57*, p. 177-184.

Schleifer, M. Shultz, T.-R., Lefebvre-Pinard, M. (1983). Judgments of causality, responsibility, and punishment in cases of harm due to omission. *British Journal of Developmental Psychology, 1*(2), p. 87-97.

Shultz, T.-R., Schleifer, M., Altman, I. (1981). Judgments of causation, responsibility, and punishment in cases of harm-doing. *Canadian Journal of Behavioral Science/Revue canadienne des sciences du comportement*, 13(3), p. 238-253.

[11]Keillor, G. (2004). Daughter Dearest: The Little One Adores You Now Dad, But Brace Yourself for the Next Chapter. *Time Magazine*, August 30, p.64.

[12]Ethical problems related to the Internet have forced the American Psychological Association, and other similar groups to provide new guidelines on how to cope with the dangers.

[13]Turiel, E. (1983). Domains and Categories in Social Cognitive Development. In W. Overton (Ed.). *The relationship between social and cognitive development*. Hillsdale, NJ: Lawrence Erlbaum Associates Inc.

Turiel, E. (1983). The Development Morality. In W. Damon (Ed.) Book of child psychology (5th ed.), vol. 3, N. Eisenberg (Ed.), *Social, Emotional and Personality Development*. New York: Wiley.

14 Schleifer, M., Douglas, V. (1973). Moral judgments, behavior, and cognitive style in young children. *Canadian Journal of Behavioral Science, 5*(2), p. 133-144.

Schleifer, M., Douglas, V. (1973). Effects of training on the moral judgment of young children. *Journal of Personality and Social Psychology, 28*(1), p. 62-68.

15Thomas, A., & Chess, S. (1977). *Temperament and development.* New York.: Brunner & Mazzel

Miller, P. & Jansen, M.A. (1997) Emotional, cognitive, behavioural, and temperament characteristics of high-empathy children. *Motivation and Emotion. 21*, pgs 109-125.

Izard, C.E. (2002). Translating emotion theory and research into preventive interventions. *Psychological Bulletin*, vol. 128, no 5, pp. 796-824.

16See Schleifer, M., Audet, F. (1987). L'enfant de 8-9 ans, un philosophe ou un imbécile? Arrimages, (3), printemps, p. 27-35. See also Gazzard, A. (1983). Philosophy for children and the Piagetian frameword, *Thinking,* vol. 5, no 1, pp. 10-14.

17See notes 1, 2, 5 and 6.

18Piaget, J. (1968). *The moral judgment of the child.* Routledge and Kegan Paul. Originally Piaget, J. (1932) *Le jugement morale chez l'enfant.*

19Bryant, P.E. (1984). Piaget, teachers and psychologists, *Oxford Review of Education*, vol. 10, no 3, pp. 251-259.

20Ibid.

21Shultz, T.-R., Wright, K., Schleifer, M. (1986). Assignment of moral responsibility and punishment. *Child Development, 57,* p. 177-184.

22Daniel, M.-F., Schleifer, M. (dir.) (1996). *La coopération dans la classe/Cooperation in the classroom.* Montréal: Éditions Logiques, 303 p. See especially Tock Keng Lim Cooperative learning in action: experiences of the philosophy for children programme, pp. 101-124 and Margaret Sharp Some philosophical presuppositions of philosophy for children, pp. 59-100 and Michael Schleifer La cooperation: une perspective piatégienne (Cooperation: A Piagetian Perspective), pp. 49-58.

Schleifer, M., Daniel, M.-F., Lafortune, L. et Pallascio, R. (1999). Concepts of Cooperation in the Classroom. *Païdeusis,* vol. 12, n° 2, p. 45-56.

Garnier, C., Schleifer, M., Carbonneau, F. et Sykes, P. (1998). "La coopération existe-t-elle dans les classes de philosophie pour enfants". dans: *Canadian Journal of Education/Revue canadienne de l'éducation,* vol. 23, n°4, p. 373-389.

Conference Papers (available on request) E-mail: schleifer.michael@uqam.ca

Schleifer, M. (1998). Concepts of cooperation in the classroom. Annual Meeting of the Canadian Society for Studies in Education (CSEE), Ottawa, June.

Schleifer, M. (1993). Cooperation in education: a moral perspective. Annual Meeting of the Canadian Society for Studies in Education (CSEE), Ottawa, June.

Schleifer, M., Fitch, T. (1993). The development of the concept of cooperation. Society for research in child development, New Orleans, April, (Abstracts IX, p. 585).

23Children from around age 2 onwards begin to put words to some of these emotions, and very soon (by around 3 years of age) others like disgust, surprise, hope, guilt, shame, jealousy, envy, love and hate begin to appear.

Fridja, Plutchik, Nussbaum (see Bibliography).

24Montessori, M. (1914). *Dr. Montessori's own handbook.* New York: Frederick A. Stokes.

Montessori, M. (1965a). The Montessori elementary material. Cambridge, Mass.: Robert Bentley.

Montessori, M. (1965b). *Spontaneous activity in education.* Cambridge, MA: Robert Bentley.

Montessori, M. (1957). *The absorbent mind.* New York: Holt, Rinehart and Winston.

[25]For more on philosophical discussions with children, see Bibliography. Also the website for Philosophy for Children. In the present book I have included some of the present material which we use in the Philosophy for Children approach, both as exercises for developing judgment (Chapter 2) and empathy (Chapter 6) and as instruments we use to measure these variables (see Appendice B, pp. 163-165).

[26]The notion of "development" is clearest in biology, it refers to an invariant order of things, for example, in the foetus, the heart develops before the limbs, this is universally true. Piaget and Montessori applied this notion to psychology, reminding us that certain abilities and concepts must be mastered before others. Here too, we have an invariant order and a universality. So for example, in regard to the topics of the present book, a child will have to understand the truth before understanding lying (see Chapter 3); he will comprehend anger before jealousy and disgust before guilt (see Chapter 7). In the development of judgment, similarity must be mastered before difference (see Chapter 2).

[27]Mogel, W. (2001). *The blessing of a skinned knee.* New York: Penguin Putnam Inc., 302 p.

Faber, A. & Mazlich, E. (2002). How to talk so kids will listen & Listen so kids will talk. New York: HarperCollins Publisher, 286 p.

Burba, M. (2001), *Moral Intelligence.* See note 4.

Coles, R. (1997). *The moral intelligence of children.* New York: Random House, 217 p.

Shulman, M. and Mekler, E. (1985). *Bringing up a moral child.* Reading, Mass.: Addison-Wesley, 359 p.

Coloroso, Barbara (1995). *Kids are worth it giving your child the gift of inner discipline.* Harper Collins.

Lickona, Thomas (1983). *Raising good children.* New York: Simon and Shuster.

Lickona, Thomas (1990). *Educating for character: How schools can teach respect and responsibility.* New York: Simon and Shuster.

Lickona, Thomas (2004). *Character matters: How to help our children develop good judgment, integrity and other essential virtues.* New York: Simon and Shuster. Lickona's most recent book, which has just appeared at the time of writing this one, does not provide, despite the title, any specific suggestions for improving judgment.

Mellor, Christie (2004). *The three-martini play date: A practical guide to happy parenting.* Raincoast Books. Mellor tells parents to take more time, leave their toddlers alone. This is a fine message. Our message, however, is in opposition to hers. We feel more time is needed with preschoolers in order to talk to them.

Wolf, Anthony (2003). *Mom, Jason's breathing on me!: The Solution to Sibling Bickering.* Ballantine Books, 203 p.

Wolf, Anthony (2000). *Secret of parenting: How to be in charge of today's kids – From toddlers to preteens – Without Threats of Punishment.* Farrar Straus & Giroux, 233 p. This book is about negative behaviour, tantrums and back-talk.

Wolf, Anthony (1996). *It's not fair, Jeremy Spencer's parents let him stay up all night!: A guide to the tougher parts of parenting.* Farrar Straus & Giroux. This one is about family disputes and fights.

Wolf, Anthony (1998). *Why did you have to get a divorce? And when can I get a hamster?: A guide to parenting through divorce.* Farrar Straus & Giroux, 208 p.

[28]For example, Mogel, op. cit., and Telushkin's (see Bibliography) wonderful books are within the Orthodox Jewish Tradition. On the issue of honesty, Telushkin's advice is interesting but restricted (I return in detail to this in Chapter 3). Similarly, Mogel's advice about autonomy is quite extreme (this is discussed in Chapter 4). Thomas Lickona's excellent books on moral character are within the Catholic Tradition. On issues of homosexuality, abortion, and pre-marital sexual activity, his discussion takes a

definite conservative and rigid stance (these issues will be discussed in Part IV of the present book). As noted in the text, educators want to avoid indoctrination; Lickona is not successful in doing this because of his specific limiting perspective.

See also Gellman, Rabbi M. & Hartman, Monsignor ("The God Squad") (2002). *Religion for dummies.* New York: Wiley, Chapter 10 "Personal Virtues," pp. 181-198. See particularly Section "The Golden Rule: A Universal Principle," pp. 181-182.

[29]Schleifer, M. (1976). Moral education and indoctrination. *Ethics,* 86(2), p. 154-163.

See also Olivier Reboul's book *Endoctrinement* (1980). Presses Universitaires de France.

[30]Faber, A. & Mazlich, E., op. cit.

Ginott, H.G. (1969). *Between parent and child.* New York: Avon.

Ginott, H.G. (1971). *Between parent and teenager.* New York: Avon.

Ginott, H.G. (1975). *Teacher and child.* New York: Avon.

Ann Hulbert's book, (see note 7 above) illustrates the evolution of expert advice on children. She profiles two key experts in each generation, each of whom falls into a distinct "camp." One exemplifies "child-centred" or "soft" parenting, a proponent of letting "nature take its course in childhood" and an advocate of parent-child bonding. The other, "parent-centred expert instead advises strict discipline, believing in the power of parental nurture to shape child behavior for good or ill.

The first generation of parenting experts, Hulbert contends, came to prominence when early twentieth-century mothers, who viewed themselves as raising their children in a new and sometimes terrifying modern world, no longer trusted the time-honored "experts" of previous generations – their own mothers and grandmothers. Instead, these modern mothers, eager to equip their children for twentieth-century success, looked to two male experts for advice. G. Stanley Hall, the "soft" expert, was a psychologist who viewed childhood, especially adolescence, as a fragile, almost spiritual time – a "new birth." His counterpart, L. Emmett Holt, was a pediatrician who advocated strict schedules and developed complicated feeding regimens for infants.

Hall and Holt's successors, too, provided polarizing advice to parents. From the strict behaviorist Watson, who famously conditioned a young child to fear not only rats but all other cute furry animals, to Gesell, whose timetables of child development were the precursors of the milestones that today's parents obsess over, to Spock, whose parenting advice defined the baby boomer generation.

[31]Thanks to Annette Werk M.S.W. for reminding me of this example, one of her favorites in clinical practice, as it is mine.

[32]Goleman, D. (1995). *Emotional Intelligence.* New York: Bantam Books, pp. 80-82 and 193.

[33]For example, early preschool programs can have an important impact. See

Schleifer, M. (1995). Commentary on Richard Herrnstein and Charles Murray's The Bell Curve. The *Alberta journal of educational research,* vol. 41 (1), p. 355-359.

Interventions with impulsive and hyperactive children in early years have also proven to have an influence many years later. See for example

Schleifer, M. (1975). Hyperactivity in preschool children. Research relating to children, *Bulletin (34),* (abrégé), U.S. Department of health, education and welfare, p. 88.

Schleifer, M., Weiss, G., Cohen, N., Elman, M., Cveijic, H., Kruger, E. (1975). Hyperactivity in preschoolers and the effect of methyphinidate. *American Journal of Orthopsychiatry, 45,* p. 38-50.

Schleifer, M., Campbell, S., Weiss, G. (1978). Continuities in maternal reports and child behaviours over time in hyperactive and comparison groups. *Journal of Abnormal & Child Psychology, 6*(1), p. 33-45.

Schleifer, M., Campbell, S., Weiss, G., Perlman, T. (1977). A two-year follow-up of hyperactive preschoolers. *American Journal of Orthopsychiatry, 47,* p. 149-162.

Psychological research concerning children's beliefs and attributions at preschool level have also shown to have an effect in later years. See for example

Allen, T. I Think, Therefore I can: Attribution and philosophy for children, *Thinking,* vol. 8, no 1, pp. 14-19.

Goddard, W.H. & Miller, B.C. (1993). Adding attribution to parenting programs. *The Journal of Contemporary Human Services,* pp. 84-92.

Shapp, L.C., Thurman, S.K. & Ducette, J.P. (1992). The relationship of attributions and personal well-being in parents of preschool children with disabilities. *Journal of Early Intervention,* vol. 16, no 4, pp. 293-303.

Jaspars, J., Fincham, F.D. & Hewstone, M. (1983). *Attribution theory and research: Conceptual, developmental and social dimensions.* London: London Academic Press, 415 p. See especially Chapter 5, Frank D. Fincham "Developmental Dimensions of Attribution Theory," pp. 117-164 and Chapter 2, Thomas R. Shultz and Michael Schleifer "Towards a Refinement of Attribution Concepts," pp. 37-62.

[34]Schleifer, M., Daniel, M.-F., Peyronnet, E. et Lecompte, S. (2003). The impact of philosophical discussions on moral autonomy, judgment, empathy and the recognition of emotion in five year olds. *Thinking,* vol. 16, no 4, pp. 1-19.

[35]For more on the importance of modelling, see Bandura and Walters (1963). *Social learning and personality development.* New York: Holt, Rinehart and Winston, 329 p.

For the dangers of relying on role models in moral education see Kristjan Kristjansson (2005). Emulation and the use of role models in moral education. Paper presented at the annual meeting of the British Society for Philosophy and Education.

[36]Lipman, M., Sharp, A. M. et Oscanyan, F. S., (1980). *Philosophy in the classroom* (2e éd.). Philadelphia, PA: Temple University Press. p. xiii.

[37]Milgram, S. (1963). Behavioural study of obedience. *The Journal of Abnormal and Social Psychology*: vol. 67(4), p.371-378. This important study highlights the dangers of young people following the orders of an authority.

On this issue see:

Tisak, M. (1986). Children's conceptions of parental authority. *Child Development 57*: pp.166-176.

Laupa, M. & Turiel, E. (1986). Children's conceptions of adult and peer authority. *Child Development:57,* pp.405-412.

Kohlberg, L. (1984). *The psychology of moral development.* Vol 2. Harper & Row, San Fransisco.

Kohlberg, L. & Candee, D. (1984). The relationship of moral judgment to moral action. Kurtines W.M. & Gewirtz, J (eds.). *Morality, moral behaviour, and moral development.* New York: Wiley, pp.52-73.

See also Melanie Killen and Daniel Heart (Eds.) (1999). *Morality in everyday life.* Cambridge University Press. Especially Chapter 4.

These articles highlight the importance of adolescents and adults thinking for themselves, including those few who could resist Milgram's orders. One of the main aims of the present book is to help young children learn to think for themselves.

[38]See note 27 above.

[39]The concept of "dialogue" is discussed in the Philosophy for Children approach. See recommended reading for books and articles related to this perspective.

[40]Lipman, M., Sharp, A.M. et Oscanyan, F. S., (1980). *Philosophy in the classroom* (2e éd.). Philadelphia, PA: Temple University Press. p. 39.

[41]For example, Nussbaum, op. cit. as well as Robert Solomon and Michael Stocker (see Bibliography).

[42]For example, Carole Izard and Francisco Pons.

Izard, C.E. (2002). Translating emotion theory and research into preventive interventions, *Psychological Bulletin,* vol. 128, no 5, pp. 796-824.

Pons, F., Harris, P.L. and Doudin, P.A. (2002). Teaching emotion understanding. *European Journal of Psychology of Education,* vol. 17, no 3, pp. 293-304.

[43]See Recommended reading for a list in this book, pp. 201-206.

[44]See notes 1 and 2 above.

[45]LeDoux, J. (1993). *The emotional brain: The mysterious underpinnings of emotional life.* New York: Simon and Schuster.

Abbot, J. & Ryan, T. (1999). Learning to go with the grain of the brain. *Education Canada*, vol. 39, no 1, reprinted in Paciorek, K.M. & Munro, J.H. (eds.). *Annual edition early childhood education,* 2001, McGraw-Hill.

[46]Schleifer, M. (2004). *Moods, emotions and morality.* Annual Meeting of the American Philosophical Association, Pacific Division, Pasadena, California, March.

[47]Shultz, T.-R., Schleifer, M., Jaggi, C. (1987). Assigning vicarious responsibility. *European Journal of Social Psychology*, XVII, p. 377-380.

Shultz, T.-R., Wright, K., Schleifer, M. (1986). Assignment of moral responsibility and punishment. *Child Development, 57*, p. 177-184.

Schleifer, M. Shultz, T.-R., Lefebvre-Pinard, M. (1983). Judgments of causality, responsibility, and punishment in cases of harm due to omission. *British Journal of Developmental Psychology, 1*(2), p. 87-97.

Shultz, T.-R., Schleifer, M., Altman, I. (1981). Judgments of causation, responsibility, and punishment in cases of harm-doing. *Canadian Journal of Behavioral Science/Revue canadienne des sciences du comportement, 13*(3), p. 238-253.

Schleifer, M., Douglas, V. (1973). Moral judgments, behavior, and cognitive style in young children. *Canadian Journal of Behavioral Science, 5*(2), p. 133-144.

Schleifer, M., Douglas, V. (1973). Effects of Training on the Moral Judgment of Young Children. *Journal of Personality and Social Psychology, 28*(1), p. 62-68.

[48]Schleifer, M. (1995). Commentary on Richard Herrnstein and Charles Murray's "The Bell Curve." *The Alberta journal of educational research*, vol. 41 (1), p. 355-359.

Schleifer, M. (1976). Moral education and indoctrination. *Ethics, 86*(2), p. 154-163.

Part I – Values

Chapter 1. Which values?

[1]Skinner, B.F. (1971). *Beyond Freedom and Dignity*, p. 103.

[2]Skinner, B.F. (op. Cit., Chapter 6). See especially pages 104 to 126.

[3]Schleifer, M. (1977). Le behaviourisme en psychologie. Philosophiques, IV(2), p. 327 334.

[4]See bibliography for a list of references

[5]In 1958 Carl Rogers, the clinical psychologist, debated Skinner on this very point. This clash between the leading humanist and leading behaviorist is commonly used in Foundation of Education courses.

[6]Goleman, D. (1995). Emotional Intelligence, p. 80-82.

[7]In 1958 Noam Chomsky confronted Skinner in another famous debate about differing perspectives concerning language. Chomsky and most psycholinguists see language as uniquely human, in opposition to behaviorists who treat it as a form of communication shared by other species. See also Alison Gopnik's book *The Scientist in the Crib.*

The wonder dog Rico, trained by Julia Fisher at the Max Plank Institute, knows the meaning of about two-hundred words. This smartest of all dogs can fetched, by name, objects he has never seen before. A month after seeing them once, he still remembered and fetched new objects on demand. Fisher argues, following Skinner that language acquisition is not uniquely human. This claim must be put in perspective. Rico may understand two-hundred words, but a nine-year-old knows tens of thousands of words. Paul Bloom, of Yale University, writes in the journal *Science* that Rico's abilities are fascinating. Following Chomsky however, Bloom summarizes: "Children can speak, Rico cannot."

[8]Feyerabend, Paul (1999). *Conquest of abundance*. Chicago: University of Chicago Press.

Rorty, R. (1989). *Contingency, irony and solidarity*. Cambridge, Mass.: Cambridge University Press.

[9]Lipman, M., Sharp, A.M. et Oscanyan, F.S., (1980). *Philosophy in the classroom* (2e éd.). Philadelphia, PA: Temple University Press.

Schleifer, M. (1997). *Philosophy and community in education: A critique of Richard Rorty. Analytic teaching,* vol. 17 (2), p. 27-34.

Schleifer, M. (2001). Objectivity in discussions about values. Annual Meeting of the Canadian Society for Education (CSEE), Québec, June.

Schleifer, M. & Thesée, G. (2000). Philosophy for Children and Values as Objective and Universal. World Conference on violence, Montréal, July.

[10]Feyerabend, Paul (1999). *Conquest of abundance*. Chicago: University of Chicago Press.

[11]Lipman, M., Sharp, A.M. et Oscanyan, F.S., (1980). *Philosophy in the classroom* (2e éd.). Philadelphia, PA: Temple University Press p. 164.

[12]See Montefiore, A. (1966). Fact, value and ideology. in Williams, B. & Montefiore, A. (1966). *British analytical philosophy*. Routledge & Kegan Paul, London: p. 179-204. See also:Johnson, P. (1991). *Modern times*. New York: Harper and Row.

[13]See note 8 above.

[14]Schleifer, M. (2003). Philosophy of Education Courses. Annual Meeting of the Canadian Society for Studies and Education (CSEE), Halifax, May.

Blackburn, S. (2003). Relatively speaking. Think, *Journal of the Royal Institute of Philosophy*. Available on website.

[15]This controversy is discussed in the book by Paul Kropp (1998). *I'll be the parent, You be the kid*. Random House.

[16]See Simon Blackburn's article "Relatively Speaking" available on the internet. Blackburn's argument, with which I completely agree, was applied to the issue of fox hunting, an important British controversy.

[17]See Olivier Reboul (1971). La Philosophie de L'education. Presses Universitaires de France. See also Gohier, C., Schleifer, M. (ed.) (1993). *La question de l'identité*. Qui suis-je? Qui est l'autre? Montréal: Éditions Logiques, 264 pages. English Version, *The Question of Identity* available on request. Particularly "Universalism and Toleration" Chapter 5.

[18]See note 16.

[19]See notes 8 and 9 above.

[20]Lipman, M., Sharp, A. M. et Oscanyan, F. S., (1980). *Philosophy in the classroom* (2e éd.). Philadelphia, PA: Temple University Press. p. 163-164.

[21]Schleifer, M. (1995). Commentary on Richard Herrnstein and Charles Murray's "The Bell Curve. *The Alberta Journal of Educational Research,* vol. 41 (1), p. 355-359.

Schleifer, M. (1973). The Flew-Jensen uproar. *Philosophy,* 48(186), p. 386-390.

Hilary Putnam (2004). *The Collapse of the Fact/Value Dichotomy*. Harvard University Press.

[22]Ginsberg, M. (1956) *On the diversity of morals* Heinemann, London. See especially Chapter 7.

[23]Shultz, T.R., Wright, K., Schleifer, M. (1986). Assignment of moral responsibility and punishment. *Child Development, 57,* p. 177-184.

[24]See note 7 above. For a defense of universalism, see Olivier Reboul (1971). *La Philosophie de l'Éducation.* Presses Universitaires de France. See also Gohier, C., Schleifer, M. (ed.) (1993). *La question de l'identité. Qui suis-je? Qui est l'autre? Montréal:* Éditions Logiques, 264 pages. English Version, *The question of identity* available on request. Particularly "Universalism and Toleration," Chapter 5.

Charles Schulz's Peanuts cartoons exemplify this universalist aspect: People across the globe can appreciate the humor and pathos of his characters. William Shakespeare's genius, likewise, is to portray universal emotions common to all of human nature.

Another example of the universal comes from music. Although there are cultural differences, music has certain features for all human beings.

See Bernstein, L. (1959). *The joy of music.* New York: Simon & Schuster, 303 p.

Storr, A. (1992). *Music and the mind.* New York: The Free Press, 212 p.

Bernstein, L. (1973). *The unanswered question.* Cambridge, MA.: The Harvard University Press, 428 p.

[25]Ibid.

[26]Turiel, E. (1983). Domains and categories in social cognitive development. In W. Overton (Ed.) *The relationship between social and cognitive development.* Hillsdale, NJ: Lawrence Erlbaum Associates Inc.

Turiel, E. (1983). The development morality. In W. Damon (Ed.) *Book of child psychology* (5th ed.).Vol. 3, N. Eisenberg (Ed.), *Social, Emotional and Personality Development.* New York: Wiley.

[27]Lipman, M. & Sharp, A.M. (1978) *Growing up with philosophy.* Temple University Press. See particularly pps. (374-375).

[28]Peters, R. (1966). *Ethics and education.* Routledge and Kegan Paul Reboul, O. (1971) *La Philosophie de l'éducation.* Presses universitaires de France.

Chapter 2. How to discuss values: The role of judgment

[1]Schleifer, M., Daniel, M.-F., Peyronnet, E. et Lecompte, S. (2003). The Impact of philosophical discussions on moral autonomy, judgment, empathy and the recognition of emotion in five year olds. *Thinking,* vol. 16, no 4, pp. 1-19. Only a few of the five year olds could cope with these examples, especially example 4. At the end of the year, those children exposed to philosophical discussions improved their performance significantly compared to a control group. 95% of the children were able to pick the correct items, and justify their choices.

[2]Example 1: Hammer (inanimate object); Example 2: Horse (animal, non human); Example 3: Peacock (living creature); Example 4: Violence (violence with dominance and submission). Other tests on pages 164 and 165.

[3]Merleau-Ponty, M. (1962). *Phenomenology of perceptions.* London: Routledge & Kegan Paul, cited in Dreyfus, H.L. (1979). *What computers can't do: The limits of artificial intelligence.* (Revised edition). New York: Harper & Row. (First edition, 1972).

[4]Neisser, P. 1(990). Cognitive psychology. cited in Dreyfus, H.L. (1979). *What computers can't do: The limits of artificial intelligence.* (Revised edition). New York: Harper & Row. (First edition, 1972).

[5]Crick, B. (1994). *The astonishing hypothesis.* New York: Scrabner's, pp. 178-179.

[6]Horgan, J. (1993). The death of proof, *Scientific American,* Vol. 269, no 4, p. 93-103.

Byers, W. 2002. Mathematics and Computers (unpublished manuscript).

[7]Crick, op. cit. Byers, op. cit.

[8]See appendices C to H.

[9]See Schleifer, M. (1992). *La formation du jugement*. Montréal: Éditions Logiques. Particularly chapter 5, Judgment and Reasoning.

[10]Lipman, M. (1993). *Thinking children and education*. Iowa: Kendall Publications, 745 p.

Lipman, M. (1992). L'éducation au jugement, in *La formation du jugement,*ouvrage collectif sous la direction de Michael Schleifer. Montréal: Les Éditions Logiques, pp. 99-123. (Available in English translation)

Lipman, M. (1992). "Judgment and Person," Montclair State University, New Jersey, unpublished paper, 20 pages.

Schleifer, M., Neveu, F. and Poissant, H. (1999). "Le programme de philosophie pour enfants: son impact sur le discours argumentatif chez les élèves du primaire," 17 pages, dans: Louise Guilbert, Jacques Boisvert et Nicole Ferguson (dir.), *Enseigner et comprendre*. Québec: Les presses de l'Université Laval, p. 128-143.

[11]Hare, W. (2001). Bertrand Russell on critical thinking. *Journal of Thought*, p. 7-16.

Bruneau, S. (1996). Is there a political agenda behind critical thinking?. Paper presented at Canadian Society for the Study of Education, Brock University.

Bailin, S., Case, R., Coombs, J.R. and Daniels, LB. (1999). Conceptualising Critical Thinking. *Journal of Curriculum Studies,* vol. 31, no 3, p. 285-302. Giroux, A. 1990. "Enseigner à penser: passer de maître à mentor," *Revue canadienne de l'éducation,* vol. 15, no 3, p. 229-244.

[12]Schleifer, op. cit. Lipman, 1995, op. cit.

[13]Schleifer, *op. cit.*, pp. 227-268.

[14]Aristotle *Nicomochean Ethics*. Chapter 7.

[15]Wong, D. (2002) Crossing cultures in moral psychology. *Philosophy Now.* June v.36: pp 7-11.

[16]See Introduction, note 37.

[17]Glazer, J. Reason and the reasoner p. 664-674. in Lipman *Thinking children and education* (1993). Kendall-Hunt.

[18]Matthews, Garrett. (1976) *Dialogue With Children*. pp 91-191. see also Shklar, Judice. *Op. cit* p.193.

[19]Lipman, Sharp p. 200. this is also discussed in Piaget's *Moral Judgment of the Child*.

[20]See Chapter 4 for a further discussion of etiquette.

[21]Beck, op. cit., p.106.

[22]See section in this chapter on Counselling and Therapy: Judgment and Work.

[23]Lipman et al. p. 201. This distinction is discussed by the children in Chapter 10 in the novelette *Lisa*, used in Philosophy for Children (see Recommended Reading and Appendices).

[24]Sklar, J.N (1984). *Ordinary vices*. Harvard University Press. 268 pages.

[25]Aristotle, *Nicomochean Ethics*.

[26]Ibid.

[27]Lipman, M., Sharp, A.M. et Oscanyan, F.S., (1980). *Philosophy in the classroom* (2e éd.). Philadelphia, PA: Temple University Press. p. 192-193.

[28]Pavlicek, R. Mapping Bridge Deals, Article 7Z68. http://rpbridge.net/7z68.htm

[29]"Heuristics" is defined in Webster's dictionary (from the Greek root word for "discovery") as "problem-solving by experimental and especially trial and error methods." It also lists a second definition: "exploratory techniques of the computer program which includes evaluation of *feedback*" AI uses this latter meaning.

[30]Schleifer, M. (2004). The Human Mind and Artificial Intelligence: Why Computers Cannot Play Bridge. *The Bridge Bulletin,* May. Full article available on request. E-mail: schleifer.michael@uqam.ca

[31]e.g. Newborn, 2002, see note 2 above.

[32]Artificial intelligence expert, Steve Smith, has informed me that up to now they have had difficulty with bridge, and also surprisingly with the game Go. (Personal correspondence).

[33]Stocker, see Recommended reading, pp. 201-206.

[34]Nussbaum M. (2001). Upheavals of thought: the intelligence of emotions. Cambridge: Cambridge University Press.

[35]Ibid.

[36]The pre-testing items for form and color can be found in the Appendix. See p. 162.

[37]These easier items were difficult for many children aged 3 to 5, although most can be helped with training.

[38]See Schleifer *The question of identity, op. cit.*

[39]See appendix D.

[40]See Frances Aboud, Concerning stereotype and prejudices in Gohier & Schleifer. *The Question of identity.*

[41]Ibid.

[42]See Recommended Reading, pp. 201-206.

[43]See footnote no. 27.

[44]See appendix H for test of moral autonomy, p. 287.

[45]See Saltzstein, H. op. cit.

[46]Many phobias, like fear of flying are found among children and adults whose imagination is particularly strong. One part of the most effective cognitive therapy used with phobias is to delineate the line between reality and fantasy.

[47]See Chapter 7, note 25.

[48]Ibid.

[49]Schleifer, M., Poirier, G. (1996). The effect of philosophical discussions in the classroom on respect for others and non-stereotypic attitudes. *Thinking.* vol. 12, no 4, p. 32-34.

[50]Race is different than gender. In fact, the word race should be avoided. See Zack, N. (2002) *Philosophy of science and race.* Routledge.

[51]Bohm, D. (1992). Insight and reason: The role of ratio in education. in Lipman (ed.) op.cit. pp. 654-658.

[52]Chopra, D. (1993). *Ageless body, timeless mind: The quantum alternative to growing old.* New York. Harcourt. See especially chapter 2 and part 4. Chopra speaks of the dread of uncertainty which leads many parents to be dogmatic with their young children, often leaving long-term, harmful psychological consequences.

[53]Wendy Mogel. (2001). The Blessing of a skinned knee. New York: Penguin Putnam Inc., 302 p.

Part II Specific Values

Chapter 3. Honesty

[1]Philosophers of course often see The Truth as central to their activity. Emanuel Kant, Jean Jacques Rousseau, and more recently Richard Peters and Margaret Sharp's (see Recommended reading for references) put truth telling as a core value and cardinal virtue for educators. I side with these defenders of truth against the post-modernists like Richard Rorty and Paul Feyerabend (see Recommended reading), who deny that any truth exists in science or morality (see Chapter 1, section on objectivity where this is

discussed). Despite this, teaching our children to tell the literal truth will not be helpful for their emotional, social or cognitive development. This will be discussed in the sections following. For more on this debate see Jeremy Campbell's (2001) book *The liar's tale: A history of falsehood.* Norton. New York. London. Especially Chapter 20, p. 302-314.

[2]Canal Vie Montreal, (February 2004). The panel was asked to talk about the pathology of lying. Although the two psychiatrists were happy to link lying to mental illness (particularly social maladjustment), the student participant and I insisted that everyone sometimes lies. Two recent studies have demonstrated that we were correct. The first study:

DePaulo, B.M., Kashy, D.A., Kirkendol, S.E., & Wyer, M.M. (1996). Lying in everyday life. *Journal of Personality and Social Psychology:* vol 70 (5), 979-995. looked at the diaries of hundreds of college students who report telling at least three lies a day. The second study:

Kashy, D., & DePaulo, B. (1996). Who lies? *Journal of Personality and Social Psychology:* Vol 70 (5), 1037-1051. Reports that people who tell more lies are more sociable as well as having higher quality same sex relationships.

[3]Wimmer, H. (1984). Young children's conception of lying: Lexical realism-moral subjectivism. *Journal of Experimental Child Psychology: 37*, 1-30.

[4]Kant, Immanuel (1994). On a supposed right to lie from benevolent motives, In *The Critique of Practical Reason,* translated and edited by Lewis White Beck. Chicago: University of Chicago Press, pp. 346-350.

Augustine, Saint (1952). On Lying. In R.J. Defarrari, ed., *Treatises on various subjects,* vol. 14. New York: Catholic University of America Press.

[5]For an excellent discussion of this perspective within Judaism, see Rabbi Joseph Telushkin. (2000). *The book of Jewish values.* New York: Random House, 519 p. See particularly section 71. See also: Bok, S. (1989). *Lying: Moral choice in public and private life.* New York: Vintage Books.

[6]Piaget, J. (1968). *The moral judgment of the child.* Routledge and Kegan Paul. Originally Piaget, J. (1932) Le jugement moral chez l'enfant. For ways in which Piaget underestimated the capacities of the young child. See the introduction and particularly note 17.

[7]Bussey, K. (1992). Lying and truthfulness: Children's definitions, standards, and evaluative reactions. *Child Development: 63,* 129-137.

[8]Rabbi Joseph Telushkin. (2000). *The book of Jewish values.* New York: Random House, 519 p. See particularly sections 70 to 73.

[9]Shklar, J.N. (1994). *Ordinary vices.* Harvard University Press, 268 p.

[10]Op Cit p.73.

[11]Ibid p.78.

[12]Lewis, M., Stanger, C. & Sullivan, M.W. (1989). Deception in 3-Year-Olds. *Developmental Psychology* vol 25, (1): pp. 439-443.

Dr. Ekman, P. (1989). *Why kids lie?* Scribner.

Peisach, E., & Hardeman, M. (1983). Moral reasoning in early childhood lying and stealing. *The Journal of Genetic Psychology:* vol 142, 107-120.

Webley, P., & Burke, M. (1984). Children's understanding of motives for deception. *European Journal of Social Psychology:* vol 14, 455-458.

Keyes, R. (2004). *The post-truth era: Dishonesty and deception in contemporary life.* St. Martin's Press.

[13]Matthews, G. (2004). Augustine and the Parable of the Pears. American Philosophical Association Annual Meeting, Pasadina. Augustine's views as well as Plato's and Kant's (eighteenth century), represent the absolutist view about lying being wrong. The group of philosophers who are in opposition include

Aristotle (Plato's favorite student), David Hume (eighteenth century) and Nietzche (nineteenth century). An excellent discussion about the debate between these two sets of philosophical opponents appear in Nussbaum and Telushkin (see Recommended reading).

[14]For a discussion of this see: Rabbi Joseph Telushkin. (2000). *The book of Jewish values.* New York: Random House, 519 p.

Chapter 4. Politeness

[1]American Philosophical Association annual meeting in March 2003 in Pasadina, California. Some other recent books on etiquette include one by Peter Post, the great grandson of Emily Post (pioneer of the rules about table manners, invitations and so on), entitled *Essential manners for men: What to do, When to do it and why?* Another book discussing this is by psychologist John Gottman entitled *Raising an emotionally intelligent child: The heart of parenting.* Some schools in California and the city of Washington have adopted the etiquette lessons, coaching children on the proper way to greet an adult ("Give him a firm hand shake, look him in the eye, smile and say something nice"). It is of interest that the new curriculum on etiquette stresses social skills and common courtesy rather than the mini-finishing school lessons of our grandmothers that dwelt on cutlery and curtsies.

As a contrast to the focusing on etiquette, (which can be relatively unimportant and even, as we discuss in the text, sexist or racist) is the kind of politeness which Robert Keeshan, known better as Captain Kangaroo, stressed. Captain Kangaroo, who passed away in 2004 talked about the power of two "magic phrases." The first being "please" and the second being "thank-you." Early on, he taught vocabulary and skills like crossing the street. Later, as divorce rates and family instability grew, he taught about love, pride, and self-confidence.

[2]See: Martha Nussbaum (2001). *Upheavals of thought: The intelligence of emotions.* Cambridge: Cambridge University Press. p. 200-206. The importance of the emotion of disgust in child development in regard to moral values will be discussed in Chapter 8 of the present book.

[3]Schleifer, M. (2004). Moods, Emotions and Morality. Annual Meeting of the American Philosophical Association, Pacific Division, Pasadena, California, March.

[4]Strawson, P.F. (1968). *Freedom and resentment. Studies in the philosophy of thought and action.* London Oxford University Press. Stawson's essay is discussed by Jay A. Brook in his article, "How to treat Persons as persons," as well as by myself in my article, "Psychological explanation and interpersonal relations." Both Brook's article and my own appear in Allan Montefiore's collection 1973) entitled *Philosophy and personal relations.* London: Routledge and Kegan Paul, Chapter 4 (pages 62-83) and chapter 8 (pages 170-191).

[5]Emmons, R.A. & McCullough, M.E. 2003. Counting blessings versus burdens: An experimental investigation of gratitude and subjective well-being in daily life. *Journal of Personality and Social Psychology,* vol. 84, no 2, pp. 377-389.

[6]From Philosophy for Children. See appendices.

[7]Shultz, T.-R., Schleifer, M. (1983). Towards a refinement of attribution concepts, in M. Hewstone, F.D. Fincham et J. Jaspars (Eds): *Attribution theory and research: conceptual, developmental, and social dimensions.* New York: Academic Press, p. 37-62.

Forgas, J.P., Bower, G.H., & Moylan, S.J. (2003). Praise or blame? Affective influences on attributions for achievement. *Journal of Personality and Social Psychology.*

Zuckerman, M., Larrance, D., Porac, J. & Blanck, P. (1980). Effects of fear of success on intrinsic motivation, causal attribution, and choice behaviour. *Journal of Personality and Social Psychology;* vol. 39 (3), 503-513.

[8]For further discussion of greetings, see Rabbi Joseph Telushkin. (2000). *The book of Jewish values.* New York: Random House, 519 p. See particularly sections 70 to 73.

[9]Turiel, E. (1983). Domains and categories in social cognitive development. In W. Overton (Ed.) *The relationship between social and cognitive development.* Hillsdale, NJ: Lawrence Erlbaum Associates Inc.

Turiel, E. (1983). The Development Morality. In W. Damon (Ed.) Book of child psychology (5th ed.).Vol. 3, N. Eisenberg (Ed.), *Social, Emotional and Personality Development.* New York: Wiley.

[10]Rabbi Joseph Telushkin. (2000). *The book of Jewish values.* New York: Random House, 519 p. See particularly sections 70 to 73.

[11]Ayim, M. (1994). Political Correctness-The Debate Continues. Paper presented at the Canadian Philosophy of Education Annual Meeting, Calgary.

Wetering, V. (1991). *Political correctness: The insult and the injury, vital speeches of the day,* vol 58 (4), p100-103.

[12]Katwinkler, W., & Murray, G. (2004). *Walter the farting dog.* Nutton: New York.

[13]Daniel Goleman. (2003). *Healing emotions.* New York: Random House, 277 p.

Chapter 5. Responsibility

[1]For the psychological aspect, see: Jean Piaget (1968). *The moral judgment of the child.* Routledge and Kegan Paul. (Originally *Le jugement moral chez l'enfant.* 1932).

For the moral and legal aspects of the concept of responsibility here is a list of some of my publications:

Shultz, T.-R., Schleifer, M., Jaggi, C. (1987). Assigning vicarious responsibility. *European Journal of Social Psychology,* XVII, p. 377-380.

Shultz, T.-R., Wright, K., Schleifer, M. (1986). Assignment of moral responsibility and punishment. *Child Development, 57,* p. 177-184.

Schleifer, M. Shultz, T.-R., Lefebvre-Pinard, M. (1983). Judgments of causality, responsibility, and punishment in cases of harm due to omission. *British Journal of Developmental Psychology, 1*(2), p. 87-97.

Shultz, T.-R., Schleifer, M., Altman, I. (1981). Judgments of causation, responsibility, and punishment in cases of harm-doing. *Canadian Journal of Behavioral Science/Revue canadienne des sciences du comportement, 13*(3), p. 238-253.

Schleifer, M. (1970). The responsibility of the psychopath. *Philosophy, 45*(173), p. 231 232.

Schleifer, M. (1973). Psychological explanations and personal relations, in A. Montefiore (Ed.): *Philosophy and personal relations.* Routledge and Kegan Paul, p. 170-190.

[2]More on "pride – and its counterpart humility" – in Chapter 8.

[3]Jean Piaget (1968). *The moral judgment of the child.* Routledge and Kegan Paul. (Originally Le jugement moral chez l'enfant. 1932).

[4]See Shultz, T.-R., Wright, K., Schleifer, M. (1986). Assignment of moral responsibility and punishment. *Child Development, 57,* p. 177-184.

[5]More in Chapter 11.

[6]See Shultz, T.-R., Wright, K., Schleifer, M. (1986). Assignment of moral responsibility and punishment. *Child Development, 57,* p. 177-184.

[7]For a discussion on this topic, see: P.F. Strawson (1968). *Freedom and resentment. Studies in the philosophy of thought and action.* London, Oxford University Press. As well as my article Schleifer, M. (1973). Psychological explanations and personal relations, in A. Montefiore (Ed.): *Philosophy and personal relations.* Routledge and Kegan Paul, p. 170-190. and that of J.A. Brook (1973) entitled *How to treat person's as person's,* Chapter 4 in the same collection as my article.

See also:

Flew, A. (1973). *Crime or disease.* Macmillan Press. London.

Lucas, J.R. (1970). *The freedom of the will.* Clarendon Press, Oxford. Especially chapter 2 Responsibility and Freedom.

Schleifer, M. (1970). The responsibility of the psychopath. *Philosophy, 45*(173), p. 231 232.

[8]Baxter, J.S., Macrae, C.N., Manstead, A.S.R., Stradling, D., & Parker, D. (1990). Attributional biases and driver behaviour. *Social behaviour;* vol 5, 185-192.

Shaw, J. & Skolnick, P. (1971). Attribution of responsibility for a happy accident. *Journal of Personality and Social Psychology;* vol. 18 (3), 380-383.

[9]Schleifer, M., McCormick, M. (1991). The concept of foreseeability in judgments of moral responsibility. Society for research in child development, Seattle, April, (Abstracts VIII, p. 441).

[10]Schleifer, M., Shultz, T.-R. (1988). Severity of consequences and mitigating factors in judgments of blame/punishment and praise/reward. 5th Biennial University of Waterloo conference on child development, May.

[11]See Chapter 2.

[12]See Introduction.

[13]White, P. (2002). What should we teach children about forgiveness? *Journal of Philosophy of Education,* Vol. 36 (1), 57-67.

[14]Gross, D., & Thompson, C. (2004). Children's understanding of apology and forgiveness in peer relationships. Unpublished manuscript.

[15]Ibid.

[16]An excellent example of people refusing to forgive, because of the absence of apology concerns Pete Rose, who apparently gambled while playing baseball. See Vincent, F. (January 19, 2004). No bloom on this rose. *Time Magazine.*

[17] Spring, J. (2004). *How can I forgive you? The courage to forgive, the freedom not to.* Harper Collins, 255 pages.

[18]Telushkin, J. (2000). *The book of Jewish values.* New York: Random House, p. 464.

[19]See references in note 7 above.

[20]See Chapter 1.

[21]Barker, G.P. & Graham, S. (1987). Developmental Study of Praise and Blame as Attributional Cues. *Journal of Educational Psychology,* vol. 79 (1), 62-66.

Carlton, M.P. & Winsler, A. (1998). Fostering Intrinsic Motivation in Early Childhood Classrooms. *Early Childhood Education Journal,* vol. 25 (3), 159-166.

[22]See Chapter 4, footnote 7.

Interlude. To speak or to keep silent

[1]In the *Nicomochean ethics,* Aristotle does talk about instilling moral virtues without wisdom (Chapter 3). It is wrong, however, to interpret him as being against offering explanations and justifications for every moral virtue. Although Aristotle tells us "moral virtue comes about as a result of habit" (Book 2 Chapter 1, 1103A17), he also reminds us that "the agents themselves, must in each case consider what is appropriate to the occasion (1104A9). Aristotle states that "actions are called just and temperate when they are such as the just or temperate man would do it." (1105b8-10). Moral virtue for Aristotle is never simply "habit" or "automatic behavior." Moral virtue must involve some element of judgment, if only to understand what is appropriate.

[2]Eskritt, M. & Lee, K. (2003). Do Actions Speak Louder Than Words? Preschool Children's Use of the Verbal-Nonverbal Consistency Principle During Inconsistent Communications. *Journal of Non-verbal Behaviour: 27*(1), 25-41.

Ellis, C.R. et al. (1997). *Recognition of facial expressions of emotion by children with emotional and behavioural disorders.*

Rosenthal, R. et al., (1977). The Pons test: Measuring sensitivity to non-verbal cues. In P. McReynolds (Ed.) *Advances in Psychological Assessment.* San Fransisco, Jossey-Bass.

Brothers, L. (1989). A biological perspective on empathy. *American Journal of Psychiatry;* 146(1).

Steinberg, S.,& Laird, J. (1989). Parent attributions of emotion to their children and the cues children use in perceiving their own emotions. *Motivation and Emotion;* vol 13(3), 179-191.

Daniel Goleman. (1995). *Emotional intelligence.* New York: Bantam Books, pp 96-104.

[3]Telushkin, J. (2000). *The book of Jewish values.* New York: Random House, p. 57.

[4]For example, in the novel *The island walkers,* by John Bemrose (2003) the hero struggles with wanting to apologize for something he said to hurt a friend, but unable because he would be admitting he was wrong.

[5]Apology is discussed in Chapter 5; gratitude and greetings in Chapter 4.

[6]For more on this issue, see:

Ayim, M. (1994). *Political correctness, the debate continues.* The Canadian Philosophy of Education Society, Calgary. Agreeing with Ayim is John Vander Wetering (1991). *Political correctness-The insult and the injury. Vital Speeches of the Day;* vol. 58(4), p.100-103. On the other side of the issue are those who claim that racist and sexist language may be rude, but even rude language must be protected by a right to freedom of expression. See for example, Dinesh, D'souza (1991). *Illiberal education: The politics of race and sex on campus.* New York, the Free Press. and Nat, N (1992). Who's on first? Hurt feelings and free speech. *The Progressive;* vol.56(2), pp. 16-17.

See also Diane Ravitch (2003). The language police and Robin Barrow (2005). On the duty of not taking offence. Paper presented at the annual meeting of the British Society Philosophy and Education.

[7]Bissonnette, V., Rusbult, C., & Kilpatrick, S. (1997). Empathic accuracy and marital conflict resolution. In Ickes, W. (Ed.) *Empathic accuracy.* New York, London: Guilford Press.

[8]Ibid.

[9]Telushkin Op.Cit. p.12.

[10]Telushkin, Op. Cit. p.129.

[11]Montessori, M. (1914). *Dr. Montessori's own handbook.* New York: Frederick A. Stokes.

[12]Telushkin Ibid, p.127.

[13]See Wood, D. chapter 9 on honesty in Allan Montefiore's collection (1973) entitled *Philosophy and personal relations.* London: Routledge and Kegan Paul, p191-224.

[14]Schleifer, M., McCormick, M. (1991). The concept of foreseeability in judgments of moral responsibility. Society for research in child development, Seattle, April, (Abstracts VIII, p. 441).

Part III – Feeling

Chapter 6. Caring

[1]See Chapter 5

[2]See Noddings, N. (1988). An Ethic of Caring and its implications for instructional arrangements. In *American Journal of Education,* vol. 96, no 2, pp. 215-229.

Skoe, E.E.A. (2003).:The ethic of care. Issues in moral development, In *Personality development in adolescence: A cross cultural and life span perspective.* London: Routledge, pp. 144-171.

[3]See Noddings, N. (op. cit., p. 218).

[4]See Gilligan, Carol (1982). *In a different voice*. Cambridge, Mass.: Harvard University Press.

[5]See Skoe, E.E.A. in note 2.

[6]See Goleman, D. (1995). *Emotional intelligence*. New York: Bantam Books, p. 98.

[7]See Gallese, V. (2003). The roots of empathy: The shared manifold hypothesis and the neural basis of intersubjectivity. *Psychopathology,* vol 36, p171-180.

[8]Meltzoff, A. (2002). *The imitative mind: Development, evolution and brain bases*. Cambridge: Cambridge University Press.

[9]See Stern, D. (1987). *The interpersonal world of the infant*. New York: Basic Books, p. 30. See also Pickens, J. and Field, T. (1993). Facial expressivity in infants of depressed mothers in *Developmental Psychology,* vol. 29, no 6. See also Goleman, op. cit, chapter 7.

[10]See Rabbi Joseph Telushkin. (2000). *The book of Jewish values*. New York: Random House, p. 8.

[11]Ibid. p. 12.

[12]See Goleman, op. cit., chapter 14. We will return to this question in chapter 7.

[13]See Schleifer, M., Weiss, G., Cohen, N., Elman, M., Cveijic, H., Kruger, E. (1975). Hyperactivity in preschoolers and the effect of methyphinidate. *American Journal of Orthopsychiatry, 45*, p. 38-50.

[14]Ibid.

[15]Ibid.

[16]See Schleifer, M., Campbell, S., Weiss, G. (1978). Continuities in maternal reports and child behaviours over time in hyperactive and comparison groups. *Journal of Abnormal & Child Psychology, 6*(1), p. 33-45.

Schleifer, M., Campbell, S., Weiss, G., Perlman, T. (1977). A two-year follow-up of hyperactive preschoolers. *American Journal of Orthopsychiatry, 47,* p. 149-162.

[17]Brazelton, T. (2004). Raising happy kids in hectic times. *Family Circle Magazine,* November, p. 31.

[18]See Nussbaum, M. (2001). *Upheavals of thought: the intelligence of emotions*. Cambridge: Cambridge University Press, p. 301.

[19]Ibid.

[20]A primary example is Emmanuel Kant. See *Groundings for the metaphysics of morals*. Trans. J.W. Ellington, Indianapolis: Hackett. As Kant states: "Such benevolence is called soft heartedness and should not occur at all among human beings." Another example of a philosopher against compassion is Plato in *The Republic*. See Nussbaum, op. cit., chapter 7, pp 354-400 on the philosophical debate between Plato and Kant on the one hand, and Aristotle and his followers on the other.

[21]Nussbaum, *op. cit.,* p. 301.

[22]This is Nusbaum's reason. See p. 329. See also Ickes, W. (Ed.) *Emphatic accuracy*. (pp. 73-116). New York: Guildofrd Press.

[23]Martiny, C. (2002). Non-verbal behavior and empathy in the communicational context: indications for training helping-practitioners. Unpublished doctoral thesis. Université du Québec à Montréal.

[24]Ibid.

[25]Ibid.

[26]See Eisenberg, N. & Strayer, J. (1987). *Empathy and its development*. Cambridge: Cambridge University Press.

Eisenberg, N., Murphy, B. & Shepard, S. (1996). The development of emphatic accuracy. In William Ickes (Ed.) *Emphatic accuracy*. (pp. 73-116). New York: Guilford Press.

Eisenberg, N. & Mussen, P. (1989). *The roots of prosocial behavior in children*. Cambridge: Cambridge University Press.

[27]See discussion of Piaget and his errors in the Introduction.

[28]Cited by Rabbi Telushkin, p. 12.

[29]Daniel, M.-F., Schleifer, M. (dir.) (1996). *La coopération dans la classe/Cooperation in the classroom.* Montréal: Éditions Logiques, 303 p.

[30]Piaget, J. (1968). *The moral judgment of the child.* Routledge and Kegan Paul. Originally Piaget, J. (1932) Le jugement moral chez l'enfant.

[31]See Introduction.

[32]Ibid.

[33]See note 25.

[34]Ibid.

[35]Ibid.

[36]Bronwen, L. & Howe, N. (2003). Solitary play and convergent and divergent thinking skills in pre-school children. *Early Childhood Research Quarterly;* vol. 18(1), p. 22-42.

[37]Ibid.

[38]Nussbaum, M. (2001). *Upheavals of thought: the intelligence of emotions.* Cambridge: Cambridge University Press.

Winnicott, D. (1965). *The maturational process and the facilitating environment.* New York: International Universities Press.

[39]See Chapter 8.

[40]See Chapter 8.

[41]See Perner, J. & Wimmer, H. (1985). John thinks that Mary thinks that…Attribution of second-order beliefs by 5-10 year old children. *Journal of Experimental Child Psychology,;* vol. 39, p 437-471.

Chapter 7. Understanding Emotions

[1]On Kant versus Aristotle see Stark, S. (2004). A Change of Heart: Moral Emotions, Transformation, and Moral Virtue; Conference given at the American Philosophical Association Annual Meeting, Pasadena. Also: Martha Nussbaum (2001). *Upheavals of thought: the intelligence of emotions.* Cambridge: Cambridge University Press. p.463.

[2]For example, Nussbaum, Stocker, Solomon. See Recommended Reading.

[3]For a good example of this view, see Beck, C. (1972). *Ethics.* Toronto. McGraw-Hill, Chapter 9.

[4]Ibid.

[5]Bailin, S. (1991). Rationality and intuition. *Paideusis: Journal of the Canadian Philosophy of Education Society;* vol. 4(2), spring,p.17-27.

[6]Egan, K. (1992). *Imagination and education.* New York Teachers College Press.

[7]Interview in the *Montreal Gazette,* May 2004.

[8]See Recommended Reading, pp. 201-206.

[9]Nussbaum, M. (2001). *Upheavals of thought: The intelligence of Emotions.* Cambridge: Cambridge University Press. p. 19-88.

[10]Among philosophers Paul Griffiths is a representative of this view, see his book *What emotions really are.* (1977). University of Chicago Press. Another representative is Jenefer Robinson in her 2005 book entitled *Deeper than reason.* Oxford University Press. Among psychologists the leading representative would be Nico Fridja (1986). *The emotions.* Cambridge: Cambridge University Press.

[11]Pitcher, G. (1995). *The dogs who came to stay.* New York. Dutton.

[12]See Paul Ledoux (1993). *The emotional brain: The mysterious underpinnings of emotional life.* New York: Simon and Schuster.

[13]For more on pride see Chapter 8.

[14]For shame also Chapter 8.

[15]Nussbaum, M. (op. cit., p.132-135).

[16]Nussbaum, M. (op. cit., p. 61).

[17]Nussbaum, M. (op. cit., p. 133).

[18]Nussbaum, M. (op. cit., p. 134).

Two of her examples which illustrates her thesis are worth considering. The first concerns a ´positive` emotion and mood, the second a ´negative` pair. Nussbaum argues that joy, an emotion, must have an object, although often this object is very vague and indistinct.

"One may have a very general joy about how one's life is going, or how the world is, and that will be an emotion with a very general object;" on the other hand, "joy may be truly moodlike, and truly objectless, a kind of euphoria that doesn't focus on anything." (p. 133)

The example of a ´negative` emotion would be depression, where, following Seligman's work with animals, Nussbaum speaks of emotional depression as opposed to moodlike or endogenous depression.

"Although there are many cases of depression that are genuine moods, caused by chemistry without the intervention of belief, and unresponsive to changes in situation or belief, there are also many cases in which the general symptoms of depression are about something in the person's life." (p. 132)

[19]e.g. Freud, S. (1917). *Mourning and melancholia.* Collected Papers, vol. 4, New York: Basic Books (1959).

[20]Ledoux, J. (1996). *The emotional brain: The mysterious underpinnings of emotional life.* New York: Simon and Shuster.

Edelman, G.M. and Tononi, G. (2000). *A universe of consciousness,* New York: Basic Books.

[21]Nussbaum, M. (op. cit., p. 67 ff).

[22]Freud, (op. cit.).

Wender, P.H., Klein, F. 1981. *Mind, mood and medicine: A guide to do biopsychiatry.* McGraw Hill.

[23]See Pinker, S. 1997. *How the mind works,* New York: Norton, pp. 386-387.

[24] Nussbaum, M. (op. cit., p. 133).

Nussbaum has argued that brain process should not be included in the criteria of emotions. The evidence is overwhelming, however, that the brain is functioning in certain ways whenever (and without exception) human beings experience moods or emotions. What neurologists seem to have a consensus about is the following:

1. The amygdala is involved in all mood and emotion experiences for humans.

2. The emotional brain has much "plasticity," that is lived experience alters the neural networks activated when we experience any mood or emotion.

3. The neural networks are not identical for different (main) emotions, such as fear, anger, or sadness. There seems to be a neural network for each emotion. (Ledoux, 1996. *The emotional brain,* New York: Simon and Shuster)

One's conceptual analysis must be consistent with at least the above three propositions until more experiment leads to a more refined, or even different theory. The philosophical account must cohere with the neurological "phenomena."

Ledoux, like Edelman and Pinker, is an avowed materialist: thoughts and feelings are brain processes. The thorny problem of "consciousness" remains a separate issue for these scientists, working in physiology, medicine and cognitive science (Ledoux, Edelman and Pinker respectively). They also have complex and divergent views concerning Artificial Intelligence, and the extent to which any computer could ever mimic the human brain, including emotion and judgment. Although Nussbaum does not take an explicit stand concerning AI's claims, my guess is that her analysis of emotions would provide an argument against the AI's contention (for example, by Newborn, M. 2002. Interview with La Presse, oct. 18.) His new book *Deep blue: An artificial intelligence milestone* is apparently about to appear).

The revised conceptual analysis that I have suggested paper should provide an even stronger case against AI, since it resurrects moods, temperament and subjective feeling as important to one's understanding of emotions, in addition to the cognitive component stressed by Nussbaum.

Nussbaum cites Ledoux's work, but interprets him differently than I do. She claims that Ledoux only offers a "cautious conclusion" concerning whether physiological information should be included in the definition of emotion. I think that it is quite clear that Ledoux insists that the physiological phenomena must be included (see Ledoux, J. 1996. *The emotional brain,* New York: Simon and Shuster). This is particularly so in his more recent book (Ledoux, J. 2002. *Synaptic self: How our brains become who we are,* New York: Penguin-Putnam).

On another point, Ledoux insists that for every main emotion (fear, anger, joy, sadness), there is a separate "neural network." This, too, does not square with Nussbaum's interpretation of his views (see particularly pages 114-115).

The other major phenomenon to be considered is the universal occurrence of specific reported "feelings" associated at least with the principal moods and emotions. Children (and sometimes even adults) may be confused about what they are feeling (see for example, Holm, O., Greaker, E. & Strömberg, A. 2002. Experiences of longing in Norwegian and Swedish 4- and 5-year-old children. *The Journal of Psychology*, 136(6), pp. 608-612; Sherri, C.W. and Russel, J.A. 2003. A closer look at preschooler's freely produced labels for facial expression. *Developmental Psychology*, vol. 39, no 1, pp. 114-128.). Nevertheless, they report confidently on feeling mad, glad, and sad at very early ages (see Widen, S.C. and Russell, J.A. 2003. Children also recognize, despite Nussbaum's doubts (see p. 158), facial expressions universally and cross-culturally (Martiny, C. 2002. Empathy in counseling, unpublished doctoral thesis, Université du Québec à Montréal).

Thus to summarize, Nussbaum's general thesis, that emotions are only individualized by their cognitive component, seems to fail to jive with at least three sets of phenomena: the universal (subjective) reports about feelings, the research on cross-cultural facial expressions recognition, and the neurological consensus discussed above.

[25]One area where Nussbaum goes astray is in regard to music. In her discussion of certain philosophical issues, she makes use of too clear-cut a distinction between emotions and moods, emphasizing the presence and role of the former, and entirely neglecting the latter. Nussbaum does not mention the word "mood" in her entire Chapter entitled "Music and Emotions"'" (chapter 5, pp. 249-294). Yet some of the philosophical problems she discusses can be illuminated by considering the function and role of mood as it interacts with emotion. One of these questions is: "How can we have real emotions when listening to a musical work if there is no real-world object for those emotions to be about?" (p. 239).

[26]Schleifer, M. (2004). Moods, Emotions and Morality. Annual Meeting of the American Philosophical Association, Pacific Division, Pasadena, California, March.

[27]See Recommended Reading, pp. 201-206.

[28]Nussbaum, M. (op. cit., p. 133).

Endogenous depression is defined in Webster's as "a psychic depression caused by factors within the organism or system; it is produced or synthesized within the organism or system." The term derives analogically from its use with hormones, which can either be produced by our body (or brain) and transported to various other parts (like sap) or can be artificial hormones injected from the outside. This analogy lacks force in at least one way. Unlike any of the known hormones, there is no one depressive chemical produced by the body, nor can any kind of deep clinical depression ever be entirely divorced from the person's interaction with the world.

[29]Nussbaum, M. (op. cit., p. 88). In fact, grief connected to loss via death, or radical changes, often shift into clinical depression of the severest kind. One of the most effective cognitive-behavioral approaches is to suggest strategies to the client on preventing grief in various forms from turning into depression.

[30]Nussbaum, M. (op. cit., p. 133).

[31]For example, see Wender, op. cit., 1981, pp. 39-65. Here Nussbaum invokes the authority of Graham's article on "epistemic melancholy" (1990, Synthese 83: pp. 399-422) as well as Oatley and Bolton work on depression. Neither of these authors, however, support Nussbaum's conceptual distinctions between endogenous and reactive depression. Graham is arguing against Beck that both so-called "intentional and non-intentional depressions" overlap in certain ways. Depressive reasoning is not, he wants to contend, flawed or distorted in any kind of depressions. Oatley and Bolton (A social-cognitive theory of depression in reaction to life events, *Psychological Review,* 1985, vol. 92, no 3, pp. 372-388) also insist on the great overlap between life events and so-called "chemical" depression (see p. 381 and p. 385).

[32]Ledoux, op. cit.

Edelman, op. cit.

Pinker, S. (1997). *How the mind works,* New York: Norton.

[33]Wender (op. cit, p. 45).

[34]Ursin, H. and Eriksen, H.R. (2002). *The cognitive activation theory of stress.* University of Bergen. Internet Article.

Ursin, H. & Murison, R. eds. (1983). *Biological and psychological basis of psychosomatic disease.* Oxford: Pergamon Press.

Ursin, H., Baade, E. & Levine, S. eds. (1978). *Psychobiology of stress: A study of coping men.* New York: Academic Press.

See also Wender, op. cit.

[35]Lange, C. & James, W. (1922). *The Emotions.* Baltimore: Williams and Wilkins.

[36]Cannon, W.B. (1929). *Bodily changes in pain, hunger, fear and rage.* New York: Appleton.

[37]Goleman, D. (1995). *Emotional intelligence.* New York: Bantam Books, pp. 80-82 and 193.

[38]Kagan, J. (2000). *Galen's Prophecy.*

[39]Goleman opus. cit. Chapter 14.

[40]Davidson, R. (1994). Asymmetric brain function, affective style and psychopathology: The role of early experience and plasticity. *Development and Psychopathology;* vol. 6, p.741-758.

[41]Ibid.

[42]Thomas, A. & Chess, S. (1997). *Temperament and development.* New York, Brunner.

[43]Miller, P. & Haar, M. (1997). Emotional, cognitive, behavioural and temperament characteristics of children. *Motivation and Emotion,* vol. 21, p.109-125.

[44]The modern definition of "temperament" is "characteristic or habitual inclination or mode of emotional response" as in "nervous temperament." A "temperamental" person is "marked by excessive sensitivity and impulsive changes of mood as a temperamental opera singer or university professor" (both prima donnas?) (Webster's). "Temperament" in its obsolete form refers to "the peculiar or distinguishing mental or physical characteristics determined by the relative proportions of the humours according to medieval physiology" (Webster's).

"Humor" as a word only exists in the English language. The modern French dictionary includes the word "Humor" referring to an idiosyncratic English notion, not easily translated or even understood as an idea in the French language. "Humeur" (sic!) in French retains the original medieval meaning of "mood." The theory was that the "humors" were those four Cardinal fluids: blood, phlegm, choler (yellow or green bile) and black (sometimes called melancholy) bile which were secreted by the liver, although, for some reason, the spleen was the centre of emotion. These fluids coursed around the body and according to the relative strengths determined a person's mental or physical state. When one of the fluids predominated, then a person's character was dominated by that particular "humor" so he would become overpassionate (too much blood) or dull and droopy (overdose of phlegm), quick tempered and irascible (choler flowing too strongly), or gloomy and dejected (too much of the melancholy or black bile). Such a man was said to be "in a humor." If he carried on peculiarly he was a "humorist." Ben Johnson wrote two plays entitled: Every man in his humour (Shakespeare was an actor) and Every man out of his Humour (1598 and 1599). By the 18th century, at the time of Addison and Steele, the humourist was not the eccentric person but the one who wrote about the eccentricity (Oxford Book of Humorous Prose, Frank Muir, 1990, Oxford U. Press. p. xxvii-xxvix, xxx).

One of the most consistent findings in psychological research (see for example, Eisenberg, N., Fabes, R., & Losoya, S., 1997, Emotional responding: Regulation, social correlates, and socialization, In P. Salovey & D. Sluyter (Eds.), *Emotional development and emotional intelligence:* Educational implications (pp. 129-167) and Izard, C.E. 2002, Translating emotion theory and research into preventive interventions, *Psychological Bulletin,* vol. 128, no 5, p. 796-824) is that people are stably different in regard to certain personality dimensions, such as being extraverted-intraverted, or aggressive-nonaggressive, as well as being more or less prone to certain emotional or mental illnesses, including schizophrenia and mood disorders. These are determined by heredity; one's genetic background is crucial much as with baldness and age expectancy. These genetic determinants of "personality" characteristics are not, of course, uninfluenced by experience and the environment. This again parallels the fact that all the longevity genes in the world may not help if one abuses one's body or suffers an accident. Similarly, a tendency to aggression (or emotionality or moodiness) might have different life manifestations depending upon the individual's history. In this way heredity and genetics contribute to temperament, but not in the same way as they determine eye colour or hand preference, for example (these can also be influenced by extreme measures, as used to be the case for left-handed people being forced by ignorant teachers to use their right hand).

[45]Paul Harris (1989). *Children and emotions.* Oxford: Blackwell.

[46]Holm, O., Greaker, E., Strömberg, A. (2002). Experiences of longing in Norwegian and Swedish 4- and 5-year-old children. *The Journal of Psychology,* vol. 136, no 6, pp. 608-612.

[47]Solomon, R.C. & Stone, L.D. (1994). On "Positive " and " Negative" *Emotions. Journal for the Theory of Social Behaviour,* vol. 32, p. 417-435.

[48]Daniel Goleman. (2003). *Destructive emotions.* New York: Bantam Books, 424 p.

Daniel Goleman. (2003). *Healing Emotions.* New York: Random House, 277 p.

[49]Ibid.

[50]See note 9.

Chapter 8. Emotions and Morality

[1]See Swanton, C. (2002) book called *Virtue ethics.* New York: Oxford Press.

[2]See for example: Rabbi Marc Gellman & Monsignor Thomas Hartman ("The God Squad") (2002). *Religion for dummies.* New York: Wiley, 400 p. See Chapters 10 and 11.

[3]Ibid.

[4]Solomon, R.C. (2003). *Living with Nietzche.* Oxford New York: Oxford University Press.

[5]Aristotle's analysis in the Eudaimedian Ethics is somewhat more complicated, making use of the emotion of confidence interacting with the emotion of fear (see EE III, 1, 1229 and EE, III, 7, 1224b2).

[6]This is explained by Aristotle via an analogy in regard to food (1106b); where 10 pounds is a lot and 2 a little, 6 is not the mean we seek (although it is the arithmetical one). This is because the relevant mean depends on whether we are talking about Milo the trained athlete or a relative beginner. I believe that we can best capture Aristotle's idea of the "mean" by substituting the expression "a happy medium." In seeking this happy medium, in regard to the food example, we must focus on the relevant factors. In this case, these factors might include the relative needs of Milo and the less experienced wrestler.

Aristotle applies this version of the mean in an interesting way to what he calls "mildness," (praotes) which is the virtue concerned with anger: "The person who is angry at the right things and towards the right people, and also in the right way, at the right time, and for the right length of time, is praised" (1126a).

In more modern terms, we might talk of the virtue of "patience" which is a mean between impatience and wishy-washiness. The crucial emotion is still anger, which we will feel, but must decide how much, if at all, is appropriate, and how to convey or display. (This anger may come in the form of indignation, resentment, frustration, jealousy, envy and other varieties).

[7] See for example: Goleman, D. (1995). *Emotional intelligence*. New York: Bantam Books, particularly Chapter 5, entitled P*assion's slaves*. Also Paul Harris's (1989). *Children and emotions*. Oxford: Blackwell. Also: Eisenberg, N., Fabes, R., & Losoya, S., 1997, Emotional responding: Regulation, social correlates, and socialization, In P. Salovey & D. Sluyter (Eds.), Emotional development and emotional intelligence: *Educational implications* (pp. 129-167).

[8]Ibid.

[9]LeDoux, J. (1993). *The emotional brain: The mysterious underpinnings of emotional life*. New York: Simon and Schuster.

[10]Ibid.

[11]See for example: Tangney, J. & Wagner, P. (2003). Shame, guilt and psychopathology in Tangney, P & Fisher, P. (Ed.) *Self conscious emotions: Shame, guilt, embarrassment and pride*. Also in the same book, Fergusson, T. & Stegge, H. Emotional states and traits in children: The case of guilt and shame.

[12]Nussbaum M. (2001). *Upheavals of thought: the intelligence of emotions*. Cambridge: Cambridge University Press. Chapter 6.

[13]See Recommended Reading, pp. 201-206.

[14]Daniel Goleman. (2003). *Destructive emotions*. New York: Bantam Books, 424 p.

[15]Nussbaum M. (2001). *Upheavals of thought: the intelligence of emotions*. Cambridge: Cambridge University Press. Chapter 4.

[16]For example: Proust, M. *Rememberance of things Past,* 3 vols. Trans. C.K. Scott & Kilmartin, T. New York: Vintage Press.

[17]See for example: Rabbi Marc Gellman & Monsignor Thomas Hartman ("The God Squad") (2002). *Religion for dummies*. New York: Wiley, 400 p. See Chapters 10 and 11.

[18]See for example: Biddle, S. & Hill, A. (1988). Causal attributions and emotional reactions to outcome in a sporting contest. *Personality and Individual Differences;* vol. 9(2), p. 213-223.

[19]See for example: Belsky, J. & Crnic, K. (1997). Temperament and parenting Antecedents of individual differences in three-year-old's pride and shame reactions. *Child Development,* vol. 68(3), p. 456-466.

[20]Rabbi Joseph Telushkin. (2000). *The book of Jewish values*. New York: Random House, p. 342.

[21]Mann, T. (1944). *Joseph and his brothers*. Translated from the German by Lowe Porter. New York: Albert A. Knopf.

[22]For example: *Ramban commentary in the Torah* translated by Rabbi Dr. Charles Chavel (1971). New York, Shilo Publishing. And Zornberg, A. (1995). *The beginning of desire: Reflections on Genesis.* New York. Doubleday.

[23]See Bok, S. (1989). *Lying: Moral choice in public and private life.* New York: Vintage Books.

Also see Baier, A. Ethics as trusting and trust in great traditions in *Ethics.* White, N. & Theodore, D. (Eds) (2002). Wadsworth. P. 326-341. Baier links her analyses to Carol Gilligan's psychological work on caring. However, she does not accept that the ethics of trust is primarily feminine. She does, however, mention that David Hume and John Stewart Mill were better able to understand trust in asymmetrical relations, because there were important women in their lives. This is the opposite of lives of Jeremy Benthem and Emanuel Kant, who had no contact with women.

Part IV – The Most Difficult Subjects

Chapter 9. Separation

[1]Piaget, J. (1929). *The child's conception of the world.* New York. Harcourt, Brace and Co.

[2]See Sharp, K. (1985). Children's judgment and reasoning about aliveness. *Merrill-Palmer Quarterly;* vol. 31(1), p.47-65. and Candy-Gibbs, S.E. (1985). The affects of age, object, and cultural/religious background on children's concepts of death. *Omega,* vol.15(4), p.329-346.

Chapter 10. Illness

[1]See Kato, P., Lyon, T. & Rasco, C. (1998). Reasoning about moral aspects of illness and treatment by preschoolers who are healthy or who have a chronic illness. *Developmental and Behavioural Pediatrics,* vol. 19(2), p.68-76.

Chapter 11. Touching

[1]Schleifer, M., Daniel, M.-F., Peyronnet, E. et Lecompte, S. (2003). The impact of philosophical discussions on moral autonomy, judgment, empathy and the recognition of emotion in five year olds. *Thinking,* vol. 16, no 4, pp. 1-19.

[2]Smith, E., Clance, P. & Imes, S. (1998). *Touch in psychotherapy: Theory, research, and practice.* New York: The Gilford Press.

Chapter 12. Beliefs

[1]See McCormick, M. and Schleifer, M. (2005). Responsibility for emotions and beliefs. Annual Meeting of the Canadian Society for Education (CSEE). London, May.

Appendix A

Episode 3 Audrey-Anne's Tales
(created by Marie-France Daniel)

The Butterfly

Alexis and Audrey-Anne are on an outing with their school. They are chasing butterflies . . .. Not for keeps! Not to kill them! Just to get a look at them up close. An itty-bitty light yellow butterfly sets down on a flower close to Alexis's net. The butterfly seems comfortable on the flower's crown. The flower is dark yellow, almost orange. Alexis wants to try and tame the butterfly. He whispers to it:

— *Hello little butterfly, what is your name? How old are you? You are so tiny!*

The little butterfly is afraid of being caught. It flies away. But it comes back. Once again, Alexis tries to tame it:

— *My name is Alexis. I'm small, just like you.*

The butterfly doesn't answer. But its antennas are moving very fast. Alexis wonders:

— *Do butterflies talk by moving their antennas?*

The butterfly's wings are moving too, but not so fast. Their movement is slow and regular. They look like tiny lace fans. Audrey-Anne and Alexis observe their movement. They start laughing. They feel happy.

All of a sudden, their eyes are attracted to a small detail: The butterfly's wings are not the same. One of them is torn. Audrey-Anne worries about this difference.

— *Little butterfly, does your wing hurt? How did you tear your wing?*

The little butterfly crosses its front legs and then explains with a pout:

— *Over here, the adult butterflies are mean*

Alexis is surprised:

— *Oh really? Why?*

The itty-bitty light yellow butterfly explains:

— *Because an adult butterfly tore my wing.*

Alexis doesn't understand. He answers:

— *My parents are adults and they are not mean.*

— *You're lucky! Replies the little butterfly.*

But from his tone of voice, it doesn't seem to believe what Alexis is saying.

Alexis continues:

— *No, no adult has ever hurt me…Nor my friend Audrey-Anne.*

— *That's true, continues the yellow butterfly, I should have said that some adults are mean.*

Audrey-Anne heard the whole conversation between Alexis and the little yellow butterfly. She is feeling sad. Big fat tears rolled down her cheeks.

— *This morning, my friend Jeanne pulled on my dolls arms, just because I wouldn't lend her my skip-rope. She pulled so hard that the arms came out.*

Audrey-Anne turns towards the pretty, light yellow butterfly and asks:

— *What do you think of that? Do you think some children can also be mean?*

Since the little butterfly doesn't answer, Audrey-Anne continues to explain:

— *This morning, my doll cried.*

Alexis butts in:

— *Come on Audrey-Anne, dolls don't cry. Dolls aren't real people. Her name is Louiselle.*

Audrey-Anne adds:

— *I cried when I saw my doll without arms. Now, when I look at her, I don't recognize her. She isn't the same anymore!*

Appendix B
Exercises on Similarities and Differences (P₄C)

Discussion Plan: Contrasts

1. Do we have to be sad sometimes in order to be happy at other times?

2. Could the whole world be red?

3. Could everyone be tall?

4. Do you have to make mistakes in arithmetic to do better?

5. Do some people have to suffer so that others can see how lucky that they are?

6. Can everyone be rich?

7. Could everyone always lie?

Exercise: Similarities and Differences

When you try to compare the things, sometimes similarities are important and sometimes differences are important. Yet, not all similarities are important, for instance, both trucks and whales are big, but that's not usually an important similarity for comparing the two. Again, not all differences are important, for instance, one book has 120 pages, while another has 130 pages. See if you can tell whether the similarities and differences in the following are important. Can you think of other similarities and differences that would be more important?

1. Whales and fish are similar because they both live in the ocean.

2. Typewriters and pencils are different because typewriters are large with many parts, while pencils are small with few parts.

3. Windup watches and digital watches are similar because they both tell time.

4. Identical twins are similar because they are both born at the same time.

5. Baseball and football are different because they are played different seasons of the year.

6. Spelling and arithmetic are similar because you have to memorize the answers for both.

7. Children and adults are different because of their ages.

8. All pets are similar because we have a responsibility to take care of them.

9. Games are similar because they all have rules.

Exercise: Alike and not alike

Which of the following would you say are alike, and which would you say are not alike:

                                    Alike   Not Alike   ?

1. Tweedledum and Tweedledee
2. The five letter e's in the word Tweedledee
3. Two cans of Campbell's Vegetable Soup
4. Four copies of Pixie
5. Two snowflakes.
6. Two fingerprints from the same person
7. Two grains of sand in the desert
8. Two stars in the sky
9. Two sides of your face
10. Isabel and Miranda

Practice Items for Judgment Test: Which is not like the other? Why?

For 2-year-olds

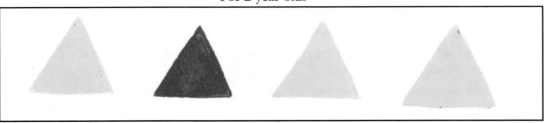

Judgment Test: Which is not like the other? Why? (For Ages 3 to 5)

Example 1

Example 2

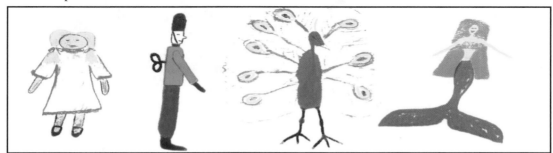

Example 3

Example 4

see page 142, note 2 for "correct" answers

Judgment Test. Which is not like the other? Why? (Age 5 to adult)

Example 1

Example 2

"Correct" answers: Example 1, Item 42 (unequal violence)
Example 2, Item 32 (non-religious)

Appendix C
Exercises on Ambiguity (P$_4$C)

Exercise: Ambiguities

Each of the following sentences can be read at least two different ways. Tell what the different meanings are in each case:

Part I

1. The actor with the broken leg was placed in a large cast.

2. Lulu: "You can always count on the cafeteria: there is nothing fresh here but the boys."

3. Prisoner: "I am tired of being cooped up all the time in this same cell. I think it's time for a break."

4. The elephant helped the circus get packed, by lifting the tree by the trunk.

5 Judge: "I feel out of practice, so maybe I better hold lots of trials."

6. When he finished peeling the potatoes, John lifted his eyes from the plate.

7. She was greatly thrilled and watched the oil well gushing.

8. The policemen jumped up when they heard the report.

9. The swimmers didn't want the lifeguard to catch them, so they ducked him.

10. Everyone but the umpires saw the play.

Part II

1. Teacher: "I took this exercise out of the Teacher's Manual."
   Phyllis: That's good! It should never have been there in the first place."

2. Salesman: "This freezer will soon pay for itself"
   Mrs. Jones: "Fine! As soon as it does, send it over."

3. Visitor: "Well, son, have you lived here all your life?"
   Archie: "Not yet."

4. Clerk: "Is there a certain kind of blanket you are looking for?"
   Mitzi: "Not really. I'm just looking for a friend."
   Clerk: "Have you tried asking for your friend at the information desk?"

5. Carol: "Do you like visiting relatives?"
   Ginger: "Yes, but not too many at a time."

6. Nicole: "Does everyone here have enough money to get into the movies?"
   Arnold: "Well, Gail's a little short."
   Nicole: "Then maybe they'll let her in at the children's rate."

Exercise: Teakettle (practice in working with ambiguities)

When a word can mean several different things in a given sentence, we call it "ambiguous." For example, "in the mornings, before his golf game, Dr. Wilson engages in his practice."

Here are a number of words which can have a variety of meanings. No doubt you can think of a great many more.

draw	root	page	lie	place	break
solution	race	rough	post	time	save
good	state	stand	will	house	wash
right	man	account	succeed	grave	kid

A volunteer goes out of the room, and the remainder of the group chooses a word that can have several meanings. When the volunteer returns, the members of the group, in turn, offer sentences in which the mystery word could be used. But instead of using the secret word, they always use the word "teakettle."

The person who's sentence leads to the discovery of the secret word becomes the next to go out of the room.

Exercise: Ambiguities

Identify the words that can have two different meanings, and say what the different meanings are:

1. One parent of a baby firefly says to the other:
   "She's bright for her age, isn't she?"

2. Teacher: "Who was Atlas?"
   Fred: "The world's first hold-up man."

3. Judge: "Since you're charged with battery, I'm going to put you into a dry cell."

4. Dog-owner to man: "Why did you just kick my dog?"
   Man: "Because he's mad."
   Dog-owner: "That's ridiculous! He's not mad!"
   Man: "He isn't? That's funny – I know I'd be if someone kicked me like that!"

5. Police chief: "This hill is quite a location for a police station."
   Policeman: "Why is that chief?"
   Police chief: "It overlooks the area where there's the most crime."

6. Newspaper editorial: "Since the birth rate has started to decline, the population had become less dense."

7. Professor (Facing bull in a field): "Let's be reasonable about this."
   Bull: "O.kay., I'll toss you for it."

8. Bert: "Don't you find it a great strain to let your mustache grow like that?"
   Harry: "Only when I drink vegetable soup."

9. Butcher: "I don't like to scratch myself in the freeze, because there's nothing I hate more than cold cuts."

10. Lost boy in amusement park: "I can't find my father."
    Policeman: "What's he like?"
    Boy: "Beer."

Appendix D
Exercises on rules (P$_4$C)

Discussion Plan: Rules

1. What is a rule?

2. Do all families have the same rules?

3. Are all rules in families made up by the parents?

4. Do children ever invent rules?

5. Have you ever played a game in which you made up the rules?

6. Are there rules which it is all right to break?

7. Are there rules telling you to do things which you're unable to do?
   If there are, should you be punished for not obeying such rules?

8. Do rules in a family remain the same, whether the parents are present or not?

9. What happens to rules that no one obeys?

10. Does every rule have a good reason?

Exercise: Rules

Do you agree or disagree with the following statements? If so, why? If not, why not?

	Agree	**Disagree**	**?**

1. All families have the same rules.

2. Rules are made only by parents.

3. Children sometimes invent rules.

4. Only parents can enforce rules.

5. It is never right to break a rule.

6. If a person is unwilling to obey a rule,
   the rule applies to him just the same.

7. If a person is unable to obey a rule,
   the rule doesn't apply to him.

8. Family rules remain the same, whether
   or not adults are present.

9. Some rules are imposed on us by others.

10. Some rules we invent and impose on others.

11. Some rules we invent and impose upon ourselves.

12. Some rules are invented by others,
    but we accept them and impose them upon ourselves.

Discussion Plan: Are there exceptions to rules?

1. John woke up in the morning with a bad cold. Does he have to go to school?
2. Tommy's bed time is at 9:00, but Star Wars is on T.V. from 7:30 to 9:30. Can he stay up until 9:30?
3. Susan is on a diet. Should she have ice cream and cake on her birthday?
4. Mr. Jones is driving on an empty highway. Should he go 20 miles per hour faster than the speed limit?
5. The ice cream man is outside and Mary's father has left a bit of change on his dresser.
6. Mary's mother has left a big plate of cookies on the table. They are for her women's group, and Mary's mother has told Mary not to take any.
7. Joan gets a bad headache. Should Sue give her medicine?
8. Aunt Sally has a new baby boy, and she wants to paint his bedroom pink.
9. If you got an A on a test by cheating, and nobody finds out, does the A count?
10. Can you make up some new rules while playing hop-scotch?
11. Can you invent a new way to play tag?
12. Do you have to stay within the lines in a coloring book?
13. Does a finger painting have to look like anything?
14. Can you spell your name in a different way?
15. Can you play baseball with 12 on a team?

Discussion Plan: Freedom

1. What do you think Pixie means when she yells, "We're free!"?
2. Are we free when there is no one over us to tell us how to live?
3. Are we free when we have to make up our own rules instead of having them already made up for us?
4. Are Pixie and Miranda free when their parents go away?
5. Are we free when nothing stops us from doing what we want to do?
6. Are we free if no one prevents us from hurting ourselves?
7. Would we be free if there were no laws to prevent other people from hurting us?
8. Would we be free if the laws applied only to some people and not to everyone?
9. If you were the only person in the world, could you live without rules?
10. Can a large number of people live together in the world without rules?

Discussion Plan Living with and without rules

1. Jenny says there's "no such thing as a game without rules." Is she right?

2. Can there be a family without rules?

3. Can there be a school without rules?

4. Can there be a friendship without rules?

5. Is it possible that there are rules in a friendship, but they just aren't ever spelled out?

6. Can a country have rules but no laws?

7. Can a country have laws but no rules?

8. When you are impolite, are you breaking a rule?

9. When you do the wrong thing, are you breaking a rule?

10. When you commit a crime, are you breaking a rule?

Exercise: Rules and principles

Mr. Mulligan tells Rusty that his comment was not a rule, but a principle. But Mr. Mulligan doesn't explain the difference.

Pixie, however, has already suggested what the difference might be: rules tell us how we should act; principles tell us how things do happen.

Thus, gravitation is a principle of physical science. It doesn't tell people how they ought to behave. Instead, it is part of our general understanding of how things work in the world. And a principle of mathematics is part of our general understanding of how things work in mathematics.

Would you classify the following as illustrations of rules or principles?

	Rule	Principle
1. Mr. Smith: "Johnny, I want you to be in bed every night by nine o'clock and not a minute later."		
2. Mr. Smith: "As a rule, I go to bed every night at 11:15."		
3. Glenda: "There goes my balloon! I filled it with hydrogen and the string broke!"		
4. Ted: "This ship floats on water, even though it carries A heavy load of steel."		
5. Gary: "This submarine sinks to the bottom of the ocean, Even though it's filled with air."		
6. Fred: "When swimming, breath through your mouth."		
7. Zelda: "I'll say this for water: it sure is wet."		
8. Mike: "When an odd number is added to an odd number, the result is an even number."		
9. Lou: "Stay out of drafts."		
10. Nell: "The longer you live, the older you get."		

Chapter Seven Episode 3

Different kinds of rules

Prior to the zoo trip, Mr. Mulligan and the class have a discussion of rules. Mr. Mulligan agrees with Kate that school rules and zoo rules are different. He also points out that many rules apply to grown-ups as well as children, and he give the rules of grammar as an example.

Jenny suggests that there is no such thing as a game without rules. This is probably so, but one should not conclude that rules are a defining characteristic of games, because games are not the only things that have rules.

The children in the class then give examples of rules in each of the academic areas that they study in school. Pixie objects to Rusty's example. She claims that rules tell us how to act. She says that Rusty's example doesn't tell them what to do; it merely tells how numbers act. Mr. Mulligan thereupon explains that Pixie is right and that what Rusty proposed was not a rule but a principle of arithmetic.

Rules and principles

Chita takes the distinction between rules and principles into consideration and raises a question as to which of the two is to be found in spelling. Rather surprisingly, Mr. Mulligan evades the question, possibly because the distinction between rules and principles breaks down. For example, spelling is both a descriptive and a prescriptive discipline. Principles are descriptive: they are laws which describe natural or human behavior. There are principles of magnetism and combustion in nature, and presumably there are principles also of the social, psychological, and linguistic behavior of human beings. When we learn to spell, we follow the traditional practices in our culture, which are both descriptive and prescriptive.

Discussion Plan: Whose rule is it?

Whose rule is it?

1. Don't play with matches.

2. No talking during the fire drill.

3. Boys and girls take turns cleaning the board.

4. The children set the table.

5. No driving over 55 mph.

6. Don't feed the animals.

7. Love thy neighbor as thyself.

8. All men are created equal.

9. Don't say "ain't."

10. Cross only at corners.

Exercise: Freedom

Do you agree or disagree with the following statements? If you agree, why? If you don't agree, why not?

Agree   Disagree   ?

1. We are free if no one tells us how to live.
2. We are free if we make up and follow our own rules for how to live.
3. We are free when nothing gets in our way.
4. We are free if we think we are free.
5. We are free when we can do what we think best.
6. We are free if we are healthy.
7. We are free if we are intelligent.
8. We are free only when everyone is free.
9. We are free if we are ourselves.
10. We are free when all the above statements are combined.

Discussion Plan: Rules

1. Why isn't there a rule against flying around the living room?
2. Can there be a rule against sneezing when you have a cold?
3. Do we need a rule to make us breathe?
4. Why isn't there a rule against eating breakfast?
5. When do we need a rule to have a good time at a birthday party?
6. Should there be rules about cleaning your room?
7. Do you need rules on spending your allowance?

Appendix E
The Golden Rule (Modified):
Questions from Philosophy for Children (P₄C)

Discussion Plan: Should the way we treat others resemble the way we would like them to treat us?

Pixie plays a trick on Tommy by suggesting that his mystery creature be a unicorn. But she gets very upset when Neil seems to be giving away the identity of her mystery creature. Perhaps she has learned a lesson from this (but will she get the lesson straight?)

Suppose the lesson is that we should treat others as we would like them to treat us. Are there any circumstances under which this rule would not apply? Could the rule be formulated differently? Perhaps you will be in a better position to answer these questions if you first discuss the following:

1. Do other people treat you the way you treat them?

2. Do you treat others the way they treat you?

3. Do you act the way you ought to act?

4. Would you like to act the way you ought to act?

5. Would you like to act the way you would like others to act?

6. Should you act the way others should act?

7. Should you act the way you would like others to act?

8. Should you not act the way you would not want others to act?

9. Should you not act the way others do not act?

10. Should you not act the way others should not act?

11. Which of the following formulations do you prefer:
    (Rank them if you can.)

a. Treat others as they treat you.

b. Do not treat others as they treat you.

c. Do not treat others in ways they do not treat you.

d. Treat others as you would like them to treat you.

e. Do not do to others what you would not like them to do to you.

f. Treat others as they ought to treat you.

g. Don't do to others what you would like to do to them.

Appendix F
Stories Related to Truth Telling and Lying

The shower was over, and Harry, Mark and Luther balanced on the curb outside the school, observing the flooded street corner.

"The drain's clogged," Luther remarked.

"Yeah," Mark replied. "Lemme poke it a little with this branch." But the soaked leaves were so compacted that Mark was unable to move them. Luther found a piece of wood and began to help.

Soon two older boys came by. Mark recognized them as the boys who'd bothered Maria on her way home from school the week before. They didn't know Mark was her brother. One of them asked, "Any of you guys seen Maria?"

Luther and Harry shook their heads.

The other boy said, "We want to have some fun with her." His friend snickered.

Mark said, "I think I saw her leaving school about ten minutes ago. She said she had to go straight home."

The two boys stared at Mark for a moment, then continued on their way. Luther resumed poking at the clogged leaves. After a while, Millie came by. "Mark," she called out in her high-pitched voice, "you seen Maria?"

Mark nodded. "Yeah, she's still in school. She's doing some kind of special assignment with Lisa and Fran." Millie went back into the school.

"They asked you exactly the same question," Luther said to Mark, "but you gave them exactly opposite answers."

Mark nodded. "Different situations," he said.

Just then, Maria Fran, Millie and Lisa came out of the school building. Mark told Maria what had happened. The others listened attentively. Then Luther remarked, "It was kind of funny hearing Mark get the same question twice in a row, and once he answered it with a lie, and the other time he answered it with the truth."

Lisa couldn't help teasing Mark a bit, "You done good, Mark. But you don't get very high grades for consistency."

Mark flushed, and no one seemed to have anything to say, until finally Harry came out with "Well-"

Lisa looked at him questioningly.

"What I mean is," said Harry slowly, "Mark would have been inconsistent only if the two situations were the same. But they weren't. They were miles apart."

"You measured the distance between them?" Lisa inquired, still mischievous. "Can you tell us your criteria?"

Harry ransacked his mind and was on the point of giving up when he remembered the Three Heads of the Giant. But before he could say anything, Millie had exclaimed, "Those boys — they were up to no good, I'll bet. They didn't have a right to an honest answer! Only an honest question deserves an honest answer!"

"Does that mean," Fran asked, "that before you answer anybody's question, you have to know whether they have good or bad intentions?"

Harry couldn't contain himself any longer. "Hold on!" he exclaimed, hands out, palms up, fingers wide apart. "It's not all that difficult! Yes, there are criteria: truth, consequences and intentions." The others just stared at him, aware that Harry would not have to be urged to continue. "Look, take the case of those two guys. They asked a question, but their intention – their purpose in asking it – wasn't good. Their bad intention disqualified their question – this is where I agree with Millie. And the consequences of Mark's answering it honestly might have been bad."

"Okay," said Lisa, "but what about Mark's answer to Millie?"

"Same three criteria," Harry retorted. "Millie's intention was okay, and the consequences of answering her honestly seemed okay, so Mark told the truth. I see nothing wrong with what he did."

"But what about his inconsistency?" Lisa persisted.

Harry shrugged. "I don't think he was inconsistent. We all agree that the two situations were completely different. If they had been the same and he'd said one thing one time and the opposite the next time, then he'd have been inconsistent."

Later, Fran and Lisa walked off together. Lisa said, "I really had nothing against what Mark did. I just wanted to push him to give reasons for doing what he did."

"Lying's not a problem for you?"

"It's not a personal problem for me," Lisa responded quickly. "I mean, I'm just not often tempted to lie. I hate lying, and I really enjoy telling the truth. But why do we do it?"

"Why do we do what?"

"Why do we tell the truth? Funny – I can't remember my parents ever telling me never to lie and always to tell the truth."

"You wonder why we tell the truth, and I wonder how we can tell what's true." Fran thought for a moment, then added, "Anyhow, maybe we learn more from the way we see our parents live than from what we hear them tell us."

Lisa grinned. "And maybe I'm just a worry-wart. That's what my father calls me."

Fran suddenly recalled that she had a biology assignment to hand in the next day.

"Hey Lisa," she said, "will you remind me of something tomorrow?"

"That depends on what I look like tomorrow," Lisa replied.

Summary

The Trouble With Truth is a two-part sound filmstrip presentation. Each part dramatizes an unresolved situation inviting classroom discussion about the problem of whether or not to tell the truth.

In Part 1 Patrick and six of his friends visit the local fishing area with Dave, their camp counsellor. As a special treat, Dave has made arrangements with a lobster fisherman to take the children out in his boat for a ride.

When Dave and Captain Conner leave for a few minutes to check weather conditions at the Coast Guard Station, they put Patrick in charge; but before they go, Captain Conner explains his rules about the boat. NOBODY is to set foot on his boat unless he is present. He warns the children that if this important rule is broken, the whole trip is off, and no one will get a ride.

Tempted by gauges, levers, the steering wheel, and some fishing lines on the boat, three children climb aboard. However, the others eventually persuade them to get off before Dave and Captain Conner return.

The children ask Patrick what he intends to do about the kids who got on the boat. Will he tell or not? Patrick's decision is a complicated one because his desire to tell the truth conflicts with several other values strongly held by children Patrick's age. Concern about having and keeping friends, doing things that are fun such as going on a fishing trip, and being fair in regard to the children who stayed off the boat as they had been told, are issues that must be considered.

The viewers as well as Patrick must make up their minds — what is the right thing for Patrick to do? Careful consideration of all conflicting reasons is encouraged before final judgments are made.

Part 2 dramatizes a completely different moral situation. For her seventh birthday Debbie's father has promised to take her to the fair. She may also choose five rides as part of her present. Debbie and her father arrive at the fairgrounds and walk along outside the fair to the ticket gate. They see many of the rides, hear the music, and even get to see part of a parade through the fence.

When Debbie and her father approach the gate to buy their tickets, Debbie's father discovers he has left his wallet at home. He has just enough pocket change for two admission tickets, but that means no money left over for rides. Debbie is so disappointed that her father suggests she might say that is she six years old instead of seven. That way she can get in for half-price and use the money left over for rides. Of course, this would mean Debbie would have to lie about her age, and so on second thought her father wonders if that is such a good idea. The final decision is left up to Debbie.

Discussion Plan: Making things up

1. If you make up an excuse, is that a fib?

2. If you make up a story, is that a fib?

3. If you draw a picture of someone, and your picture doesn't look at all like that person, is your picture a lie?

4. Can there be a make-believe story about real people?

5. Can there be a true story about make-believe people?

6. Is it possible to make up a story that doesn't have any people in it at all?

7. Is it possible to make up a story in which nothing happens?

8. Would it be possible for someone to make up a story, and the story turns out to be true?

9. If someone tells you a make-believe story, can you disbelieve it?

10. If someone tells you a true story, can you disbelieve it?

Appendix G
Stories and Questions For Children 2-5 About Values and Feelings

The general outline;

Each theme should begin with a dialogue, acted out by the puppets or cartoon figures. The adults will usually begin by manipulating the figures, and tell the story or stories. One adapts the language to the comprehension-level of the child The drama can be repeated if necessary, so that everyone grasps the essentials of the story: Who is who (each character will have a name), and who said, thought or did what. Then one begins with a few general leading questions. During the discussion, all the children are encouraged to talk, but some will probably talk more than others, and a few may even say nothing. They will, however, be paying attention. If they have said nothing after most of the time-period (40 minutes?) then the educator can gently ask their opinion on some matter discussed. There will be a list of guidelines and sample questions for follow-up for each theme. Any of these can be used to stimulate further reflection and discussion. Each theme (for example Gratitude) might carry over into a second session – not a problem! The children at all ages will inevitably ask the educator. "What do you think?" Here one usually wants to say, truthfully. "I am thinking about these things, sometimes I am not sure. Maybe this, maybe that." One might at some point judge that giving one's own views about each of the themes is appropriate, but not too soon, and it is always a danger that the children will simply take the adult view as the "right answer" and stymie thinking for themselves. Although there will be differences of opinion, one encourages respectful language, and grasping what the other child said, or tried to say. There is lots of repetition and synthesis by the discussion leader or leaders. For example, Billy thinks that Little Bear should always say 'thank you' but Sally thinks that he shouldn't. What do others think?"

Theme 1- Gratitude

Story 1

One character, usually older, (Aunt Minnie?), brings a gift for some little cute puppet character (Little Bear ?).So let us say, a bit of string was the gift, with Aunt Minnie choosing it quickly, saying "I am in a hurry, I don't have time to pick a gift." Little Bear, was hoping for a book, toy or whatever. He gets the string. It is clear that the recipient doesn't like the gift. He mutters his discontent, disappointment. There will then be a third character, (Big Bear?) who will remind the recipient to say "thank you." Which, he did not do. Little Bear says "I do not want to say thank you." A fourth character (Miss Turtle ?) will say "Give Aunt Minnie a hug, or kiss, or peck on the cheek." Little Bear will not do this. Little Bear will be thinking about what do. He will say "What shall I do?"

Initial Questions;

How does Little Bear feel when he gets the gift? How does Aunt Minnie feel when Little Bear doesn't say "Thank you?" Or give her the expected kiss or hug? Should Little Bear say "Thank you" even if he doesn't like the gift? Why or why not? Should he give Aunt Minnie the hug or kiss?

Follow-up questions:

Has anybody received a gift he/she didn't like? Has anybody given a gift for someone where the person didn't like it? (Each example can be the basis of further discussion) Do people kiss or hug others? When? Who? If we don't feel "thank you" should we say it? Should we say what we don't mean or feel? Would we be angry or sad if we were a person who gave a gift and the other didn't say "Thank you"? How would we feel? Does it make a difference if someone has given a nice or good gift, has thought about what the person would like, or has given very little thought? Why do we say "thank you"? If a person tells a child "say x" (fill in any word or phrase – could be nonsensical) should the child say it? If an adult says "say 'thank you'" should the child do it? If one is told "kiss the aunt" should we do it? Is there something else one could do? If no suggestions come from kids, one can say "What about looking them in the eye, and shaking their hand ? "Should one remind a person to say "thank you."? When to do it? Would a person (child) be embarassed if the reminder is done right away and out loud in front of the gift-giver? When would be the best time to remind someone to say "thank you"? Is it better to tell them quietly before or after rather than right away ?

Story 2

A puppet character, Michael, loses dog (dies, or whatever). Then a friend, Bob, thinks of getting him a dog as a gift for his birthday. A second friend, Cindy, suggests this is not a good idea. Bob must decide what to do. Bob gets the dog. Then Bob gives it to Michael who had lost his dog. The recipient, Michael, shows negative emotion (to himself or a third party) such as, sadness, perhaps a bit of anger. He does not say "thank you." Another puppet (Miss Goose?) reminds him: "You should say 'thank you'." He still does not want to say thank you. Another puppet, Miss Turtle, says "Give him a hug." He hesitates.

Initial Questions.

Will getting a dog make the recipient sad or happy? How does Michael feel? How does Bob feel? Should the recipient say "Thank You"? Does anybody have an example of giving a gift the other didn't like? Or getting a gift that made one sad, maybe because it reminded one of something sad, or whatever. Should one say "Thank You" even if one doesn't feel it or mean it?

General Follow-up questions

Can one say "thank you" even if one didn't get a gift? Can anybody think of some examples during this day (yesterday, this week) where one would have wanted to say "thank you" for something somebody did? Were there times one didn't say "thank you" but would have wanted to? Why didn't one? Too hurried? Didn't think of it? Didn't want to be too polite, a wimp etc.?

Can one feel gratitude when there has been no birthday, no gift, no present? Can anyone think of something they are grateful for, feel thanks for even if it is not a gift? If there are no examples, the educator perhaps can suggest. How about something very nice that happened today? What about nature, or health, or a fun activity? Can we be grateful even though we do not thank anyone particularly? If there is a child who cannot think of at least one thing he feels grateful for that day, maybe others can have suggestions? If we are sick or sad, can we still feel grateful?

What is the feeling one has which goes with the words "thank you"? If there is no answer, (young children . . . 3 to 5 . . . even 7)ask "Have you heard of the word "gratitude"? Or "grateful?" One can write this down, and children can practice saying it? What is the word for "thank you" in Spanish, Hebrew? Any other languages we know? Is there any language which doesn't have this word? When someone says "thank you," is there something one should say in return? In some places we say "you are welcome." Are there other things one could say? Is it necessary? Can a smile do the job after the thank you? Can a smile replace the words? Is it best to have a smile and the words? How important is it to look at the person when doing it? What about a little hug? Or a little touch on the shoulder? Is it okay. to do this? Should one touch the other person if one doesn't feel good about it? Is this different in different countries? In different parts of the country? Do some liked to be touched or hugged more than others?

Can animals feel grateful? Even if a dog cannot talk, is he feeling "thank you"? What about a hamster? Is it the same for people, or different? Can a dog, or cat or hamster feel gratitude of the general sort, as people can? Why or why not? Are there other emotions (one can explain the word as a special kind of feeling something about something) which dogs and other animals cannot have, but only people? Can dogs (or hamsters or insects etc.) feel sadness, loneliness, anger? What about shame, guilt, disgust, hope? What about love? Pride? Jealousy? Are there some emotions which need an understanding of time, an idea of the future? Can animals other than human beings have these more complicated emotions? Does gratitude go along with awe and wonder? Can we have this thing called "awe" or "wonder." Has anybody heard the word "wonderful"? Can an animal have the emotion of awe or wonder? Why or why not?

Theme 2: Honesty

Story 1

Puppet A sees an elephant behind a fence. He then meets a friend, Puppet B., who asks, "What animal is behind the fence?" Puppet A tells Puppet B "It is a dog." Now Puppet B meets puppet C, who asks, "What animal is behind the fence? Puppet B says. "A dog" Puppet C looks behind the fence, and says (surprised) "It is not a dog, it is an elephant!"

Note: Puppets should be named, but preferably not animals, to avoid confusion.

Initial Questions

Did Puppet A tell a lie to Puppet B? Did Puppet B tell a lie to Puppet C? Did Puppet A, or B do anything wrong? What did Puppet C believe? Why was he surprised? What is a lie? Did they tell the truth?

Story 2

Puppet A sees an ostrich behind the fence. He meets Puppet B, who asks "What animal is that behind the fence?" Puppet A tells Puppet B, "It is a cat" Puppet B meets Puppet C, who asks "What animal?" Puppet B tells puppet C "It is an ostrich." Puppet C now looks and sees the ostrich.

Initial Questions

Did A tell a lie to B? Did B tell a lie to C ? What did C believe? What did B believe? Did A do anything wrong? Did B do anything wrong? What is a lie? Did they tell the truth?

Follow-up Questions

How do we know if someone has told a lie? Is it okay to lie sometimes? Have you ever told a lie, a fib which was the right thing to do? If we tell a joke, is that a lie? How can we tell if someone is lying, or joking? If a friend asks you what you think of a new toy, or dress, or whatever, do you tell the truth? If you don't like it, will you tell them? How will they feel if you tell them the truth, which they don't want to hear? How will they feel if you don't tell them the truth? Are there different ways of telling the truth? Is it okay to tell part of the truth, but not the whole truth? If one doesn't answer a question, is one lying? Can we fool people by not lying? If a very bad person says "where is he?" should you tell the truth, if we know where he is hiding? Is it better sometimes not to tell the truth if someone will get hurt? If one does something bad, should one tell the truth? Do parents, teachers, other adults sometimes not tell the truth? Can you think of examples? Have you heard of a "white lie"? Are there good lies? Are there times when telling the truth is bad? Is it more important to tell the truth to a friend, than to someone one doesn't know well? What about a stranger? Do you know the word "trust"? Is it good to trust a friend, a relative, other people? If we promise something, should we keep our promise? Why? If we promise something, but can't do it, is it our fault? If we break our promise, is that a lie? Can you think of an example, where someone promised something, but didn't do it? Is this a lie? Does it matter if they tried to do it, but couldn't manage? Does it matter how hard they tried? Does one have to mean what one says, when one says "I promise"? Can I say it, but not mean it? Is that a lie? Can I change my mind? Should we say how we feel? Always? Can one sometimes hurt somebody by saying how one feels? Any examples?

Theme 3 Pride

Story One

One puppet (Little Bear?) is trying to solve a puzzle which is very hard and gets it. All the others couldn't get it even though they tried for a long time. A character (Miss Goose?) says: "that was very good, how did you get to solve the puzzle?" The puppet says "I am good at this." Miss Rabbit, overhearing, says, "You should not say you are good. It is not nice." To Miss Goose.."You should not say he was very good at solving puzzles with other puppets listening." Miss Goose and Little Bear think about this.

Questions

Should Little Bear say "I am good at puzzles" if he is good at them? Did he do anything bad, or wrong? Did Miss Goose say anything bad or wrong, when she was proud of Little Bear? Is it good to be proud of what we do? Is it good to be proud of what others do? If we are good at something, should we say that we are not good at it? How did Little Bear feel? How did the other puppets feel? Have you done things where you are proud? Are parents or teachers sometimes proud of what children do? Is it good to say that we are proud of others? Do you know what boasting is? Is pride the same as boasting? How do we say "pride," "proud" in French, Spanish and other languages?

Story Two

A group of characters are about to play a game, and choose teams. They see one puppet, Little Miss Bear, and ask "Are you good at soccer?" Miss Bear is very good at it, and says. "Yes, I am." Miss Goose hears this and says: "You shouldn't say that, it isn't nice." Little Miss Bear thinks about this. She is good at soccer. Should she say that she is not good at it?

Questions

Should Little Miss Bear say that she is good at soccer, or say she is not good, or say nothing? How does Miss Goose feel? How do the other puppets feel? If you are good at something, and people ask you, will you say that you are good at it? Do you have examples where you are good at something? Can you say it? Is this a bad thing? Is Miss Goose right or wrong? Do you think that saying you are good at something is "boasting"? Can we sometimes tell people we are good at something, before they ask? If we did something nice, or made something beautiful, should we tell people about it? Is this bad pride or good pride? Is there a nice way of talking about the things we are proud of? Do we have to think about how others will feel? Do you feel bad when somebody else is good at something? Can you think of an example where someone said another person was good at something, they were proud of them, and that made you feel bad? If one does not have bad pride, sometimes this is called being humble.

Follow-up questions

Do you know what "humble" means? If no response (likely from 2-5) one can say "humble means not having bad pride." Humble can also be replaced by the idea of wonder. Educator can ask: "Do you understand how it feels to think one is very small compared to other things? Did you ever think everything was very big? The stars? The whole world? The sky? How do you feel when you see huge things and think how small you are? Do you know what it means to "wonder"? Have you ever wondered about things? Do you ever think things are wonderful? How do you feel when you wonder, or when you think something is wonderful? What examples do you have? Anything you ever ate, tasted, smelled and said "this is wonderful!?" One can say "Some of this feeling about these wonderful things is what we mean by "humble" or "humility." When we think how much we do not know, how much there is to learn, this can also mean being humble. If people say, be humble and don't be proud, what would you do? Can we be proud and humble? Should we pretend to be humble even if we don't feel humble? Should we bow down to people? Should we lower our heads? Is there a bad humility and a good humility?

Theme 4: Apology

Story One

A group of puppets are riding on a train, or bus. The bus shakes and Little Bear bumps into a second puppet, Little Rabbit. Miss Goose says: "Say you are sorry" Little Bear doesn't know if he should say this. He didn't do anything wrong. The bus pushed him into the second puppet Little Rabbit.

Initial Questions

Should Little Bear say "I am sorry"? Why should he say this? How does Little Rabbit feel? How does he feel if Little Bear doesn't say "sorry"? How does he feel if Little Bear does say "sorry" (or "pardon me" or excuse me"?) Why should Little Bear say "sorry" if he didn't do anything bad? (It was the bus that pushed him, an accident.) How did Little Bear feel when Miss Goose said " Say sorry"? Did Little Bear feel embarrassed? Should Miss Goose explain to Little Bear why he should say sorry?

Story Two

Two puppets are playing. Puppet B snatches a puzzle from Puppet A. Puppet A grabs it back, and hurts puppet B a bit. Puppet B is angry and sad. Miss Goose says to puppet A. "Say sorry" Puppet A does not feel sorry. Should he say it anyway? Why should he say it, or not say it? How will puppet B feel if he says it, or doesn't say it?

Further Questions

Should one say "sorry" if one doesn't mean it? Should one feel "sorry" when you say it? Do you have any examples where you wanted to say "sorry" or didn't want to? Or wanted someone else to say "sorry"? When we say things, should we mean them, and feel them, or not? Any examples? If someone says "sorry" but in a grumpy way, and you know they don't mean it, or feel it, how does that make you feel? If you say "sorry but I don't know what for" is that really being sorry? Do you know the word "apology" and "forgive"? If someone has done something wrong to you, do you forgive them? Do you stay angry and sad? Is it easier to forgive if the person says "sorry"? How do you feel when you say " I forgive you" or "that's o.k. no big deal" Can one stay friends with someone even if one did something bad? Do parents and teachers say "sorry" to children? Do you have examples where adults said sorry? Or when they didn't ? How does one feel when an adult says "sorry" or when they don't? Does one have to say "sorry" right away, or is it okay to say it later? How much later? If you don't think you did anything wrong, should you ever say "sorry" anyways?

Theme 5 Responsibility

Story One

A bigger puppet tells a smaller puppet to throw a stone. Puppet B (the smaller one) does it. It breaks a glass window. Puppet B says "It is not my fault, you told me to do it" A third puppet C sees the damage.

Initial Questions

Was anybody bad? Who? Why? Who was bad? Puppet A or puppet B? When young children choose one or the other, continue. Was the other puppet bad too? Who was more bad? How does Puppet C feel? If he is angry, is it more at Puppet A or Puppet B? Why? If one talks of punishment, who should get punished? How ? How much? Who punished more, A or B? Why?

Story Two (With thanks to Saint Augustine)

Five puppets are in front of a pear tree belonging to a farmer. Four puppets want to take the pear, but it is not theirs. They tell Puppet A to take the pear, urging him to do it. He is the smallest puppet. He doesn't like pears, and hesitates, and then takes one. The farmer sees it. Exit puppets.

Initial Questions

Who was bad? Why? Were puppets B, C, D, E at all bad? How does puppet A feel? How did the others feel? How did the farmer feel? If he is angry, who is he angry at? If there is punishment, who will he punish? If they are all bad, who is baddest? Who should get punished more?

Follow-up Questions

If a group does something bad, who is to blame? If someone tells another to do something bad, who is to blame? Who should be punished, or punished more?? Do you have examples where someone tells another? What if an adult tells a child to do something which is bad? Should we punish the child or the adult? Who more? What about a captain of a boat, or a general in the army? What about a teacher or a rabbi? Do you know the word "responsible"? What does it mean? One can explain that the person who does something is "responsible" that means, if there is blame or praise or punishment or reward they are a candidate. Consequences are theirs. What about people who tell others to do things? Are they responsible? More or less? If a person in authority (explain this as adult to child, or captain to crew etc.) tells another to do it, can they say "no.?"

Theme 6 Jealousy

Story 1

One puppet, Little Bear is making a drawing, and the teacher or parent puppet (Miss Goose) praises it. A second puppet, Little Rabbit, is also making a picture, and says, to himself, "I don't like Little Bear, I have a good picture too." " I don't want to be friends with Little Bear any more."

Initial Questions

What is Little Rabbit feeling? Is he sad? Is he angry? Did the teacher/adult puppet (Miss Goose?) do or say anything bad? Why does Little Rabbit not want to be friends with Little Bear? Do you know the word "jealous"? Is Little Rabbit feeling jealous? Is that like being angry or sad? Were you ever jealous? Does it feel good to be jealous? What about angry or sad? What feelings feel good, and which feel bad? How does Little Bear feel?

Story 2

Adult puppet (Miss Goose?) gives out candies. She gives more to Little Bear than to Little Rabbit. Miss Goose also hugs and talks to Little Bear, and not to Little Rabbit. Little Rabbit says. "I don't like Little Bear." "I don't want to be his friend anymore."

Initial Questions

How does Little Rabbit feel? Is he angry? Sad? If children don't say it, one suggests. Jealous?

Why does Little Rabbit feel jealous? Did Little Bear do anything wrong? Bad? Did Miss Goose do or say something bad? How does Little Bear feel?

Follow-up questions

Have you ever felt jealous? Why? When? What examples? Is it good or bad to feel jealous? Are there any children who are not ever jealous? Are there any people who are not ever jealous? Is there a good jealous and a bad jealous? In story 1 is it right for Little Rabbit to feel jealous? What about story 2? What is the difference? If your friend wins a prize do you feel good or bad? If your friend wins a contest, and you do not, do you feel good or bad? Why do we feel good? Why do we feel bad? Can we stop feeling jealous? What should we do or say when we are feeling jealous? Are there other words for jealous? Do you know the word "envy"? What about in French, Spanish, other languages? Are there any languages which do not have a word for "jealous"?

Appendix H
Test of Moral Autonomy
(From Saltzstein, 1994)

Moral Dilemmas and Counter-Probes

1. (teasing story) All the children are always making fun of Pat, who's a new student in school. Chris is Pat's friend and feels sorry for him/her, and promises to back him/her up whatever s/he says. Pat is really upset and says, "I won a big prize at my other school." The other students start laughing and they say to Chris, "Did Pat really win a prize, Chris?" Chris knows that Pat never won a prize at his/her old school.

What should Chris do? Why?

Weak probes:

If child says: keep promise – lie,

"What about the fact that Chris would be lying to the other students?" (weak probe)

"But are you sure that Chris should lie to the other kids? Don't you think that Chris should tell the truth?" followed by "But what about the fact that Chris is friends with the other students, too?" followed by "But what about the fact that the other students trust Chris?" (strong probes)

If child says: break promise – don't lie,

What about the fact that Chris promised to back up Pat? (weak probe)

"But are you sure that Chris should break his/her promise to Pat? Don't you think that Chris should keep his/her promise to back Pat up?" followed by "but what about the fact that Chris and Pat are friends?" ". . . Pat is being teased?" ". . . Pat trusts Chris?" (strong probes)

2. (cheating story) Nicki tells his/her best friend Shawn that s/he was afraid that s/he was going to fail the test that they just took in class and so s/he had to cheat on the test. Nicki asks Shawn not to tell anyone, and Shawn promises not to tell. The next day, the teacher suspects that Nicki cheated and asks Shawn if Nicki cheated.

3. (hiding story) Gene tells his twin brother/her twin sister Alex about a secret hiding place that s/he has in the apartment, and asks him/her not to tell anyone. Alex promises not to tell anyone about Gene's secret hiding place. Later the same day, their parents haven't seen Gene and ask Alex if s/he knows where Gene is.

Appendix I
Test and Discussion Questions About Empathy

Levels of Empathy (Perspective Taking)

(from Selman, 1971, 1974)

Perspective taking proceeds in levels. Studies of children form four years of age through young adulthood show that there is a sequence of levels through which individuals go in their understanding of the relationship between their own and other's points of view. Each level stems from the preceding level and paves the way for the next one. Children may go through the levels at different rates but always in the same order.

The child's approach to perspective taking changes as he moves through each level. These changes are illustrated by the following sample responses to this typical perspective taking dilemma: A boy named Tom must decide whether to give his friend Mike a puppy for his birthday. Mike's own dog disappeared two weeks ago, and Mike is so sad that he says he never wants to see another dog.

Level One: Egocentric perspective taking (about ages four to six). The child has difficulty distinguishing between his view and that of others. He reasons that his point of view is the true perspective, not because he is right and others are wrong, but because he is unaware that others may have a different perspective. He may say in response to the puppy dilemma, "Tom should give Mike a puppy. I like puppies. Puppies are fun." He does not consider the possibility that Mike may not want a puppy.

Level Two: Information perspective taking (about ages six to eight). The child sees himself and other people as having possibly different interpretations of the same social situation, depending upon how much information each has. However, he cannot put himself in another's place because he does not realize that another person can think about what he is thinking. A child at this level may respond to the puppy story like this, "Mike said he doesn't want a puppy. Tom likes puppies, but he shouldn't get one for Mike."

Level Three: Self-reflective perspective taking (about ages eight to ten). The child becomes aware that people think or feel differently from one another, not only because they have different information, but also because they have different values. The child can put himself in other people's shoes, and, in doing this, he can see himself through their eyes. He understands that one person can think about another's view. A child at this level may answer, "If I were Mike, I'd want a puppy. Maybe Mike just doesn't know how he would feel if he had a new dog."

Level Four: Mutual perspective taking (about ages ten to twelve). The child realizes that both he and other people are thinking about each other's views at the same time. The child can view his own interaction with people as if he were a bystander. A child at the level of mutual perspective taking may say, "Well, if Tom gets Mike a puppy and Mike doesn't like it, Tom still knows Mike will understand that he was only trying to make him happy." At this level the child understands that people can be simultaneously and mutually aware of their own and others' motivations.

Episode from Lisa novelette

After dinner, Lisa went outside. She had hardly reached the sidewalk when Mr. Johnson came along with his dog on a leash. Mr. Johnson was new to the neighborhood; Lisa really didn't know him at all. When he and the dog got in front of Lisa's house, the dog spotted a squirrel by a tree and started after it. Mr. Johnson pulled up on the leash and the dog went sprawling. Then it was up again, growling and straining after the squirrel which had disappeared behind the tree. Mr. Johnson started to walk on, but the dog stayed put. The more the leash was pulled and yanked, the more the dog resisted. Mr. Johnson called to his dog, he shouted at it, but the dog did not move. Finally he picked up a small stick from a nearby bush and began to hit the dog which crouched, motionless, absorbing the blows. Lisa stared at the two of them in horror. She couldn't even cry out. Suddenly she sprang forward and tried to grab the stick. "You stop doing that!" she commanded furiously. Surprised, Mr. Johnson snatched the stick clear and turned, saying: "What's it to you?" Beside herself with rage, she blurted out, "I'm a dog too!" He shrugged his shoulder and began pulling on the leash again. Now the dog ended its resistance and began walking alongside Mr. Johnson; soon they were out of sight.

In school next day, Randy Garlock said, "Boy, did I have a great time this weekend! My father took me duck hunting."

"Takes lotsa guts to hunt ducks," said Mark sarcastically. "They're always so heavily armed."

"Very funny," Randy replied.

"You don't even eat those birds, so why do you kill them?" Mark persisted.

"There's too many of them," Randy snapped. "Unless hunters kill off the oversupply, there'll be ducks all over the place."

"Sure, sure. I'll bet it's only the hunters who claim to have counted how many there are, and who've decided there are too many, just so they can keep shooting them. I'll bet the hunters will keep on killing animals until they're all wiped out."

"So what?" put in Mickey. "Good riddance."

"People got a right to hunt," Randy said to Mark. "It's in the Constitution."

"The Constitution doesn't say anything about hunting," Mark retorted. "It just says that men have a right to bear arms for purposes of defense. Next you'll be telling me that people have the right to hunt whatever they like, even other people. I once saw a movie like that, and I've never forgotten it."

"That's ridiculous!" Randy retorted. "Killing people is altogether different than killing animals."

"But if we can exterminate animals because we say there are too many of them, what's to keep us from exterminating people because we think there's too many of them?"

Lisa had been listening to the conversation without saying anything. But now she remarked, "Right, because once we get in the habit of killing animals, we may find it hard to stop when it comes to people."

Randy shook his head vigorously. "People and animals are completely different. It doesn't matter what you do to animals, but you just have to remember you shouldn't do the same things to people."

The conversation drifted off to other topics, but Lisa was troubled. "Why is it," she asked herself, "that everything looks so simple, and then when you start talking about it, it always turns out to be so difficult? Mark's right: it's horrible the way we slaughter animals all the time. But in order to eat them, we have to kill them first. I don't understand — how can I be against killing birds and animals, when I love roast chicken and roast beef so much? Shouldn't I refuse to touch such food? Oh, I'm so confused!"

Lisa's father was in his study, listening to his stereo. She sat down on a hassock alongside his lounging chair, waiting for the music to end. (When she would sit like that in class, with her knees drawn up to her chin and her long hair falling down straight behind her, she looked, Harry Stottlemeier once remarked, like the letter M.)

"Beethoven," said Mr. Terry.

Lisa said nothing.

"String quartet," said Mr. Terry.

Again Lisa said nothing. But she thought to herself, "He knows I can't tell one piece of music from the next. But I remember everything he tells me; I just wish he'd tell me more." Then she remembered her problem. "Maybe I should become a vegetarian," she concluded, after telling her father about the conversation with Randy, Mickey and Mark.

"And you've got two reasons, as I understand you. First, you feel sorry for animals. And second, you believe that if you can kill animals, you might think killing human beings is okay."

"That's right. But are my reasons any good? Randy said they weren't."

"Oh? Why was that?"

"He said animals have to be killed off because there are too many of them. And he also said that if we didn't have animals to kill, we'd be even more likely to kill people than we are now."

"Did Randy claim that animals have no feelings?"

"He didn't say one way or the other."

"Do you believe that animals have a right to live?"

"Oh, daddy, how should I know? Animal rights? I never heard of such a thing."

Lisa's father regarded her soberly. "Your mother's calling you," he remarked. Lisa twisted her arms in front of her and interlaced her fingers backwards, then undid them. She stretched and bounded out of the room, her father watching her mildly until she was out of sight, down the long hall into the kitchen.

Exercise: Empathy

In the following situations, tell what the person is thinking or feeling:

1. Yesterday, you were scolded for something that you didn't do. You cry. Today you saw Jimmy being scolded for something he didn't do. How do you think he feels?

2. Last week you got an F on your arithmetic test. You feel very badly. But you know you didn't study. This morning, Irene got an F on her spelling test. She told you at recess that she didn't study. How do you think she feels?

3. Today at gym practice, you managed to get 5 baskets. You felt very proud. Carol got 6 baskets. How do you think she felt?

4. Last Monday, your mother asked you to go to the store and get some groceries. You remembered everything except the milk. Today, you meet Robert. He tells you he is on his way home, having bought some groceries for his mother. While talking to you, he remembers that he forgot the eggs. How do you think he felt?

5. This morning you were late for school. When you got there, the teacher was annoyed. She asked you for a note from your parents. But you had none. You felt very guilty. A few minutes later, Kevin came into the room. The teacher asked him if he had a note from his parents as to why he was late. He did and gave it to the teacher. How do you think he felt?

6. Last Tuesday was his mother's birthday. You bought her 6 carnations and had them on the table with a card when she came home from work. You felt so happy when she exclaimed, "Oh, what beautiful flowers. Thank you. Thank you." Today you met Carl coming home from basketball practice. He tells you that yesterday was his mother's birthday and he forgot all about it. How do you think he felt?"

7. Karen is your best friend. She promised to see the new Mr. Spock movie with you as soon as it came to town. This Saturday it will be at the local theatre. You call up Karen and she tells you that she can't go on Saturday because she has to go visit her grandmother. How do you think Karen felt?

8. Everyone in your class is planning on going to Gerard's birthday party. They've been talking about it all week. The day before the party, your classmate, Sam, gets sick. As a result he can't go to the party. How do you think Sam felt?

9. On your way home from school, you meet your older brother. He looks like he has been crying. You say, "what's the matter?" He tells you that someone stole his bike. How do you think he feels?

10. You invite your friend, Jennifer, over to play at your house. While she is there, she accidentally hits one of your mother's glass vases. It falls to the floor and breaks. How do you think Jennifer feels?

Leading Idea No. 4: "I'm a dog, too."

In a previous episode, Lisa is so disturbed by the way the man treats his dog that she tries to stop him, and cries out, "I'm a dog too!"

Lisa's identification with the victim, in this case a dog, is intense and articulate. She puts herself in the dogs place. In terms of inquiry skills, this is a matter of taking another's perspective. It can also be considered an act of empathy, if the psychological and affective components are stressed.

To a considerable extent, one's ability to put oneself in another person's place is essential for ethical experience. Taking another's perspective is important for ethical inquiry in that it permits one greater objectivity, in the sense that astronomers will observe a planet from different positions on earth in order to obtain a more objective and more comprehensive understanding of it.

Exercise: Putting oneself in another's place

Sometimes we put ourselves in another person's place, and we ask ourselves how we would feel if we were that other person.

Sometimes we tell ourselves this is what we've done, but we haven't really done so. In the following cases, each individual claims to have put himself or herself in another persons place. You are asked if you agree or disagree, and why.

	Agree	Disagree	?

1. Sonya: "Since Margaret and I swapped seats in class, I understand perfectly how she feels about arithmetic."

2. Phyllis: "Margaret and I always seems to dress alike, so she must feel the same way about clothes that I do."

3. Jordan: "I know just how Margaret feels about me. She likes me tremendously. After all, I'm very likeable, and if I were in her shoes, how could I feel otherwise?"

4. Jorge: "I love making Margaret laugh, and whenever Margaret laughs, Eve laughs, so she must feel the same way about Margaret as I do."

5. Albert: "I once shook hands with Margaret. I squeezed her hand and she squeezed mine. It told me a lot about how she feels."

6. Laurie: "I once saw Jordan make fun of the way Phyllis dresses, and I felt so badly for Phyllis, because he could just as easily have made fun of any of us."

Discussion Plan: On children and animals

1. Have you ever felt that other people didn't understand you, so that you turned to a cat or dog or horse for comfort and consolation?

2. Have you ever felt that animals which like to play and have fun are closer to children than they are to adults?

3. Have you ever felt that human beings will never be able to understand what it is like to be an animal?

4. Have you ever felt that animals will ever be able to understand what it is like to be a human being?

5. Do you think that young animals think about what they will be like when they grow up, the way young people do?

6. Do you think kittens want to be cats and puppies can't wait to be dogs?

7. Do you think that young animals ever want to be different animals — that a kitten might want to be a puppy, or a puppy might want to be a kitten?

8. Do you think that young animals ever want to be able to read and write?

9. When animals are what we call good — gentle, kind, loving — is it because we made them that way?

10. When animals are not what we call good — when they are dangerous and destructive — is it always because that's the way they naturally are?

Discussion Plan: Reasoning analogically in ethics

Perhaps Lisa is able to imagine how the dog feels. (This is what is sometimes called moral imagination.)

Now, an act of moral imagination may very well involve analogical reasoning. Consider and discuss the problem situations that follow. Do they involve analogies?

1. When someone accidentally dropped a wastepaper basket on Neil's toe, Isabel tried to remember how it felt when she got her thumb caught in the car door.

2. Tommy's father has lost his job, and his family is having a hard time. Jenny says: "I can't imagine what it must be like! My parents have always had jobs!"

3. Chita's brother steps on the cat's foot by accident, and the cat lets out a loud screech. Chita picks up the cat and hugs it, while saying to her brother, "You hurt it!" "Oh, no," he replies, "animals can't feel pain."

4. Kate speaks lovingly everyday to her plants. Her sister says to her, "why bother?" "Funny," Kate replies, "that's the same thing people say to my English teacher."

Appendix J
Sharing

Discussion Plan: Accepting help and asking for help

Who should you help? Who should you accept help from?

1. Should you help a classmate think up a topic for a paper?

2. Should you let someone copy your homework?

3. Should you let someone see the paper you're working on?

4. Should you explain how to do a paper to a classmate?

5. If your best friend wants to copy from your paper, should you let her?

6. Your grandmother has given you 6 photos for a term paper, and you need only 4. Should you give the other 2 to your friends?

7. You have to collect news articles from the paper and your mother gives you 10.

8. Your aunt gets 100 orders for school candy from the office in which she works.

Discussion Plan: Sharing

I.　Can two people share the same

1. room?	6. relatives?
2. book?	7. pleasures?
3. body?	8. pains?
4. ideas?	9. pet flee?
5. friends?	10. mind?

II.

1. Suppose you and your friend are going to share a piece of pie. If you demand a larger share, will that mean your friend's share will have to be smaller?

2. Suppose you and your friend are reading in class from the same book. Does it follow that, the more you read, the less your friend will be able to read?

3. Can some things be shared only if you each take portions? (Give examples)

4. Can some things be shared only if you each take turns? (Give examples)

5. Can some things be shared, and yet each person's share be the same as if he or she had the thing all to himself? (Give examples)

Appendix K
Tests About Emotion

Test of emotion understanding

(from Pons, Harris & Doudin, 2002)

Test of Emotion Comprehension (TEC)

The TEC consists of a picture book with a simple cartoon scenario on the top of each page (size of the book = 21 cm by 29.7 cm). Beneath each scenario, on the bottom part of the page, are four emotional outcomes, typically represented as facial expressions.

Testing is conducted on an individual basis. The general procedure is divided into two steps: (1) While showing a given cartoon scenario, the experimenter reads the accompanying story about the depicted character(s); (the face(s) of the characters in the cartoon are left blank). (2) After hearing the story, the child is asked to make an emotion attribution to the main character by pointing to the most appropriate of the four possible emotional outcomes (the children's responses are non-verbal). The test is divided in 9 blocks presented in a fixed order. Each block assesses a particular component of the understanding of emotion: (I) Recognition of emotions on the basis of facial expression (e.g. recognition of the face of a happy person); (II) Understanding of external causes of emotions (e.g. attribution of an emotion to a character being chased by a monster); (III) Understanding of desire-based emotions (e.g. attribution of an emotion to two characters in the same situation but having opposite desires); (IV) Understanding of belief-based emotions (e.g. attribution of an emotion to a rabbit who is enjoying a carrot without knowing that a fox is hiding behind the bushes); (V) Understanding the influence of a reminder on a present emotional state (e.g. attribution of an emotion to a character who is reminded of the loss of one of a pet); (VI) Understanding of the possibility of regulating an experienced emotion (e.g. attribution of an psychological strategy such as "think about someone else" to a character who wants to stop feeling sad); (VII) Understanding of the possibility of hiding an underlying or true emotional state (e.g. attribution of an emotion to a character who is smiling in order to hide his or her distress from another child engaged in teasing); (VIII) Understanding of mixed emotions (e.g. attribution of an emotion to a character who has just received a bicycle for his or her birthday but is wondering, as a novice, if he or she might fall off and get hurt); and (IX) Understanding of moral emotions (e.g. attribution of an emotion to a character who has done something naughty and who fails to confess to his or her mother). One point is assigned for each component answered correctly. This produces a level of emotion understanding with a minimum of 0 points and a maximum of 9 points.

Stories for Emotion Recognition

(based on Freeman, 1984)

Happiness

1. Today is Peter's birthday. He is having a birthday party for his friends. They will play lots of games and eat cake and ice cream.

2. Today Peter is going to his favorite place, the zoo. His mother has packed a picnic lunch so they can eat outside. Peter will see the animals he likes.

Sadness

1. Peter lives on a street with many children. Peter and his friends play together all the time. One day, Peter's mother tells him that they are moving to another street and he will not be able to play with his friends anymore.

2. Peter has a dog which he loves very much. Peter and his dog play together all the time. One day, the dog runs away and no one can find it.

Fear

1. Peter and his mother go to the grocery store. Peter helps pick out the food. When Peter turns around, he does not see his mother anywhere.

2.. Peter is sound asleep. He dreams that a big monster is chasing him. Peter wakes up screaming.

Anger

1. Peter goes to preschool. He plays with his favorite toy, the "peoples." Then a boy comes over and grabs all the "peoples" away.

2. Peter wants to watch Sesame Street. He has been waiting to watch it all day. But Peter's big brother wants to watch a different program so Peter and his big brother start fighting over which program to watch.

The emotion-recognition test was based on Freeman's work (1984). Two short story vignettes were written for each of four emotions: happiness, sadness, fear, and anger (see Appendix F). The children were shown the same picture for each story. The facial expression was judged neutral by three independent raters. After each vignette, the child was asked: "How does the child in the story feel?" The responses are rated as follows:

Score of 1: complete confusion of emotion or "I don't know."

Score of 2: generally correct emotion, at least on a positive-negative dimension.

Score of 3: the correct specific emotion appropriate for that story

Following Freeman's suggestion, based on her finding that gender and racial similarity/difference can have an effect on response, children were shown a picture of a child of a different gender and differing also by "racial group." Thus, a Black girl would see a White boy (4 stories) or an Asiatic boy (4 stories), and a White boy would see a Black girl (4 stories) or an Asiatic girl (4 stories).

Appendix L
Questions About Hope (P$_4$C)

Discussion Plan: Hope

In which of the following sentences would you fill in the blank with the word "hope," and in which would you fill in some other word? (What word would you use instead of "hope"?)

1. "I _____there will be a tomorrow."
2. "I _____there will be no more wars."
3. "I _____there is a tooth fairy."
4. "I _____that I will stay in good health."
5. "I _____that more things are possible than I think there are."

Discussion Plan: Corresponding mental acts

Pixie says, "That's what I hoped she was hoping." In other words, Pixie here engages in a mental act that seems to correspond to Miranda's mental act. This discussion plan deals with occasions in which several people engage in the same mental act, or the same person engages in the same act on several different occasions.

1. Could I have hope that you have hope?
2. Could I wish that you wish?
3. Could I dream that you dream?
4. Could you hope to have hope?
5. Could you wish to have wishes?
6. Could you dream that you are dreaming?
7. Could I believe that you believe?
8. Could I wonder whether you wonder?
9. Could I think that you think?
10. Could I know that you know?

Exercise: Hoping

What is the difference between hoping and

1. wishing?
2. believing?
3. expecting?
4. awaiting?
5. trusting?
6. suspecting?
7. doubting?
8. foretelling?
9. wanting?
10. predicting?

Appendix M
Questions About the Body (P$_4$C)

Discussion Plan: Do we own our bodies?

1. Do you own your books?

2. Do you own your bed?

3. Do you own your home?

4. How can you tell the difference between something your family owns and something you own?

5. How can you tell the difference between something the school owns and something you own?

6. Does anyone own the sun and the moon and the stars?

7. Does anyone own the earth?

8. How can you tell the difference between things people own and things no one owns?

9. Is your body (a) something you own?
                 (b) something other people own?
                 (c) Something no one owns?

10. Is your body the same kind of thing as your bed or your toothbrush?

11. If your body is a part of you, does that mean that you don't own it?

12. If your body is not a part of you, does that mean that you own it?

13. If you believe you own your body, does that mean it isn't a part of you?

14. If you don't believe you own your body, does that mean it's part of you?

15. Is it possible that your body is not a part of you, but that you are a part of it?

Discussion Plan: Parts of you

Say whether or not you think the following are parts of you:

1. Your feet

2. Your ears

3. Your breath

4. Your hair (before cutting)

5. Your hair (after cutting)

6. Your saliva

7. Your thoughts

8. Your feelings

9. Your memories

10. Your parents

11. Your clothes

12. Your drawings

13. Things you've written

14. Your world

15. Things you say

Discussion Plan: What is it that makes you you?

Would you still be you if

1. you had a different name?

2. you had a different face?

3. You had a different body?

4. You had a different mind?

5. You had different fingerprints?

6. You had different parents?

7. You had different grandparents?

8. You were born and raised in China?

9. Everyone in the world thought you were someone else?

Appendix N
Questions About Teasing (P4C)

Discussion Plan: Teasing

Part I: Is it any of your business to:

1. tell the teacher John is cheating?
2. Tell your sister to brush her teeth?
3. Tell your parents to begin cooking dinner?
4. Tell your teacher you've learned division already?
5. Tell your older sister you don't like her boyfriend?
6. Tell a girl to stop teasing her dog?
7. Tell a woman to stop scolding her child?
8. Tell a man not to smoke in the movies?
9. Tell the doctor you don't like the medicine?
10. Tell your mother you won't take the medicine?

Part II: Should these people be teased?

1. Johnny is the best player on the team; and he strikes out.
2. Sam, as usual, gets the lowest mark on the spelling test.
3. Johnny buys his bald father a comb with no teeth.
4. Sally's teenage brother is growing his first moustache.
5. Tommy is the only kid in fourth grade to become an uncle.
6. Mary wants a record player for her birthday and you find out that she is getting a typewriter.
7. Sam is juggling raw eggs and he drops one on his shoe.
8. Alan is convinced that he will win the lottery.
9. Judy is convinced that she will get the lead in the school play.
10. John's April Fool's joke backfires and he gets soaked with water.

Recommended Reading

Of General Interest

Hulbert, Ann (2003). *Raising America: experts, parents, and a century of advice about children.* New York: Vintage Books.

Hulbert structures her history around five key parenting and family conferences, from 1899s National Congress of Mothers to 1997s Conference on Early Childhood Development and Learning, pausing in each case to reflect on the state of parenting philosophies and advice at the time.

Piaget, Jean (1968). *The moral judgment of the child.* Routledge and Kegan Paul. (Originally Le jugement moral chez l'enfant. 1932).

Piaget's book is the "Bible" for psychologists and educators interested in moral development. Among topics covered are included: lying, responsibility, cooperation, and rule following.

Johnson, Paul (1991). *Modern times.* New York: Harper and Row.

In this history of the 20th Century, Johnson argues that the relativism of Sigmund Freud and the relativity of Albert Einstein dominated intellectual thought. The challenge of the 21st century is to defend fundamental, universal values without falling into absolutism or dogmatism.

Plato. *The meno.*

This is a Socratic dialogue about moral education, the teaching of virtue. It is still relevant and readable

Aristotle's *Nicomochean ethics*, especially Chapters 3 and 7.

About virtue, judgment, and responsibility; still readable and relevant after 2500 years.

Parental advice books about talking to children (2 to 12)

Butba, Michele (2001). *Moral intelligence.* Jossey-Bass.

Coles, Robert (1997). *The moral intelligence of children.* New York: Random House, 217 p.

This excellent book emphasises dialogue, with we educators learning from our children, as they learn from us. Coles also reminds us that we recognize a 'good' kid, even if we can't quite put into words what 'goodness' is.

Mogel, Wendy (2001). *The blessing of a skinned knee.* New York: Penguin Putnam Inc., 302 p.

A clinical psychologist offering advice based on the Jewish spiritual tradition. Fun to read. She argues strenuously for parents letting their children take risks, as opposed to the tendency to overprotection. Her view is somewhat extreme, as we discuss in Chapter 5 of the present book.

Ginott, Chaim (1969). *Between parent and child.* New York: Avon.

Ginot, Chaimt (1975). *Teacher and child.* New York: Avon.

Faber, Adele & Mazlich, Elaine (2002). *How to talk so kids will listen & Listen so kids will talk.* New York: Harper Collins, 286 p.

Faber and Mazlich continue Guinott's excellent work on communicating with kids. Great cartoons too!

Colorosa, Barbara (1995). *Kids are worth it: Giving your child the gift of inner discipline.* Harper Collins.

Shulman, Michael & Mekler,Eva (1985). *Bringing up a moral child. Reading,* MA.: Addison-Wesley, 359 p.

These two excellent books discuss communication with children

Lickona, Thomas (1983). *Raising good children.* New York: Simon & Shuster.

Lickona, Thomas (1990). *Educating for character: How schools can teach respect and responsibility.* New York: Simon and Shuster.

Lickona, Thomas (2004). *Character matters: How to help our children develop good judgment, integrity and other essential virtues.* New York: Simon and Shuster.

Lickona's most recent book, which has just appeared at the time of writing this one, does not provide, despite the title, any specific suggestions for improving judgment. He writes within the conservative, Catholic tradition, which influences his recommendations concerning sexual activity, abortion and homosexuality.

Wolf, Anthony (2003). *Mom, Jason's breathing on me!: The solution to sibling bickering.* Ballantine Books, 203 p.

Wolf, Anthony (2000). *Secret of parenting: How to be in charge of today's kids - From toddlers to preteens - without threats of punishment.* Farrar Straus & Giroux, 233 p.

These book are about negative behavior, tantrums and back-talk.

Wolf, Anthony (1996). *It's not fair, Jeremy Spencer's parents let him stay up all night!: A guide to the tougher parts of parenting.* Farrar Straus & Giroux.

This one is about family disputes and fights.

Wolf, Anthony (1998). *Why did you have to get a divorce? And when can I get a hamster?: A guide to parenting through divorce.* Farrar Straus & Giroux, 208 p.

Great advice on how to talk about these matters.

Infancy

Dr Benjamin Spock's child rearing book *Baby and child care* first published in 1946 and the latest edition is 2003. The internet versions are of course handled by Dr Spock's successors under the name the "Dr Spock Company," primarily Dr. Robert Needleman.

A recent successor book to Dr Spock is by Lu Hanessian entitled, *Let the baby drive: Navigating the road of new motherhood.*

Like Spock before her she tells mothers that they are the experts and "to trust their intuition and the babies instincts."

Winnicott, Donald (1965). *The maturational process and the facilitating environment.* New York: International Universities Press.

He discusses the early origins of guilt and concern for others. We also have the idea of the "good enough" parent.)

Bowlby, John. (1969). *Attachment and loss. Vol. 1: Attachment,* 2nd ed. New York: Basic Books.

Bowlby, John. (1973). *Attachment and loss. Vol. 2: Separation: Anxiety and anger.* New York: Basic Books.

Bowlby, John (1980). *Attachment and loss. Vol. 3: Loss: Sadness and depression.* New York: Basic Books.

Bowlby, John (1988). *A secure base: Parent-child attachment and healthy human development.* New York: Basic Books.

The books by Bowlby stress the importance of early attachment to the caregiver.

Nussbaum, Martha (2001). *Upheavals of thought: The intelligence of emotions.* Cambridge: Cambridge University Press, Chapter 4.

A leading philosopher discusses Winnicot and Bowlby

Teenagers (Not covered in this book)

Ginott, Chaim (1971). *Between parent and teenager*. New York: Avon.

Wolf, Anthony (2002). *Get out of my life. But first could you give me and Sheryl a lift to the mall?* Farrar Straus & Giroux, 212 p.

Neufeld, Gordon (2004). *Hold on to your kids: Why parents matter?* Alfred A. Knopf, 332 p.

Concerning moral values: The controversies about objectivism and relativism

Skinner, B.F. (1971). *Beyond freedom & dignity*. New York: Alfred A. Knopf, 225 p.

Skinner's book is the classical defense of subjectivism and extreme relativism.

Rorty, Richard (1989). *Contingency, irony and solidarity*. Cambridge, Mass.: Cambridge University Press.

Feyerabend, Paul (1999). *Conquest of abundance*. Chicago: University of Chicago Press.

Rorty and Feyerabend represent the "post-modernist" defense of subjectivism and relativism. For a critique of these views see Michael Schleifer (1997). Philosophy and community in education: A critique of Richard Rorty. *Analytic Teaching*, vol. 17 (2), p. 27-34. For a defense of objectivism, and arguments against relativism, see the following list:

Beck, Clive. (1972). *Ethics*. New York: McGraw-Hill Ryerson Limited, 110 p.

O'Grady, Paul. (2002). *Relativism*. Montreal-Kingston: McGill-Queen's University Press, 196 p.

Hollis, Martin & Lukes, Steve. (1982). *Rationality and relativism*. Cambridge, MA: The MIT Press, 312 p.

Rabbi Marc Gellman & Monsignor Thomas Hartman ("The God Squad") (2002). *Religion for dummies*. New York: Wiley, 400 p. See Chapters 10 and 11.

Montefior, Alan e (1958). *A modern introduction to moral philosophy*. London: Routledge & Kegan Paul.

Peters, Richard (1966). *Ethics and education*. Routledge and Kegan Paul.

Reboul, Olivier (1971) *La Philosophie de l'éducation*. Presses universitaires de France.

Foot, Philippa (1967). *Theories of ethics*. Oxford: Oxford University Press. Introduction and Chapter 6.

Warnock, Mary (1977). *Schools of thought*. London: Faber and Faber.

Forquin, Jean-Claude (1996). *École et culture: le point de vue des sociologues britanniques*. Bruxelles: De Boeck.

Bernstein, Richard. (1983). *Beyond objectivism and relativism*. Philadelphia: University of Pennsylvania Press.

Blackburn, Simon (1992). *Essays in quasi-realism*. Oxford: Oxford University Press, pp. 172-73.

Brink, David (1999). Objectivity and dialectical methods in ethics. *Inquiry, 42*, p. 195-212.

Dworkin, Ronald (1996). Objectivity and truth: You'd better believe it. In *Philosophy and Public Affairs*, p. 88-139.

Wilson, John (1967). *Introduction to moral education*. Middlesex: Penguin, Chapter 4 and 5.

Johnson, Paul (1991). *Modern times*. New York: Harper and Row.

Schleifer, M et Thésée, G. (2001). Thinking critically about subjectivism and relativism," In V. Cauchy (dir), *Coexistence humaine et développement durable*, p. 293-302.*

Philosophy for children

Lipman, M., Sharp, A.M. & Oscanyan, F.S. (1980). *Philosophy in the classroom*. Philadelphia: Temple University Press, 231 p.

Lipman, M. and Sharp, A.M. (1978). *Growing up with philosophy*. Philadelphia: Temple University Press, 410 p.

Judgment

Lipman, M. (1993). *Thinking children and education*. Montclair State: Kendall/Hunt Publishing Company. See Chapter 12 "The Cultivation of Judgment," pp. 685-741.

Schleifer, M. (ed.) (1992). *La formation du jugement. Peut-on apprendre le jugement?* Montréal: Éditions Logiques, 268 pages. English versions of selected chapters available upon request.*

Schleifer, M. (2004). The human mind and artificial intelligence: Why computers cannot play bridge. *The Bridge Bulletin, May*. Full article available on request.*

Lying and Truth Telling

Shiller, Virginia. (2003). *Rewards for kids*. Magination Press.

Shiller suggests that all kids will fib, and that parents should acknowledge this. When a child says "I brushed my teeth" she advices parent to say "I know you didn't bush them, so please do it now"

Bok, S. (1989). *Lying: Moral choice in public and private life*. New York: Vintage Books.

For Bok the crucial element is not lying or truth telling; rather it is the element of trust.

Gratitude

DeBroff, Stacy (2002). *The mum book*. Free Press.

The author stresses teaching young children to look for the positive, and make thank you sounds.

Empathy

Seligman, Martin. (2004). *Authentic happiness*. Free Press.

Seligman shows how one can increase a baby's contentment by copying him. For example, if the child bangs on the table three times after finishing his food, the parent should bang three times too. This copy cat response can teach the baby that his actions influence the behavior of someone he loves; happiness is raised by making it clear that what the child does really matters.

Martiny, Cynthia (2002). Non-Verbal Behavior and Empathy in the Communicational Context: Indications for Training Helping-Practitioners. Unpublished doctoral thesis. Université du Québec à Montréal. **Articles available on request.

Eisenberg, Nancy & Strayer, Janis (1987). *Empathy and its development*. Cambridge: Cambridge University Press.

Eisenberg, Nancy, Murphy, Bridget & Shepard, Stephanie (1996). The development of emphatic accuracy. In William Ickes (Ed.) *Emphatic accuracy*. (pp. 73-116). New York: Guilford Press.

Eisenberg, Nancy & Mussen, Paul (1989). The Roots of Prosocial Behavior in Children. Cambridge: Cambridge University Press.

Ekman, Paul (1982). *Emotion in the human face*. Cambridge: Cambridge University Press.

Rogers, Carol (1951). *Client-centered therapy.* Boston: Houghton Mifflin.

Rogers, Carol (1975). Empathic: An appreciated way of being. *The Counseling Psychologist, 5*, pp. 209-220.

Wispé (1986). The distinction between sympathy and empathy: To call forth a concept, a word is needed. *Journal of Personality and Social Psychology, 50*, (2), pp. 314-321.

Wispé (1987). History of the concept of empathy. In N. Eisenberg & J. Strayer (Eds.), *Empathy and its development* (pp. 17-37). Cambridge: Cambridge University Press.

Emotions (understanding and development)

Ledoux, Paul (1993). *The emotional brain: The mysterious underpinnings of emotional life.* New York: Simon and Schuster.

Fridja, Nico (1986). *The emotions.* Cambridge: Cambridge University Press.

Nussbaum, Martha (2001). *Upheavals of thought: The intelligence of emotions.* Cambridge: Cambridge University Press. Part I

Solomon, Robert C (2003). *What is an emotion?* New York: Oxford University Press, 305 p.

Harris, Paul (1989). *Children and emotions.* Oxford: Blackwell.

Mascolo, Michael F & Griffin, Sharon (1998). *What develops in emotional development?.* New York: Plenum Press, 352 p.

Izard, Carol (1991). *The psychology of emotions.* New York: Plenum.

Robinson, Jenefer (2005). *Deeper than reason: Emotion and its role in literature, music and art.* Oxford University Press, 516 p.

Emotions and morality

Nussbaum, Jenefer (2001). *Upheavals of thought: The intelligence of emotions.* Cambridge: Cambridge University Press, Part II.

Stocker, Michael (1996). *Valuing emotions.* New York: Cambridge University Press, 353 p.

Control of emotions

Fischer, John Martin & Ravizza, Mark. (1988). *Responsibility and control.* Cambridge University Press.

Adams, Robert. (1985). *Involuntary sins.* Philosophical Review; 94, p3-31.

Solomon, Robert C (1980). Emotions and choice. In Amélie Oksenberg Rorty *Explaining emotions.* pp. 251-283. Los Angeles-London: University of California Press.

Ledoux, Paul (1993). *The Emotional brain: The mysterious underpinnings of emotional life.* New York: Simon and Schuster.

Rabbi Abraham Cohen. (1995). *EveryMan's Talmud.* New York: Penguin Books, 405 p.

Weiss, Raymond & Butterworth, Charles. (1975). *Ethical writings of Maimonides.* New York: Dover Publications, 182 p.

Hanh, Thich Nhat. (2001). Anger: *wisdom for cooling the flames.* New York: Riverhead Books, 203 p.

Rabbi Joseph Telushkin. (2000). *The book of Jewish values.* New York: Random House, 519 p.

Frankel, Estelle (2003). *Sacred therapy.* Boston and London: Shambhala Publications, 331 p.

Goleman, Daniel. (1995). *Emotional intelligence.* New York: Bantam Books, 352 p.

Goleman, Daniel (1998). *Working with emotional intelligence.* New York: Bantam Books, 383 p.

Goleman, Daniel. (2003). *Destructive emotions.* New York: Bantam Books, 424 p.

Goleman, Daniel (2003). *Healing emotions.* New York: Random House, 277 p.

*email address: schleifer.michael@uqam.ca
**email address: martiny.cynthia@uqam.ca

Recommended Movies for talking abut emotions with children as young as 3 to 5

The Wizard of Oz (hope, fear, belief)
Miracle on 34 Street -classical or modern version-(hope, fear, belief)
Spiderman 2 (love)
Shrek 1 and 2 (love, jealousy)
Beauty and the Beast (love)
The Lion King (guilt, pride)
Pinocchio (lying)
Black Stallion (sadness, pride)
Spirit (sadness, pride)
The Ice Princess (pride, jealousy)
Stuart Little (fear, courage, pride, loneliness, love)
Babe (fear, grief, loneliness)
Finding Nemo (sadness, loneliness)
Charlotte's Web (grief)
Brother Bear (empathy)
Lies my Father told me
Bambi (grief, love)
Cinderella (jealousy, hate)
Snow White (jealousy, hate)
 For older children (6 to 12):
Kramer vs Kramer (divorce and separation)
Casablanca (love, trust
It's A Wonderful Life (depression, wonder, belief)
Chariots of Fire (pride)
Love Actually (love, trust)
The Russians are Coming; The Russians are Coming (love, fear)
Amadeus (jealousy, hate)

Index